GENDER AND AGING
IN MESOPOTAMIA

GENDER AND AGING IN MESOPOTAMIA

The *Gilgamesh Epic* and
Other Ancient Literature

Rivkah Harris

UNIVERSITY OF OKLAHOMA PRESS : NORMAN

For Monnie

Library of Congress Cataloging-in-Publication Data

Harris, Rivkah.
    Gender and aging in Mesopotamia: the Gilgamesh epic and
other ancient literature / Rivkah Harris.
      p.   cm.
    Includes bibliographical references and index.
    ISBN 0-8061-3167-5 (alk. paper)
    1. Aged women—Iraq—History—To 1500.   2. Aging—Iraq—
History—To 1500.   3. Assyro-Babylonian literature—History
and literature.   4. Sex roles—Iraq—History—To 1500.   I. Title.
HQ1064.I69H37   2000
305.26'09567—dc21   99-39923
                                                      CIP

Text design by Gail Carter.

1 2 3 4 5 6 7 8 9 10

CONTENTS

ILLUSTRATIONS

PREFACE

These studies focus on two basic aspects of ancient Mesopotamian society: the stages of life and issues of gender and sexuality. I have by no means exhaustively examined these topics, nor have I utilized all possible sources. For the most part, as Gillian Clark has noted, "all we can construct is a patchwork, piecing together scraps of material for a different purpose and to a different effect from that intended by their original makers."[1] I try to present a fairly coherent and integrated picture of the different topics emerging from fragments of data gathered, sorted, and interpreted, from a variety of texts, and at times from visual sources.

I have not attempted to follow historical changes, mainly due to the fragmentary and accidental nature of the evidence and its uneven distribution in time. Nor have I made any effort to distinguish between the perspectives of the Sumerians and the Akkadian Semites, the two main components of Mesopotamian civilization. Here I concur with Jerrold S. Cooper's view that "it usually is impossible to label any particular Mesopotamian institution or belief Sumerian or Semitic," so close was "the interaction of the two linguistic communities."[2]

My approach in these studies has been eclectic, utilizing methods and insights of the social sciences. They help in providing some kind of framework for clarifying the little-known particulars of the ancient, long-dead civilization of Mesopotamia. I have especially benefited from specialized studies of classicists, as many footnotes attest. They stimulated my asking questions of the cuneiform sources I would otherwise not have considered. Throughout I have relied on the philological work and translations of Sumerologists and Assyriologists. It is in the synthesis and bringing together of the disparate information culled from the primary sources that I hope I have made some contribution.

Tens of thousands of cuneiform tablets remain, telling of the quotidian life of Mesopotamians, from kings to shepherds. The vast majority of these relate to the administrative affairs of the temple and palace and range over a period of some three millennia. Also extant is a large corpus of letters, mostly dealing with administrative and political matters, and far fewer with private and personal concerns. I use this latter genre in a limited way; it remains to be studied in depth for what facts it can yield on the subjects here treated.

The chief source I have utilized has been myths. Despite the dangers and pitfalls of using myths, I have assumed that, like a prism, they refract and reflect societal attitudes, realities, and fantasies. But what must be underscored is that what can be learned from them are the values, sentiments, and ideals of the elite strata and not of the majority of the population, who probably were ignorant of the myths. The *Gilgamesh Epic*, too, proved to be a rich mine of information.

It must not be forgotten that throughout Mesopotamian history our sources are male-authored and male-oriented and hence androcentric in perspective. The lives of "real women, like other muted groups, are to be found not so much in the explicit text of the historical record as in its gaps and silences—a circumstance that requires the application of research methods based largely upon controlled inference."[3]

Investigating the various stages of life in Mesopotamia is no easy matter, no doubt in part due to the ancients' indifference to chronological age. Although the view that human life is made up of a series of periodizations is common in many cultures, there was little reflection on these in ancient Iraq. Nor have scholars to date found evidence of private or public rituals marking the transitions from one stage to another, and no text remains that explicitly refers to a rite of passage.

The very flexibility of and overlap in the terminology designating different age categories highlight their fluidity, which may very well have depended on one's socioeconomic status. The basic characteristics and age-appropriate behavior of the various stages can, however, be discerned and are examined in chapter 1, "The Life Course."

The *Gilgamesh Epic* is indisputably the most familiar piece of literature from Mesopotamia. Specialists and nonspecialists alike have interpreted it in a variety of ways.[4] And given the multi-dimensionality of epical literature this is not surprising. A very different interpretation—intimated by others, but never fully explored—is presented in chapter 2, "Gilgamesh's Coming of Age." Central here is the view that the changes in the Standard Babylonian Version from the Old Babylonian Version, and the additions to the Standard Babylonian Version made by the ancient poet-editor, Sin-leqi-unnini, reflect his personal experiences and professional life as an exorcist. His was a profession with a rite of initiation wherein the arcane knowledge of the initiated was transmitted to the novice. The *Gilgamesh Epic* accordingly may be "read" as a metaphorical initiation of the hero in his transition from ignorant youth to mature adult. The threefold aspects of the rite of passage from separation through liminality to incorporation are delineated in Gilgamesh's departure from Uruk to find immortality, his search for and stay with Utnapishtim, and his return to Uruk. The consummate artistry and profound insights of Sin-leqi-unnini on youth and adulthood are indirectly revealed throughout the epic.

The next four chapters are gerontological studies on aging and the elderly. The attitudes toward the elderly as well as the physiological and psychological characteristics associated with old age are treated in chapter 3, "On Aging and the Elderly." Despite the proverbial ideal of respect for the aged, ambiguities abound in the responses of the younger members of society toward the old, and of the elderly toward their own increasing decrepitudes. The same ambivalence characterizes the few literary representations of senectitude that remain.

Little wonder, then, that generational conflict resulted from the reluctance of elders to yield or at least share their power with younger men. Of significance too is the fairly late age at marriage of well-to-do men, who were usually in their mid-twenties to very early thirties before establishing their own households. In chapter 4, "The Conflict of Generations in Ancient Mesopotamian Myths," the pervasive motif of generational tension and struggle is traced in Sumerian and Akkadian myths, the *locus classicus* being the so-called Babylonian creation story, *Enuma Elish*. The pro-youth bias of the myths suggests that they may have served as an outlet for the young to vent their frustration, while protecting the diminishing authority of the elders, and hence were a means of mitigating generational antagonism.

The above studies concentrate on men; by and large they do not deal with women's lives. In chapter 5, "Gendered Old Age in *Enuma Elish*," the focus is on gender differences in aging patterns. Utilizing the pioneering work of the developmental psychologist David Gutmann, I assess the psychological aspects of aging portrayed in *Enuma Elish*. In this myth the old gods have shifted from a mode of "active mastery" in youth to the "passive mastery" of the old, from "aggressive, competitive behavior" to "apathy and immobility." In sharp contrast, in the course of the mythological events, the goddess Tiamat is transformed from a quiescent, passive, young wife and mother into an increasingly assertive and agentic old widow. *Enuma Elish* depicts the old goddess as a monstrous crone assuming masculine characteristics, a ubiquitous, misogynistic stereotype attested to cross-culturally.

Chapter 6, "Old(er) Women," is the first lengthy study on this subject in Assyriology. Scholars have only in recent years begun to examine the lives of older women in general. One may assume that in Mesopotamia, as in other traditional societies, women were considered old when they were beyond their childbearing years or when their children had children. To what extent an old woman might enjoy a greater margin of freedom than in her earlier years is open to speculation. But there is some evidence that, given the existence of the little-known impurity rules associated with menstruation and childbirth, the onset of menopause may very well have liberated her from certain social and ritual restrictions. Elderly women are likely to have taken on new roles such as mediator, intercessor, and advisor in addition to occupations such as beer brewers, dream interpreters, midwives, and caretakers. In this chapter widows are given special attention, among them dowager queens.

Male attitudes toward and fantasies about desirable female exemplars are assessed in chapter 7, "Images of Women in the *Gilgamesh Epic.*" Although the epic centers on the adventures of the hero and his intimate friend Enkidu, various women play subsidiary and supportive parts. All except the goddess Ishtar assist Gilgamesh in his search for immortality. They act maternally as women of ancient Mesopotamia were expected to. Only the goddess acts like a man, proposing marriage to the hero, a proposal he scornfully and insultingly rejects. She then responds in masculine fashion, seeking revenge. Her actions are regarded negatively. Symbolic inversion, a significant feature of the epic, is a key to understanding its humorous, comedic aspects.

In chapter 8, the two versions of the myth of *Nergal and Ereshkigal* serve as a source for recovering masculine views about appropriate relationships between the sexes, especially in the area of sexuality. These in turn are examined in light of evidence found in nonmythological contexts. In ancient Mesopotamia, the essential characteristics of masculinity were mastery and dominance. Relations with a sexually aggressive woman represented an unacceptable surrender of power. Because woman's sexual desire was viewed as stronger and more voracious than man's, the woman was expected to submit to him lest he become emasculated. Women, in contrast to men, placed a higher valuation on relationship and bonding, which made for dependence on the male. Nevertheless, the ideal spousal relationship was one of mutuality and shared sexual passion, which laid the foundation for a faithful, contented marriage.

Researchers have estimated that probably far less than one percent of all adult Mesopotamian males were literate. For women, the figure would have been considerably smaller. Chapter 9, "The Female 'Sage' in Mesopotamian Literature," is a preliminary attempt to integrate the little evidence that remains on women's contributions to cultural activities: the female scribe as bureaucrat, as poetess, as scholar. Also discussed are women as performing artists, healers, mantics, and counselors, areas that did not require literacy. One can only conclude from the extant sources that only a handful of elite women—most likely royal women, who also served as celibate priestesses—had the leisure, talent, and desire to become literate.

The most significant, long-enduring goddess of the Mesopotamian pantheon, the Sumerian Inanna, later identified with the Semitic Ishtar, has been studied for generations by specialists and nonspecialists alike. In recent years, she has been appropriated by feminists, some of whom regard her as "an image of the deity who can, perhaps, carry the suffering and redemption of modern women."[5] In chapter 10, "Inanna-Ishtar as Paradox and a Coincidence of Opposites," I present a different perspective on this complex and multifaceted goddess, viewed in light of her distinctiveness and uniqueness. In her transcendence of the boundaries characteristic of human life lies the key to her awesomeness and formidable power. The separation between the sexes, between one species and another, between categories of age and status, become blurred in her. She is a deity who incorporates both order and disorder and thereby transcends them.

During the past several years of researching and writing these studies, I have often been mindful of the concerns expressed by my teacher and mentor, the late Leo Oppenheim, in his now-classic *Ancient Mesopotamia*. He decried "the stagnation" demonstrated in "the shrinkage of topics suited for research" and urged the need for new directions in Assyriological studies, as well as for syntheses of the information yielded by the remaining sources.[6] Many have responded to his challenge. I hope that in some small measure I have too.

ACKNOWLEDGMENTS

I am greatly indebted to the scholarly work of many Assyriologists and Sumerologists and acknowledge their contributions in the notes. I am especially grateful to Robert D. Biggs for sharing with me his forthcoming study, "The Human Body and Sexuality in Mesopotamian Medical Texts," and permitting me to freely quote from it. Ann K. Guinan's written and oral communications on the issue of older women's sexuality were very helpful. Throughout I have utilized *The Assyrian Dictionary of the University of Chicago*. Indeed, without this monumental work this book would not have been possible.

These studies were written over a period of several years. Five were previously published and appear here with permission: "Images of Women in the *Gilgamesh Epic*," in *Lingering over Words: Studies in Ancient Near Eastern Literature in Honor of William L. Moran*, Harvard Semitic Studies 37, ed. T. I. Abusch, J. Huehnergard, and P. Steinkeller (Atlanta, Ga.: Scholars Press, 1990), 219–230; "The Female 'Sage' in Mesopotamian Literature," in *The Sage in Israel and the Ancient Near East*, ed. J. G. Gammie and L. G. Perdue (Winona Lake, Ind.: Eisenbrauns, 1990), 3–17; "Inanna-Ishtar as Paradox and a Coincidence of Opposites," in *History of Religions* 30:3 (February 1991): 261–278, ©1991 by The University of Chicago. All rights reserved; "The Conflict of Generations in Ancient Mesopotamian

Myths," in *Comparative Studies in Society and History* 34:4 (October 1992): 621–635, ©1992 by Cambridge University Press, reprinted with the permission of Cambridge University Press; "Gendered Old Age in *Enuma Elish*," in *The Tablet and the Scroll: Near Eastern Studies in Honor of William W. Hallo*, ed. M. E. Cohen, D. C. Snell, and D. B. Weisberg (Bethesda, Md.: CDL Press, 1993), 111–115. Slight changes have been made in some of the essays. I am grateful to their publishers for permission to republish them.

Roland Larsen, circulation librarian at the School of the Art Institute, was assiduous in the acquisition of interlibrary loan books necessary for my research. Shanna Linn, academic program coordinator of the Liberal Arts and Art History Departments of the School of the Art Institute, expedited the transcription of the early drafts of several chapters.

I am grateful to Carol Becker, dean of the School of the Art Institute, for the contribution toward secretarial services in the final draft of the manuscript. I am indebted to freelance copy editor Sally Bennett for her superb editing of the manuscript, which improved it in many ways.

Most of all, and always, I am grateful to and for my husband of more than five decades, helpmate and soul mate with whom I have shared significant stages of my life cycle as wife, student, mother, and grandmother. His abiding help and encouragement have sustained me throughout. Dedicating this book to him is but a small token of my love and gratitude.

CHRONOLOGICAL TABLE

Early dynastic periods   ca. 2900–ca. 2350 B.C.E.

Dynasty of Akkad (Agade)   ca. 2350–2193 B.C.E.
    Sargon (2334–2279 B.C.E.)
    Naram-Sin (2254–2218 B.C.E.)

Third Dynasty of Ur (Ur III)   ca. 2112–2004 B.C.E.
    Ur-Nammu (2112–2095 B.C.E.)
    Shulgi (2094–2047 B.C.E.)
    Shu-Sin (2037–2029 B.C.E.)

Isin Dynasty   2017–1794 B.C.E.

Larsa Dynasty   2025–1763 B.C.E.
    Rim-Sin (1822–1763 B.C.E.)

Old Babylonian Dynasty (Hammurapi Dynasty)   1894–1595 B.C.E.
    Hammurapi (1792–1750 B.C.E.)
    Ammisaduga (1646–1626 B.C.E.)

Kassite Dynasty   1595–1185 B.C.E.

Middle Assyrian State   ca. 1400–950 B.C.E.

Neo-Assyrian Empire   ca. 950–627 B.C.E.
   Shamshi-Adad V (823–811 B.C.E.)
   Adad-nirari III (810–783 B.C.E.)
   Sargon II (721–705 B.C.E.)
   Sennacherib (704–681 B.C.E.)
   Esarhaddon (680–669 B.C.E.)
   Ashurbanipal (668–627 B.C.E.)

Neo-Babylonian Dynasty (Chaldean Dynasty)   625–539 B.C.E.
   Nebuchadnezzar II (604–562 B.C.E.)
   Nobonidus (555–539 B.C.E.)

Fall of Babylon to Persia   539 B.C.E.
Persian domination   538–331 B.C.E.
Alexander enters Babylon   330 B.C.E.

GENDER AND AGING
IN MESOPOTAMIA

CHAPTER ONE

THE LIFE COURSE

To date scholars have done little work on the life course in ancient Mesopotamia.[1] Mesopotamia, like other preindustrial societies, had no interest in chronological age.[2] Nor was it a formally age-graded or age-set society, one in which age was the primary criterion in determining roles. This perhaps accounts for the absence of data on rites of passage; neither formal nor informal mechanisms or rituals marking the entry or exit of individuals through the different stages of life seem to have existed. Nevertheless we learn indirectly of what have been termed "age norms," especially for the young and the old. In the sources we can discern views regarding appropriate activities and behavior at particular life stages. And these norms constrained Mesopotamians to behave in acceptable ways.

The Mesopotamians seem to have viewed life as a road, a course to be traveled.[3] At the end of the road lay death. Nothing in the sources parallels the Egyptian view of life as a boat that finds safe harbor from the storm of life at death.[4] Death as an integral part of life is a significant theme of the *Gilgamesh Epic*, especially in the Old Babylonian Version. The transitoriness and brevity of human existence are referred to in a variety of poetic ways:

The whole of life is but a twinkling of the eye[5]
Whatever he possesses a man does not really possess. Death
    is the (real) owner of property[6]

> Only gods dwell forever with the sungod, mere man his days
> are numbered, whatever he may do he is but wind[7]
> Mankind, whose offshoot is snapped off like a reed in a
> canebrake . . . yet there is savage death that snaps off
> mankind[8]

Only the gods were thought to be immortal, though even they might on occasion die, as did Dumuzi and Kingu.

W. G. Lambert is of the view that man was first created without a fixed life span, but as a result of a misdemeanor death was ordained for him.[9] Perhaps embedded in *The Sumerian King List*, with its incredibly long-lived antediluvian rulers, is the perspective of a utopian age when humans lived longer and were stronger and closer to the gods than in the postdiluvian period.[10]

Although the different life stages obviously manifest themselves in physiological changes, there seems to have been little interest in these in both written and visual sources, for they are rarely described or depicted (see chapter 3). Psychological traits and age-specific behavior appear to have been of greater interest, to judge from the literary texts.

The poet-editor of the Standard Babylonian Version of the *Gilgamesh Epic*, Sin-leqi-unnini, in particular exhibits an unusual fascination with the various life stages, especially with the transition from youth to mature adulthood (see chapter 2). This is revealed in a variety of ways, including the simile used to describe the Urukians' response to Enkidu when he makes his first appearance in their city: "The populace was thronging about him, the men were clustered about him and kissed his feet as if he were a little baby."[11] B. R. Foster has insightfully commented on Gilgamesh's rejection of Ishtar's marriage proposal, saying that the hero "is talking to her as if she were still a girl in school." The hero's language, he notes, is reminiscent of debating, "a cultivated *school-boy* art [my emphasis]."[12] The goddess then proceeds to act in childish ways in responding to his repudiation, crying and weeping to the gods Anu and Antum, threatening to destroy mankind if she is not given the

Bull of Heaven to kill Gilgamesh. So too is the puerility of Enkidu called attention to when he blames others (the harlot and the trapper), cursing them for his own shortcomings (Tablet VII 78–121). Especially telling is his speaking to an inanimate object: "You stupid wooden door, with no ability to understand" (Tablet VII 33 f.). Sin-leqi-unnini conveys the depth of the love between the two coevals, Enkidu and Gilgamesh, in their kissing one another and holding hands in mutual support of one another.[13] Their contemporaneousness generates a special empathy and affection. Finally, the age category *eṭlu* "young man" is used over and over again, signaling the author's focus on age categories.[14]

Like other ancient peoples, the Mesopotamians believed that human beings (and inanimate objects, too) were allotted a fixed life span determined by the gods. To die a natural death was to die in accordance with one's destiny (*ūm šīmti*); to die prematurely was to die literally "the day not (in accordance with) the destinies (*ūm la šīmāti*), or to die before one's time (*ina la ūmēšu*), or to die in one's prime (*ina lalîšu imât, ina lalîšu iqatti*)."[15] One unusual text, discussed at length later in this chapter, views the extreme limit of human longevity as 120 years. But this perspective was not accompanied by a sentimental attitude toward such a life span. Instead it was a "bane" (*ikkibu*).

The fairly rich Akkadian vocabulary for descendants, those who represented the future of the community, attests to the centrality of family and concern for its continuity. Descendants vouchsafed support in old age and for a generation or two the promise of offerings and prayers to the dead, though it is doubtful whether a long-term cult of dead ancestors existed except for royalty.[16] The usual term for grandson was simply "son of the son" (*mār māri*). Far less common poetic terms occur, taken from the sphere of agriculture and animal husbandry: *inbu* (fruit tree, fruit, but also offspring, child); *liblibbu* (offspring, descendant, as well as offshoot of the date palm); *lillidu* (offspring of humans and animals, bud); *zēru* (seed of cereals and other plants, male descendants); and *per'u* (sprig, descendant). The most horrific of curses was the decimation of descendants so that "one's brazier was extinguished (*kinūnšu belû*)."[17]

A. L. Oppenheim found the omission in the *Gilgamesh Epic* of immortality achieved through progeny puzzling and suggested that the author of the Standard Babylonian Version may have functioned in the court of a childless ruler.[18] I attempt to demonstrate in the next chapter that the author in the first eleven tablets focused on the hero's transition from youth to maturity. The enormous importance of descendants to ensure offerings and hence vitality to the dead is the subject of the twelfth tablet: the more sons, the happier the lot of the deceased in the netherworld. The one with seven sons (i.e., many sons) "sits as a companion of the gods and listens to music," whereas the "one who has no one to care for him eats scraps of leftovers thrown away in the streets."[19]

The simplest breakdown of the life stages is twofold—young (*tur.meš, ṣiḫru*) and old (*gal.meš, rabû*)—categorizing everyone into one of two juxtaposed opposites. For example, a lament for the city of Ur speaking of its inhabitants mentions "the old men and women and the little ones."[20] A Nanshe hymn refers to "the guardian angel god of youngsters and oldsters."[21] This synecdoche for the totality of mankind perhaps incorporates the fundamental polarity between Youth and Old Age; their linking possibly denotes the devaluation of both stages of life, indicated occasionally in the texts themselves.

Far more frequently the life course is divided into three stages: (1) old men and women, (2) adult men and women, and (3) children.[22] Personnel ration lists in early and late periods are more detailed in their classification, and for good reason: the quantity of the rations differs considerably depending on the age and gender of the recipient. But here too is the common threefold breakdown: old persons, grown adults who are not old, and children.

Children pose some problems in classification, for they are often subdivided, at least into immature children and infants.[23] M. Stol notes that in Sumerian ration lists children are divided into three main subdivisions: from birth to five years, from five to ten years, and from ten to thirteen years.[24] In Middle Babylonian personnel rosters J. A. Brinkman found four main age categories: old (*sū.gi*(4)*, šību*), adult (*guruš, eṭlu*), adolescent (*guruš.tur, baṭūlu*), and child. The last is further divided into weaned (*pirsu*) and suckling (*dumu.gaba, mār irti*). But he notes that adolescents "often performed the same tasks as adults and were given correspondingly large rations." Hence one might conclude that this age category (*guruš.tur*) overlaps with the adult (*guruš*), just as the term *guruš.tur.tur* designates "children from the age of weaning to adolescence."[25] In short, we are essentially back to a basic threefold classification.

As scholars have found for European medieval societies,[26] so too in Mesopotamia there are "unfixed terminology and uncertainties about where age divisions should be located." I. J. Gelb observes that "the available information does not permit us to circumscribe their [the ration recipients'] age."[27] Nevertheless, he audaciously goes on to propose the duration of the age categories of adult (*guruš* and feminine *gemé*) as "between thirteen and forty." It would, therefore, follow that old age began at forty, though he does not add this sequitur.

Written sources do reveal some patterns in attitudes toward the Mesopotamian life stages, and what were considered to be their main characteristics. It should be added that even if the parameters of a life stage probably did not vary with time, they may well have done so depending on gender, socioeconomic status, and setting, whether urban or rural.

INFANCY AND EARLY CHILDHOOD

From conception, the fetus was surrounded by dangers of which the ancients were very well aware. One Sumerian proverb realistically voiced their concerns: "Marrying several wives is human/ Getting many children is divine."[28] Man may have had the freedom to marry over and over again, but having many children rested in the hands of the gods.

The infant mortality rate estimated for classical Athens would no doubt be equally true of ancient Mesopotamia, "perhaps 25–35 percent in the first year of life."[29] The perilous journey from the womb to light of day was believed to be eased by magical rituals and incantations. The latter might be intoned asking Asalluhi, god of magic, to save a child blocked from emerging from the womb:

> In the ocean waters, fearsome raging
> In the water of the far-off sea
> There is the little one, his arms are bound! . . .
> Asalluhi, Enki's son, saw him.
> He loosed his tight-tied bonds,
> He set him on the way,
> He opened him the path . . .
> "The lock is [fre]ed,
> The doors thrown wide, . . .
> Bring yourself out, there's a dear!"[30]

The Mesopotamian world was thought to be peopled with demons ready to snatch away the newborn from her mother. The male *lilû* was dangerous to pregnant women, and Lamashtu, a goddess of sorts, daughter of Anu, was especially feared. Her chief "victims were unborn and newly born babies; both miscarriage and cot death were attributed to her." Plaques depicting Lamashtu were believed to protect against her. She was a horrific composite monster with "the head of a lion, the teeth of a donkey, naked breasts, . . . long fingers and finger nails," and bird's feet.[31]

Numerous incantations are extant, recited by the exorcist to identify the causes of infants' and children's illnesses and rid them of their effects.[32] The variety of prophylactics and remedies available to counter the dangers confronting infants attest to the anxieties of parents' helplessness in the face of potentially fatal illness.

The *Atrahasis* myth, the story of the so-called Babylonian Noah, was one of the most popular tales in ancient times. Here the flood is described as sent by the gods to reduce overpopulation:[33]

In addition let there be one-third of the people
Among the people the women who gives birth yet does
Not give birth (successfully);
Let there be the *pašittu*-demon [Lamashtu] among the people,
To snatch the baby from its mother's lap.[34]

The myth validated the desirability of miscarriages, of infant mortality, and of vocations for women that precluded marriage and childbearing. The stillborn or premature infant, the *kūbu*, was apparently deified. Isin-Larsa and Old Babylonian clay plaques with moulded reliefs depict a goddess (probably the goddess of birth, Nintu) flanked by inverted omega emblems beneath which sit very thin human forms resembling newborn babies. E. Porada has suggested that these emaciated creatures may represent the *kūbu*.[35]

A rich vocabulary refers to infants, indeed a more detailed one than for any other age category, reflecting perhaps the enormous changes in development that mark the first year of life. A fetus, an unborn child, is referred to as a *ša libbiša*, "literally, belonging to her (the mother's) insides." The *kūbu*, as already noted, is the stillborn fetus. A malformed newborn, whether human or animal, is an *izbu*. The birth of malformed children under certain circumstances was considered highly ominous and often as bearing directly on the future of the state. Such omens were collected as early as the Old Babylonian period and were copied in places outside Mesopotamia. An idiosyncratic idiom limited to the Old Babylonian period is of interest: *ina mêšu*, an infant at birth, still literally "with its amniotic fluid." Limited too to the same period is the much-discussed idiom *šilip rēmim*, referring to an infant removed from the mother's womb after she has died.[36]

The common Akkadian term for baby is *šerru*; the Sumerian equivalent *lú.tur* appears only in medical diagnostic and literary texts, where it alternates with *šerru*. But *šerru* too is elastic in its range of meanings and might on occasion describe a young child beyond infancy. The adjective *ṣiḫru*, literally "little (one)" or "small (one)," is as flexible as *šerru*, including both an infant and a somewhat older child. It appears, for example, in Old Babylonian incantations recited to quiet a crying baby.[37]

Other far less common words for this life stage are instructive at times. The substantive adjective *daqqu*, appearing in lexical texts, basically also means small. It is equated with *enšutum* "weak," underscoring the vulnerability of this life stage. Another term for a small child, *qudādu A* (or *kudādu, gudādu*), appears only in lexical texts, as does *dumugabû* "suckling (infant)," a loanword from Sumerian. The Sumerian *tur.gaba* refers to a nursing baby, which he/she remains until weaned, usually at the age of two or three. Other terms include *lakû* "suckling, young, infant" (Sumerian *lú.bàn.da*), which is also used of the young of animals; *la'û* describes a small child and baby, as well as a young reed. The "suckling" (*mār* or *mārat irti*) is used in contrast to the "weaned child" (*pirsu*). A rare Sumerian loanword is *ginû*.[38]

Examples of specific chronological ages appear in connection with infants and young children. Census lists note the ages of slave children up to the age of five, for, as already mentioned, these lists concern the distribution of rations: the younger the child, the smaller the allotment.[39] One Neo-Babylonian adoption text records the adoption by a brother of his prostitute sister's son. The child, born out of wedlock, was seventeen days old, adopted shortly after his birth. The boy was to be the "next-(heir-)in-line to his own son." Interestingly, the infant remained in his mother's care. As soon as she legally married, the mother would be reimbursed for "the feeding and rearing" of the child. The child and his "brother" (really his cousin) would "together . . . serve the king and the 'Mistress-of-Uruk,'" the goddess Inanna-Ishtar.[40]

A child or animal under the age of a year was referred to as a *mār(at) šatti*.[41] Age was noted not only by years but on occasion by height, too (e.g., two cubits high).[42] Unique is an Old Babylonian record considered to be a "birth certificate" by its editor, J. J. Finkelstein, in which the birth date of a slave-girl's daughter is given. Finkelstein believes this unusual document was drafted at

the time of the mother's parturition to confirm her ongoing status
as a slave to her owner, a woman with the special status of *ugbabtu*.[43]

Little is known about the actual care of infants. It is possible, to
judge from Hittite sources, that children not yet toilet trained may
have worn some kind of apronlike covering.[44] Infants were usually
carried in one's arms. The term *kirimmu* describes the position of
the arms of the mother in cradling a small child: there was apparently a correct way and an incorrect way of holding a young
child.[45]

The vulnerability and helplessness of newborns is graphically
described in the Sumerian myth *Enki and Ninmah*, which relates,
among other things, the invention of human self-propagation by
the two gods. A. D. Kilmer has convincingly argued for viewing
Umul, a name meaning literally "My-day-is-far," as a newborn
baby, the first baby, rather than as an old man, the earlier assumption. Umul has weak lungs, heart, bowels, and arms. He cannot feed
himself, walk, speak, or stretch out his arms to take bread, cannot
lie down or stand up by himself. In short, he is a baby, totally
helpless and dependent.[46]

To protect the very young child from injury he was kept in the
house.[47] One wonders, though, whether at a young age fatal
accidents happened any less indoors than outdoors.[48]

Crying, not surprisingly, is the trait most often associated with
infants and the very young, disturbing the sleep of tired parents.
Incantations were recited in the hope of soothing a teething, fretful,
or ill young child.[49] Some, such as the following, remain:

> Why does he scream until his mother sobs,
> Till in heaven (the goddess) Antu herself's in tears? . . .
> Let his father lie down, to get the rest of his sleep,
> Let his mother, who has her chores to do, get her chores
>   done.[50]

The text suggests that there was some sharing by both mother and
father in tending to a crying infant.

Crying was characteristic not only of infants but of young children too. Dumuzi in the netherworld says to his sister who joins him there: "Tears like a child I am weeping, sobs like a child I sob to you."[51] Children's wailing was at times compared to the bellowing of animals, including cows, sheep, donkeys, and pigs.[52]

One lullaby from Sumer is extant. It is purported to have been sung by King Shulgi's wife to their ailing son and is a combination of joyful hopes and deep anxieties:

> *ua! aua!*
> In my song of joy—he will grow stout,
> In my song of joy—he will grow big, . . .
> My son, sleep is about to overtake you,
> Sleep is about to settle on you. . . .
> He [Sleep] will fill your lap with *emmer.*
> I—I will make sweet for you the little cheeses,
> Those little cheeses that are the healer of man, . . .
> In my song of joy—I will give him a wife,
> [I will] give him [a wife], I will give him a [son], . . .
> The wife will lie on his burning lap,
> The son will lie in his outstretched arms, . . .
> You are in pain,
> I am troubled,
> I am struck dumb, I gaze at the stars, . . .
> Your bones will be arrayed on the wall,
> The "man of the wall" will shed tears for you,
> The *keeners* will pluck the harps for you, . . .
> May you have an eloquent guardian-angel,
> May you *achieve* a reign of happy days.[53]

The baby incantations studied by W. T. Farber are probably examples of originally oral lullabies or, as he puts it, lullabies "in disguise" that were written down and incorporated into the larger corpus of magical texts. The above lullaby shares with the baby incantations a mix of feelings, including tenderness, anxiety, and anger, characteristic of lullabies everywhere.[54]

But a normal healthy baby was considered to be a happy one, a child endowed by the goddess Inanna with joy (*di₄.di₄.lá šà.ḫúl.la*),[55] a child of sweetness who appealed to all who came in contact with him or her. The usual response to the young child was to embrace and kiss the child, as the people of Uruk were said to have greeted Enkidu on first seeing him (as noted earlier).[56] A Dumuzi story describes the demonic character of those who came to seize the god by saying that "they kissed not that sweet thing, a child."[57] Theirs is unnatural behavior. A striking inclusion among the powers of the goddess Inanna is kissing the lips of a baby (along with building a house, making living quarters, and acquiring household utensils).[58] Unusual is an Old Babylonian legal text stating: "I will kiss my child's (*ṣiḫrija*) lips and make a statement to you under oath by the emblem of the god Shamash." This seems to be some kind of symbolic act.[59] Of interest too is this scholastic comment to the New Year Akitu ritual: "The king who kisses the gods, this represents Marduk whom, in his childhood (*ina ṣeḫērišu*), (the goddess) Ninlil used to carry and kiss."[60]

Young and older children are rarely depicted in Mesopotamian art. This is not surprising, given the nature of much of Mesopotamian art, which is royal and/or religious. But this contrasts with the art of the West, where children are at times depicted, as well as with ancient Egyptian art. However, children are occasionally seen on Neo-Assyrian reliefs in the scenes showing the deportation of captive families (see figure 1). At times mothers and even fathers are shown kissing children, as well as tenderly carrying them in their arms or on their shoulders, or giving them something to drink from animal skin bags. The inclusion of such scenes may have aimed at showing observers the graciousness of the victors to compliant and vulnerable prisoners.[61]

The loving and affectionate demonstrativeness of adults toward the very young finds expression in the literary topos of adults dandling children on their knee (*birku*), to be played with and

Figure 1. Detail from a seventh-century B.C.E. Neo-Assyrian relief of the siege of Lachish showing men, women, and children being led into captivity. Courtesy of the Trustees of the British Museum, neg. no. 122962.

admired. The fervent wish of kings (and surely of ordinary people too) was to live to dandle grandchildren on their knee.[62] The inhuman demons who carry Dumuzi off to the netherworld are described as making "a man's child get up from his knee."[63] The dead king Ur-Nammu sadly can no longer lift his son onto his knee once he descends to the Land of No Return.[64] In the devastating aftermath of the destruction of the city of Ur, the goddess Ningal laments: "The little ones, asleep on their mothers' laps, were carried off like fishes by the water. On their nurses of strong arms, the strong arms were (pried) open." And on a similar note, the goddess Nininsina mourns: "My house where no sweet child dwells with me."[65] The last two passages describe the frightful consequences of war, especially devastating to the very old and the very young.

Generally, children seem to have been treated with affection. A symbolic act of adoption might have been the placing of the child on the adoptive father's lap.[66] A special idiom, šerra kunnû, describes the pampering of children.[67] Toys and games were part of the joyful side of the lives of children at all ages. For infants there were "pie-crust" rattles and zoomorphic rattles with pebbles inside.[68]

But there was also a dark side to the treatment of infants and young children: abandonment and exposure by some parents, who chose to reject children with deformities or were too impoverished to care for their children. An exposed child is described in vivid idioms as one "who was found in a well," "who was taken in from the street," "who was snatched from the dog's mouth," "who was let go from the raven's mouth," and most simply "who has no/who does not know his father (and) mother." Foundlings might be identified from the names given to them: "He-of-the-dog's-mouth," "He/She-of-the-street," or "He-has-been-left-over-from-the-dog's-mouth," to mention a few such names. At times these children might have been adopted by childless couples or individuals.[69] Exposure and infanticide have likewise been known "to co-exist with solicitous care and affection for children both in societies studied by anthropologists . . . and in pre-industrial Europe."[70]

In death, as in life, infants had little impact on the community. Many were buried within the confines of houses, a practice not restricted to infants. In Ur, at least, M. van de Mieroop notes that "the intriguing aspect of domestic architecture" in the Old Baby-lonian period is the presence of burials beneath the floors, which correlate with the occupation of the houses: "They were not randomly placed in rooms but usually appeared in the second largest room of the house."[71] Some information remains on burial in early and later Nuzi. In one case, an infant of two months or less was found "lying flexed in a large potsherd." Bones of eleven infants had been placed in a large jar with a small hole at the bottom. Two were "buried under walls in flat-bottomed urns covered with lids." "A third infant . . . was placed in the blocking of a door." The number of graves at Tepe Gawra had a "dispropor-tionately large number of infants' and children's bodies," which suggests "that the majority of the population was buried else-where." Inverted jars were the type commonly used for infant burials. R. Ellis opines that the divine status of the *kūbu* may account for the special burial of some infants, such as those in the private chapels of Ur.[72] Jacobsen suggests that "Nigingar was a temple in Isin which served as a cemetery for stillborn or premature babies and as a depository for afterbirths."[73] Noteworthy is the name of the first baby, Umul, whose name literally means "My-day-is-far," implying that death would be distant for the newborn, the hope of every parent.

Did the Mesopotamians grieve when their children died, as so many did? M. Golden presents a cogent treatment of this question as it relates to the ancient Greek's response and answers with a resounding affirmative.[74] And so too should the response be for ancient Mesopotamia. Golden discusses the burial of Athenian children within the house and the far less elaborate funeral rites for the young. As for the house burial, he suggests that such a burial may be "a form of sympathetic magic, a statement that the household welcomes children; or as a mark of the parent's unwillingness to give up a treasured child completely."[75] The same might well be true of infant burial in Mesopotamia.

Though little remains to inform us, the Mesopotamians must have mourned the death of their young children with great sorrow. The laments of Dumuzi's mother at his death are for an adult child, but they probably tell us about a mother's mourning at any child's death.[76] Touching and poignant is the passage in the Sumerian Gilgamesh episode where the hero asks the dead Enkidu, "Did you see my little stillborn children (tur.tur) which never came to consciousness?" Enkidu responds "<Yes, I saw them>: they play at a table of gold and silver with honey and ghee." How consoling a response to the father who apparently had never forgotten them.[77]

Telling too is the Mari letter of one man to another: "Before the king (Zimri-Lim) reaches Mari, tell him that his infant daughter is dead, and may he understand."[78] Perhaps he was to be told before reaching home to prepare him and also to spare his wife from having to tell him the sad news. In another letter the queen informs him: "I have given birth to twins, may my lord rejoice."[79] This, in contrast, was joyous news, indeed.

LATER CHILDHOOD

We are again faced with ambiguity and uncertainty as to when a child moved beyond early childhood to a point when some responsibility and minor working obligations would be assumed. Nor is the vocabulary helpful in making a determination, for it too is elastic and overlapping, so much so that the common term *ṣiḫru* "child" (Sumerian *lú.tur; tur.tur*) applies to infants and young adults. The word *ṣuḫāru* (feminine *ṣuḫārtu;* Sumerian *tur.tur*) can mean "(male) child" and "adolescent."[80] What is common to *ṣiḫru* and the other terms used for this life stage is their derivation from the verb *ṣeḫēru* "to be small, to be young, to be a minor," in short, to be insignificant, very much like the Greek *pais*, whose root meaning is also "small" or "insignificant" and means both "child" and "young person."[81] *Ṣeḫru/ṣuḫāru* can also describe persons of subordinate status.[82] The *ṣiḫru*, G. Evans observes, was not only young "but incapable of protecting his own interests . . . or of undertaking the rights and responsibilities of a *full* [my emphasis] member of society."[83] He adds that in Babylonia a person remained young (really a minor) for many years after reaching his majority. And as D. Marcus puts it, in Mesopotamia "a minor, for all intents and purposes, was one who was living in his or her parent's house."[84]

The marginality of children, as noted in chapter 3, is seen in their frequent mention in the texts alongside old men and women. The vulnerability of a child is noted in a proverb: "Vex a boy (*[lú].tur.ra*) and he will weep."[85] A child could not give orders to an adult or hold office.[86] A grown adult might be taunted for being childish as Yasmah-Adad frequently is by his father, Shamshi-Adad, king of Mari (see example later in this chapter). And one Sumerian proverb says: "Your actions are childish, there is nothing manly about them."[87]

Children needed to be taught morality and piety by parents, for in their youthfulness (*meṣḫerūtu*) "they are too inexperienced to know whether they have committed a transgression."[88] A deprived child was one for whom "no mother lived with him, talked it over with him." The task of parents was to guide and direct children, just as a boat had to be steered in the right direction.[89]

Enkidu, like a child in his ignorance when he first appears in the Akkadian *Gilgamesh Epic*, is at home with the animals whom he resembles: "His whole body was shaggy with hair. . . . He ate grasses with the gazelles, and jostled at the watering hole with the animals; as with animals his thirst was slaked with (mere) water."[90] The harlot, like a mother, must teach him how to eat, drink beer, wash himself with water, and rub himself with oil; in short, she transforms him into a civilized human being.[91]

The strong bonds between parents and children served to define personal religion in the second millennium, when the gods were regarded as parents par excellence. Jacobsen describes this new perspective: "The religious individual sees himself standing in close personal relationship to the divine, expecting help and guidance in his personal life and personal affairs, expecting divine anger and punishment if he sins, but also profoundly trusting to divine compassion, forgiveness and love for him if he sincerely repents."[92] The task of the parent, as Siduri counsels Gilgamesh, is to "attend to the little one who holds unto your hand."[93]

One, perhaps sentimental, clause was added in a Middle Assyrian will in favor of a daughter; it provided for a further transfer of property to her brothers should she have no children. But she would have the right "to keep for herself the bed of her childhood" (*erša ša ṣeḫrūtīša*). C. Saporetti describes the addition as "a very rare example indeed with a trace of humanity and affection."[94]

As for schooling, only royal male offspring and sons of the well-to-do and professionals such as scribes, diviners, physicians, exorcists, and palace and temple administrators would be sent to school (*eduba*, literally, "house of the tablet").[95] Few Mesopotamian rulers were literate. Shulgi (2094–2047 B.C.E.), second ruler of the Ur III dynasty, boasts in his hymns of his erudition and learning, claiming to have become a skilled scribe.[96] Ashurbanipal, one of the last Assyrian kings (668–627 B.C.E.), living almost 1500 years later than Shulgi, also speaks with pride about his accomplishments:

I am versed in the craft of the sage Adapa; . . . I studied the secret lore of the entire scribal craft, I know the celestial and terrestrial portents. I discuss with competence in the circle of the masters; . . . I can solve the most complicated divisions and multiplications which do not have a solution.[97]

The schoolmaster believed that sparing the rod spoiled the child, so caning was considered the appropriate means of punishing in order to teach. The evidence of the texts, S. N. Kramer observes, attests that "the ancient pedagogues had their hands full trying to control pupils who took pleasure in pushing, shouting, quarreling, and cursing." And given that "one of the major motivating forces of Sumerian behavior [was] the drive for superiority and pre-eminence with its great stress on competition and success," one would expect an energetic, aggressive student body.[98] The severity of the punishment presupposes that schoolchildren were thought to be lacking in intelligence and self-control.

One Old Babylonian letter written by the schoolboy Iddin-Sin to his mother, Zinu (wife of the governor of Larsa), vividly captures the spirit of a clever and manipulative child who is already something of a "clothes-horse":

From year to year, the clothes of the (young) gentlemen here become better, but you let my clothes get worse from year to year. Indeed, you persisted (?) in making my clothes poorer and more scanty. At a time when in our house wool is used up like bread, you have made me poor clothes. The son of Adad-iddinam, whose father is only an assistant of my father, (has) two new sets of clothes [break] while you fuss even about a single set of clothes for me. In spite of the fact that you bore me and his mother only adopted him, his mother loves him, while you, you do not love me![99]

But only a small number of children were taught the three Rs; the best of these went on to receive further instruction, and some even a university education. Most boys were taught their father's trade or were apprenticed out to learn a trade or worked alongside their father in the fields.[100] It was believed that the god Enlil ordained that a son follow his father's profession or trade.

As M. Golden remarks about classical Athens, "children make economic contributions to their families in many cultures, in ways which differ so greatly in respect to age, social status, gender roles and organization that any except the most careful use of comparative materials is hazardous in the extreme."[101] But he adds that their indirect contributions should not be slighted. So too in Mesopotamia most sons must have gradually learned to participate in their fathers' activities in the fields and workshops. As in ancient Egypt,[102] from perhaps the age of seven on, if not earlier, their participation would become increasingly important. Girls from this age on, and perhaps even younger, must have helped their mothers with household chores and looking after younger siblings.

Children probably not much older than three or four might run errands for their mother: "Like a child (*dumu*) sent on an errand by its mother, she went [from the chamber]."[103] From Mari texts and elsewhere we know that children accompanied working mothers, who were given extra rations for them. The children might when able be given simple tasks.[104] Although few of the tasks performed are specified, some are mentioned: boys might be hired to pick up clods (*kirbānu*) in the fields or might even work in textile workshops as teaselers (*kunšillu*), which required some manual dexterity.[105]

Children, mentioned in Ur III ration lists, are usually not distinguished by gender but simply designated as *dumu* "child." But even when they are gender-differentiated, the rations do not differ, in contrast to those for adults. However, H. Waetzoldt suggests that rations did differ according to age: 10 liters of barley (and sometimes wool) for children from infancy up to age five; 15 liters for children from five to ten; 20 liters for "adolescents" from ten to thirteen. Thereafter they were usually considered adults. He thinks that children probably began performing light labor in the weaving centers when they were five or six years of age.[106] The lot of women and children working as weavers in the Ur III period was a very difficult one: as many as one-third of the women and children are recorded as having died, and at least 5 out of 224 had fled.[107] The grim life of servile laborers is also reflected in the personnel rosters of the Middle Babylonian period, in which "the principal physical conditions listed as impairments (present and past) on work rosters" are death, illness or physical handicap (blindness), and escape.[108]

Poverty and debt might compel a man to sell his children. Documentation for this is largely confined to the Ur III and Old Babylonian periods.[109] But in the Neo-Babylonian period, too, siege of the city might have driven some parents to sell their children to those who could feed them.[110] Such transactions took place in unusual and dire circumstances and were not approved of. As one proverb puts it, "The strong man lives off what is paid for his strength / The weak man off what is paid for his children."[111]

Despite the necessity of long days either at school for the elite children or at work for the vast majority of children, play was an integral part of their life before crossing the threshold into the adult world of marriage and raising a family. Children played on the streets and roads of villages and cities.[112] Ereshkigal, goddess of the netherworld, appealing to the sympathies of the gods so that they will grant her request to have Nergal return to her, says:

> Since I was a young girl (*ṣeḫrākuma*)
> I have not known the play of maidens (*ardāti*)
> Nor have I known the frolic of little girls (*ṣeḫḫerāti*)."[113]

A. D. Kilmer's study, "Games and Toys in Ancient Mesopotamia," gives us some idea of the variety of children's play. For boys there were toy weapons, toy ships, carts, wagons, chariots, and a variety of toy animals, as well as action toys such as spinning tops, yo-yos, and balls, along with dice and stone games. For girls, there were dolls and miniature furniture for playing house, skipping ropes, and perhaps action toys shared with boys.

Nothing is known about children's sexuality or about adults' views on it. However, it is believed that prepubescent boys, as well as girls who had not had sexual intercourse—like old women no longer having sexual relations—were considered pure and therefore participated in certain rituals. Their purity apparently conferred curative powers and protected them from the malevolence of witches.[114] Of interest too is this Sumerian proverb: "Bread that has not had time to mature [is like] a child(-bride) [who] will not come into her husband's embrace—that does not last long." Jacobsen interprets this proverb to mean that just as freshly baked bread cannot be eaten right away but needs time to age "so too young a wife needs time to reach sexual maturity."[115] Marrying too immature a girl was frowned on.

Examples of children in ancient Mesopotamian art are rare, as mentioned earlier, and are largely confined to the Early Dynastic and Neo-Assyrian periods. Frequently reproduced is the Early Dynastic Ur-Nanshe plaque showing the king of Lagash as paradigmatic builder of temples, carrying a basket of mud on his head to mould the first brick, while his family and some courtiers look on.[116] On the top register are depicted his daughter and four sons; in the lower register are three more sons. The daughter, wearing a flounced garment, is much taller than her brothers and therefore is presumably an adult. The clothing of the sons is not flounced; nor is that of the courtiers. The sons vary slightly in height, the tallest about the height of the man standing behind the seated Ur-Nanshe in the lower register, who looms in size above all in both his representations, in accordance with the Mesopotamian convention of "social perspective." The sons are depicted as miniature adults. Their ages are unknown; perhaps only the relative differences in height suggest the age differences.

Noteworthy too is the votive statue with only the remains of small legs of a child who must have stood alongside his mother, the wife of an Early Dynastic ruler of Eshnunna. It was found along with other votive statues in the temple of Abu.[117] The nudity of boys shown in Neo-Assyrian reliefs may be emblematic of young children already toilet-trained.[118]

The terms "adolescence" and "adolescent" are occasionally found in Assyriological studies, as is the term "teenager," most notably to translate the Akkadian *batultu* (feminine) and *batūlu* (masculine).[119] But did the Mesopotamians have a recognizable phase in the life course between childhood and adulthood, corresponding to our adolescence? The flexibility of the Akkadian terminology suggests not. Perhaps the distinction should more precisely be made between early adulthood and mature adulthood.

ADULTHOOD

Mature adulthood was the most valued life stage for the Meso-potamians, to judge from their art, which, with few exceptions, depicts most men and women as neither very youthful nor very old, a point I make in several other chapters. The *Gilgamesh Epic* is a remarkable portrait of the hero's transition from youth to mature adulthood, exploring the characteristics of the former and its shortcomings (as described in chapter 2). The eventual acceptance of responsibility to community and of the inevitability of death are features of mature adulthood.

The usual term for male adult is *eṭlu* (Sumerian *[lú.]guruš*). It has been described in *The Assyrian Dictionary* as the group between the full-grown man and the *batūlu*, the adolescent male.[120] But as the references demonstrate, the term is often more inclusive, referring also to adult, able-bodied men and therefore to both the young and the mature adult. Yasmah-Adad, one of Shamshi-Adad's two grown sons, is continually berated by his father for his lack of maturity:

As to you, how long will we have to guide you? Are you still young (*ṣeḫret*)? Are you not a grown man (*eṭlet*)? Is there no beard on your chin? How much longer will you fail to administer then your own house? Do you not see your brother commanding large armies? Administer then your palace and house![121]

This letter points up some of the expectations of adulthood: independence from another's supervision, taking responsibility for managing one's own affairs, and, for a prince, leading an army. Having a beard was one of the secondary characteristics of the adult male. Indeed, a Sumerian equivalent for the Akkadian *eṭēlu* "to grow up" is "to grow a beard on the cheeks."[122] Akkadian males had fairly elaborate beards, especially those of the royals and the elite, that underwent style changes down the centuries.[123]

When a boy became an *eṭlu*, he reached his full growth and stature (*minītu*) and was characterized by virility (*dūtu*), handsomeness (*banû*), and dignity (*baštu*).[124] The young men (*guruš*) of Agade were said to be endowed by the goddess Inanna with martial might (*á giš.tukul.la*).[125] A man was at the height of his vigor and strength, so that going to war was "a festival for young men,"[126] who sought the honor and glory that war afforded. The abstract noun *meṭlūtu*, derived from the verb *eṭēlu*, means "maturity, mature age," "prowess," and "excellence"—all attributes of adulthood. Lexical texts equate *mūtu*, the usual term for "husband," with *eṭlu*, the time of life when a man would marry. The abstract *mutūtu* "the position of a husband" also means "heroism" and "masculinity."[127]

The Mesopotamian elite may have had a concept of the well-mannered gentleman, in Akkadian *amīlu*, another term for "a grown man" as well as "a free man," at least in certain periods: "He should know how to behave with respect. He should not look greedily on food and beer. He should be a gentleman."[128] The late Thorkild Jacobsen in a recent study discerned several different shades of meaning to the Sumerian *lú*, the equivalent to Akkadian *amīlu*, linking it to mature adulthood.[129] In its basic meaning, the *lú* was a man who had "economic responsibility for and charge of others." In contrast to the *guruš*, who was a single man, the *lú* was the head of a household for which he was breadwinner. The term *lú* was also used of women. Men were expected to provide raw materials such as grain, wool, and so forth for the household; women were to process these materials by baking, spinning, weaving, and so on. Women were in charge of managing the household.

The lives of girls were from early childhood directed toward marriage and children.[130] Girls and women were, therefore, defined in relationship to men—as daughters, wives, and mothers. They did not, however, live the circumscribed lives of Greco-Roman women.[131] As for the age at marriage, M. T. Roth has demonstrated in her study of Neo-Babylonian urban and Neo-Assyrian rural texts that "males marr[ied] relatively late in life and females considerably earlier." She suggests "a range of fourteen to twenty for age at first marriage for women and of twenty-six to thirty-two for men."[132]

There seems not to be a specific term for menstruation in the medical texts. R. D. Biggs thinks this was so "probably because it was considered a normal phenomenon and not one needing medical intervention."[133] Nor is there to date any evidence of a rite of passage connected with the menarche.

Girls' coming of age, far more than boys', was closely linked, as it almost universally is, to biological changes. Secondary sexual characteristics such as body hair and the development of breasts marked the transition to adulthood. The girlfriends of the bride Inanna pridefully sing to her as she awaits her bridegroom Dumuzi:

> Now our breasts stand up!
> Now our parts have grown hair!
> Going to the bridegroom's loins, Baba,[134] let us be happy for
>   them!
> Dance! Dance!
> Baba, let us be happy for our parts![135]

For girls the most significant change in their lives related then to their sexual readiness for marriage.[136]

As for the terminology of this life stage, Roth has convincingly shown that, contrary to earlier opinions, the use of *batultu* "in the Neo-Babylonian marriage agreements . . . [is] in reference to a girl who [was] marriageable; she was an unmarried girl living in her father's or brother's household." Roth would also include "the component of physical virginity" in its range of meanings. In her discussion of a comparable age category, *nu'artu, also occurring in Neo-Babylonian marriage agreements, she states that like *batultu* it refers to "the status of a girl who [was] about to become a wife."[137] Both terms are very similar in meaning to the Greek *parthenos*, a "marriageable but unmarried" woman.[138] But as was the case with other categories, *batultu* too is flexible in range and is equated in lexical texts with *ki.sikil.tur*, "the common term for a young girl *up to* [my emphasis] puberty when she becomes a *ki.sikil=ardatum*."[139]

Another word used over a much longer period of time is *ardatu* "a young woman (girl or adult)," equated with *batultu* in the lexical texts.[140] Its Sumerian equivalent is *ki.sikil*, referring to a post-pubescent girl. In one lexical passage the *ardatu* is described as *la lamittu* "innocent girl," one who has not had sexual relations. The references to *ardatu* indicate that it too is elastic in meaning and can refer to both an unmarried girl and a married woman. But *ardatu* from Old Babylonian times on is limited to literary texts.

Most informative on the courting and marriage practices of Mesopotamia is the love poetry centering on the gods Inanna and Dumuzi. In his translation, T. Jacobsen has ordered the texts so that they take the young goddess from the arrangements made by the parents of the two, to their betrothal, courtship, and marriage.[141]

Young nubile women are characterized by attractiveness (*mašraḫū*), sweetness (*duššupu*), and charm (*kuzbu*), all having sexual connotations. The Sumerian *ḫi.li* (equated with Akkadian *kuzbu*) has a broad range of meanings and is commonly associated with the goddess Inanna as a young woman.[142] G. Leick has translated it as "irresist-ible sex appeal." The myth *Enlil and Ninlil* is especially replete with phrases describing the young Sud: "full of charm and delight" (58:6), "like a large, beautifully shaped cow" (58:8), and "luscious woman" (59:41), to name a few.[143]

Singing and dancing were typical activities of marriageable girls, as the passage quoted earlier from the song to Inanna indicates. Indeed, dancing is a stereotypical characteristic of girls in literary texts.[144] In one Sumerian song the goddess describes herself as "having whiled away the time, having danced, having sung ditties all day to evening."[145]

A. D. Kilmer has found in her study of dance that it seems that in Mesopotamia certain types of dancing were normally gender-restricted: "Men did not 'whirl' . . . women were associated with the circle dance; and only men performed the 'squat dance.'" There is no evidence for mixed dancing of the sexes at any time either in pairs or in groups. Different groups took turns. When women and girls danced, men looked on, and vice versa. Interestingly, old men apparently danced separately from young men, presumably at a slower pace.[146]

The most basic term for an adult woman is *sinništu* (Sumerian *munus sal*). When a woman married she became an *aššatu* "wife."[147] A woman's life as wife was one of responsibilities and obligations to her family and the management of the household, whether rich, royal, or poor.

Some relevant comments on women's dress were recently made by M. I. Marcus. She notes the almost exclusive association at Hasanlu of shroud pins with mature adult women. She believes that, at least in Mesopotamia, "women's pins were charged with symbolic meaning, possibly marking various stages of the female life cycle (marriageable girl or virgin, married women, and mother)." Moreover, at least in the Middle Assyrian legal codes of the second millennium B.C.E., "elite married women and marriageable girls were expected to wear a head covering to distinguish them from slaves and prostitutes."[148]

The birth of the first child, especially of a son, was joyfully welcomed by husband and wife. When Kubatum gives birth to the first child of King Shu-Suen of Ur, she is greeted with song and gifts:

> Because I hailed it, because I hailed it, the lord gave me things!
> Because I hailed it, with a cry of exultation, the lord gave me
> things!

A gold pin and a cylinder seal of lapis lazuli!—The lord gave
me things!
A gold ring and a ring silver inwrought![149]

OLD AGE

Aging and attitudes toward aging and the aged are treated in
several of the following chapters. But one intriguing text from the
seventh century B.C.E. (referred to usually as STT 400), published
more than thirty years ago, has been mentioned only in passing and
merits closer attention:

> Forty (years mean) prime of life (*lalûtum*)
> Fifty: short life (*ūmū kurûtu*)
> Sixty: maturity (*meṭlūtu*)
> Seventy: long life (*ūmū arkûtu*)
> Eighty: old age (*šībūtu*)
> Ninety: extreme old age (*littūtu*).[150]

Roth describes the text as "a literary composition [which] might
refer to chronological ages, but in an idealized context with no
consequence for life events." Furthermore, "there is no comment
upon the activities or social roles of those who reach any of these
ages."[151] There is nothing here of the decrepitudes of aging found in
Shakespeare's ages of man in *As You Like It*.[152] And it is a far cry from
the Athenian Solon's hebdomadal analysis of the life course.[153] Both
Shakespeare and Solon begin with infancy and end with man's
seventieth year.

The life stages noted in STT 400 are the late stages in a man's life.
(A woman's life course would have been classified quite differently;
age forty would certainly not have been her "prime of life," not when
her reproductive capacity may have already ceased or was close to
ending.) STT 400 is a laconic, idealized view of the life journey in the
later years. In striking contrast, for example, to Dante's view that the

apex of life is reached at thirty-five, with old age beginning at forty-five (a not uncommon outlook still later, in the Renaissance period), the ancient scribe believed or wished to believe that "life begins at forty."[154] One can only speculate as to why the author did not include the years of infancy through mature adulthood as did an Egyptian scribe, living in the Ptolemaic period, when he wrote his scheme of the ages of man.[155] Was it because these earlier years did not lend themselves to a decadal structure?[156] Or was the ancient scribe himself old, reflecting on the later years of life? The scheme appears to be a bookish reflection on old age, arranged chronologically: an attempt to define it, albeit all too briefly, in numerical sets. Only the last two decades—*šībūtu* "young–old age" and *littūtu* "old–old age"—are age categories.[157] It is an optimistic outlook, with a pro-old-age bias. But it is certainly not a profound perspective.

The time frame of STT 400, like that of the slave texts studied by M. A. Dandamaev, is first-millennium Babylonia.[158] He suggests, based on some questionable assumptions, that life expectancy at this time was "relatively high." He cites the examples of ten scribes with active careers over a period of thirty-eight to sixty-eight years (as well as five long-lived slaves). But as Roth has observed, these examples "cannot be indicative of a general demographic trend."[159] What is noteworthy, however, is that in a study of Old Babylonian Sippar in the second millennium B.C.E., I too found many scribes and administrators who functioned for decades.[160] Perhaps, especially in the case of scribes, we may be dealing with a phenomenon found elsewhere: creative activity and longevity go hand in hand. This was the case, for example, in fifth-century Athens, where Euripides, who died at the age of almost eighty, had just completed his greatest work, *The Bacchae*; a working Sophocles died at ninety; and Gorgias was lecturing and continued to do so until he was well over a hundred years old.[161] So perhaps beginning his age scheme at forty may tell us more about the author's life stage than anything else.

A closer look at STT 400 is warranted: forty years old meant the prime of life (*lalûtum*). The term *lalûtum* is a nuanced one, not only connoting a life of happiness, wealth, and charm but also implying sexual potency.[162] The author, therefore, from his perspective located the peak of sexual desire from age forty to forty-nine, at what we would consider middle age. Solon viewed ages twenty-eight to thirty-five (his fifth phase) as the age at which a young man should think of marrying and having children.[163] For this ancient Mesopotamian author, sixty to sixty-nine meant maturity, as well as excellence and prowess (*meṭlūtu*).[164] For Solon, "the mind of a man comes to full maturity" in the sixth period (from thirty-five to forty-two), but "he cannot now do as much, nor does he wish that he could." Again the pro-age bias of our author is revealed, subtly sustained in the neutral description of the subsequent three decades. How very different from Solon's last age, which ends at seventy: "Death, when it comes, can no longer be said to come too soon."

As noted in chapter 3, the Mesopotamians' fervent wish was for a very long life: to live for 3,600 years (a formulaic number of 60 × 60)[165] or to live long enough "to see the gray hairs in the beards of one's grandsons."[166] The picture presented in STT 400 is far from the pervading perspective, which, in my opinion, idealized neither youth nor old age.

As J. Bottéro opines in his essay "Intelligence and the Function of Power," it is a younger god Ea and not an "ancient" or "old man" such as the god Anu who is given the role of advisor, "as if to stress his capacities not only in knowledge but also in action, in speed and in versatility."[167] The name of the plant Gilgamesh wishes to take back with him to Uruk is "The-Old-Man-Becomes-Young" (*šību iṣṣaḫir*).[168] Old age is certainly not the desideratum.

The ideal life span, at least according to a bilingual version of a Sumerian folktale found at Ebla, was 120 years. J. Klein, who treated this text, pondered how they had arrived at this figure: "No doubt they arrived at it on the basis of two factors: empirical observation and speculative calculation."[169] In my view, only the second factor is feasible. As Klein himself observes, in a society where the numerical system was essentially sexagesimal, with some decimal influence, 2 × 60 or 120 is an ideal old age. Remarkably, some contemporary scientists believe that 120 years is the extreme limit of human longevity.[170]

But the Sumerian folktale views such longevity negatively: "One hundred and twenty years (are) the years of mankind—verily it is their *bane* [my emphasis] (*ikkibu*)." Klein interprets this to mean "as a punishment imposed on humanity, which cannot be revoked." He also suggests another possible meaning: this response to such longevity implies "the contempt and dislike whereby man relates to his mortality."[171] I think Klein overemphasizes what is a common cross-cultural ambiguity toward aging, with its increasing infirmities that even contemporary medicine and technology can only mitigate, but not eliminate. Old age was not, in my opinion, the stumbling block for the Mesopotamians that it was for the ancient Greeks, who were left "with a continuing resentment of old age and a consequential distortion of the idea of maturity."[172] "A life of many days, the satisfaction of growing very old (*littūtu*), good health, and happiness" was the fervent wish of kings, and surely of ordinary people, too.[173]

CHAPTER TWO

GILGAMESH'S COMING OF AGE

The late Thorkild Jacobsen with characteristic perspicacity con-
cluded his analysis of the *Gilgamesh Epic* with the observation that
"the Gilgamesh Epic is a story about growing up." He had noted
earlier that "Gilgamesh is fleeing death by fleeing old age, even
maturity; he is reaching back to security in childhood. The loss of
the [rejuvenating] plant . . . brings home [to Gilgamesh] the
necessity for growing up, for facing and accepting reality."[1]

Jacobsen, in my opinion, has divined the key theme of the
additions to the Standard Babylonian Version, written in the last
half or quarter of the second millennium. The new sections added
to the *Gilgamesh Epic*—the addition to the prologue, the enlarging
of the story of the flood, the addition of Tablet XII, various changes
made in the content of retained sections from the Old Babylonian
Version—totally change the import and meaning of the *Gilgamesh
Epic*, transforming it into a wholly different narrative.[2] These alterations are, in my opinion, the achievement of the immensely gifted
author, Sin-leqi-unnini. The *Gilgamesh Epic* is not only a great work
of art, it is also a cultural text informing us about Mesopotamian
society: its traditions, practices, and attitudes.

Some years ago J. D. Bing observed that the Akkadian version
of the *Gilgamesh Epic* was the result of a conscious revision of the
Sumerian epic "to emphasize the themes which were of more

universal interest, or to introduce new ideas and motifs reflecting cultural concerns which were more germane to the historical experience of the Babylonian society."³ I would maintain that the Standard Babylonian Version of the *Gilgamesh Epic* incorporates the concerns, interests, and personal and professional experience of the exorcist (*āšipu*) Sin-leqi-unnini. Although the ancients regarded him as the author of this version, it has been difficult for Assyriologists, with few exceptions, to do so.⁴ I have now to make the case for Sin-leqi-unnini's authorship or at least for his being its probable author. The main clues are to be found in the addition (I 1–16) to the prologue of the Old Babylonian Version:

> He who has seen everything, I *will make known* (?) to the
>   lands.
> I *will teach* (?) about him who experienced all things,
> . . . alike,
> Anu granted him the totality of knowledge of *all*.
> He saw the Secret, discovered the Hidden,
> he brought information of (the time) before the Flood.
> He went on a distant journey, pushing himself to
>   exhaustion,
> but then was brought to peace.
> He carved on a stone stela all of his toils,
> and built the wall of Uruk-Haven,
> the wall of the sacred Eanna Temple, the holy sanctuary.
> Look at its wall which gleams like *copper* (?), . . .
> Take hold of the threshold stone—it dates from ancient
>   times!
> Go close to the Eanna Temple, the residence of Ishtar,
> such as no later king or man ever equaled!⁵

Tigay opines that the prologue focuses not on the conventional "themes that would normally be stressed in epics and hymns," namely, Gilgamesh's quest to overcome death and the heroic adventures that occupy the first half of the epic, but rather on "the outcome of Gilgamesh's quest, the understanding that is to be gained."[6] Indeed, as noted by B. R. Foster, "the language, poetics, and thematics of the Old Babylonian poet are quite different from those of his Nineveh successor."[7]

Many have pointed to the depiction of Gilgamesh as a wisdom figure in the later version.[8] He has been described by Foster as "experienced, sad, wise, [and] endowed with special knowledge acquired through suffering . . . [as he] wrote of his travails" for posterity.[9] Elsewhere Foster has proposed that "the emphasis on knowledge and on love and sex as intermediary stages to perfect knowledge was primarily the work of the Nineveh poet."[10] Foster, it seems to me, is hellenic in his perspective. Mesopotamians always accepted sexuality as part and parcel of human life, and although there were to be restraints in its expression, sexuality was never denigrated. So too does the view of G. Buccellati sound overly modern (and hence alien to the Mesopotamian weltanschauung) when he writes, "Gilgamesh (in its latest version) is the great paradigm of this type of inner adventure. . . . The dominant themes in this respect are his recognition of weakness, his admission of fear, his emphasis on physical unkemptness and above all his newly discovered readiness to ask questions."[11] I will have more to say later about the hero's "physical unkemptness."

What is primarily communicated in the addition to the prologue (Sin-leqi-unnini's addition, I contend) is the acquisition by Gilgamesh of arcane knowledge, as clearly stated in lines 5 and 6 of the text: "He saw (*īmurma*) the Secret (*niṣirta*), discovered the Hidden (*katimtu*),/ he brought information of [the time] before the Flood." Sin-leqi-unnini was an *āšipu*, an exorcist priest, a member of a profession immersed in a tradition of secret texts and practices that were to be seen (*amāru*) only by the initiated. As A. L. Oppenheim observes, "Throughout these verses, the poet clearly plays with the two verbs *amāru* 'to see' . . . and *idû* 'to know, to comprehend.'" But whereas Oppenheim suggests that the two verbs are utilized "to show that Gilgamesh's experiences are both personal and correctly interpreted,"[12] I would locate them in the realm of the acquisition of

secret knowledge, the gnosis that would be relevant and of significance to the author, an exorcist.[13] As E. Ritter remarks, the skills of
the *āšipu* (the exorcist) "were transmitted exclusively by the initiated
to the initiated." The *āšipu* is "the man of tradition, the man of rote,
and of learning, the contemplative at home in the wide world."[14]
What the exorcist has to master is summed up in a catalog of the
exorcist's curriculum as "all the depths of wisdom . . . (and) the
secret lore of exorcism."[15] Most important, the existence of an extensive esoteric lore in the first- and second-millennium Mesopotamia,
the period within which Sin-leqi-unnini lived, is well attested.[16] The
Standard Babylonian Version of the *Gilgamesh Epic* thus incorporates the author's *sitz-im-leben* in remarkable ways.

Much later in the *Gilgamesh Epic* (XI 9–10), Utnapishtim begins
his story of the flood, saying to Gilgamesh, "I will reveal to you,
Gilgamesh, a thing that is hidden, a secret of the gods I tell you"
(*luptēka Gilgameš amat niṣirti u pirišta ša ilī kâša luqbīka*). And the
paradigm for acquiring occult knowledge is through the rite of
initiation. The addition (I 7–8) to the prologue more than hints at
Gilgamesh's initiation: "He went on a distant journey, pushing
himself to exhaustion / but then was brought to peace" (*[u]rḫa ruqta
illikamma aniḫ u šupšuḫ*). Significantly, the knowledge that Gilgamesh acquired was to be shared, and so "he carved on a stone stela
all of his toils" (line 9). The Akkadian term *mānaḫtu* "toils" implies
the arduous nature of his undertaking. Furthermore, not only does
Utnapishtim transmit secret knowledge from before the flood, but
he also communicates to Gilgamesh the realities of death, which is
inescapable for all but himself.[17] The seemingly unintegrated Tablet
XII,[18] an almost literal translation of half of the Sumerian episode
called "Gilgamesh, Enkidu, and the Netherworld," informs Gilgamesh about life after death, also part of secret knowledge (*pirištu ša
šamê u erṣeti*).

As already noted by Oppenheim, the distant journey that Gilgamesh makes is a euphemism for the journey "which everybody
must travel eventually."[19] I suggest that this phrase implies an
initiation during which Gilgamesh "dies" to one state of his life and

is "reborn" to another. To reiterate the essential point: the initiatory themes which I will be describing relate directly to the experiences of Sin-leqi-unnini's life as an exorcist who underwent secret rituals of initiation about which nothing is known except indirectly. The themes of symbolic initiation involve Gilgamesh's coming of age, as Jacobsen so rightly intuited: his passing from the state of childhood to that of a mature adult.

The classicist G. S. Kirk in his *Myth: Its Meanings and Functions in Ancient and Other Cultures* discerns that after Enkidu dies "a drastic piece of rearrangement takes place" in the *Gilgamesh Epic*. He poses two crucial questions: "Why does Gilgamesh withdraw from the world of culture into that of nature after his friend's death? Why is that idea so important that it runs even through the elaborated theme of his visit to Utnapishtim in search of personal immortality?" Kirk responds that "his rejection of the world and of the appurtenances of culture is a rejection of death itself."[20]

Various responses have been indirectly suggested to these questions by scholars both in and outside of the field of Assyriology.[21] In a recent article, T. Abusch observes that "Gilgamesh's wanderings in the steppe, away from civilization, unwashed and wearing skins, a trip, in effect, through the world of the dead, is a form or a phase of mourning; washing, dressing and then taking a woman are stages in the termination of the state of mourning."[22] In a stimulating discussion of the epic, T. Van Nortwick, like Kirk a classicist, views the journey of Gilgamesh as representing "the dark side of grieving, but dying unto oneself, being taken however vicariously back into the undifferentiated, unhierarchical limbo within ourselves, represented in this case by the world of the dead that can also be the first step to rebirth."[23] For Van Nortwick, Enkidu is Gilgamesh's "second self," representing "the wildness within himself." Grieving for Enkidu brings about "the spiritual evolution of Gilgamesh."[24]

My response to Kirk's questions is that the "drastic piece of rearrangement" that is "so important" from here on in the *Gilgamesh*

Epic involves Gilgamesh's becoming transformed through an initiatory process.[25] Although others have intimated such an interpretation, no one has fully analyzed the hero's transfiguration. For example, H. Wolfe has suggested quite rightly that the subject of the *Gilgamesh Epic* "is the life cycle of a hero, that is, his progress through definable stages of life especially from youth to manhood."[26]

But before we proceed to a discussion of the initiatory elements in the *Gilgamesh Epic*, another major issue must first be addressed: What evidence is there in the epic that Gilgamesh was indeed a youth who in the course of the story achieves adulthood? Jacobsen certainly sensed that the youthfulness of the hero was of prime importance: "Throughout the epic Gilgamesh appears as young, a mere boy, and he holds on to that status, refusing to exchange it for adulthood as represented by marriage and parenthood. . . . So when Enkidu dies he does not move forward seeking a new companionship in marriage, but backward in an imaginary flight toward the security of childhood." Citing from a study of the 1950s by the psychiatrist Harry Stack Sullivan, Jacobsen calls attention to the intense same-sex bonding with Enkidu as a marker to the hero's "preadolescence" (his term), which keeps Gilgamesh from "moving on to a heterosexual relationship such as is characteristic of adolescence and adulthood."[27]

It must be noted that chronological age, as such, seems to have been of no greater interest to Mesopotamians than it was to other ancients, as is discussed in chapter 1.[28] Despite *The Assyrian Dictionary*'s translation of certain terms as "adolescent" and "adolescence," there appears to have been no stage in the life cycle that corresponds to our adolescence, no period that centered on a search for self-identification.[29] Nor is there to my knowledge any evidence whether in Mesopotamia, as in ancient Rome, a public or private ceremony took place marking the transition from childhood to adulthood.[30]

The *Gilgamesh Epic*, especially in the Standard Babylonian Version, is replete with subtle and not so subtle indicators of

Gilgamesh's youthfulness. So, for example, the counsellors of Uruk in trying to dissuade the hero from doing battle with the monster Humbaba say: "You are young (*ṣiḫretima*), Gilgamesh, your heart carries you off—you do not know what you are talking about!" (II 282ff.). Later, Humbaba, overcome by Gilgamesh and Enkidu, pleads for his life: "You are young yet" (V 135). The implication perhaps is that Gilgamesh is therefore acting irresponsibly, as the young often do.

Foremost among the subtle indicators are the psychological markers, which others have noted.[31] A. L. Oppenheim long ago commented on the psychological sophistication of the ancient author of the Standard Babylonian Version, especially in his reuse of earlier materials.[32] A close reading of the epic underscores not only the author's consummate artistry but as well what a keen observer of human life he must have been.

The findings of social scientists can assist in some understanding of the dynamics of ancient life insofar as these are recoverable from textual sources. And so I have utilized cross-cultural anthropological studies of adolescence, the period between childhood and adulthood, in attempting to pinpoint its particular features in Mesopotamia.[33]

Antisocial activity is a common characteristic of youth down the ages.[34] At the very beginning of the story, after the prologue (I 56–62), Gilgamesh is described as indulging in rowdy and disruptive behavior about which the author is rather reticent. Gilgamesh takes "sexual advantage of the young women of Uruk," as well as oppressing its men.[35] His despicable behavior leads to the women's complaints to the gods and thus to the subsequent creation of Enkidu. Noteworthy too, before the Humbaba episode, is the conflict between young and old, between the elders and Gilgamesh, a minor theme in the epic (see chapter 4). Anthropologists have commented, as did Sullivan, on the importance of same-sex peer bonding at this time in life, especially of males.[36] And of course central to the epic is the intense, intimate relationship between Gilgamesh and Enkidu. Their friendship has been the subject of much study not only by Assyriologists, but in recent years especially by classicists.[37] Foster, in his important study of the late version, notes that friendship plays a much greater role in the Standard Version than in the Old Babylonian one, thus suggesting that the period of youth was of special interest to its author.[38] The relationship between Gilgamesh and Enkidu lies outside the domestic sphere and therefore for Mesopotomians bespoke their immaturity.

Perhaps instructive here is what one Shakespearean scholar has remarked: "A common Shakespearean paradigm for the condition of childhood is that of twins and twinned experience in which a pair of friends, usually of the same sex, appear to themselves and to others as identical and interchangeable. It need not . . . be a case of literal twins."[39] The strong resemblance between the two friends is underlined in the epic:

> Let him (Enkidu) be equal to his (Gilgamesh's) heart. (I 80)
> Let them be a match for each other.[40] (I 81)
> How the youth resembles Gilgamesh. (II 46)

Interestingly, W. G. Lambert has observed that at times seal cylinders depict the two as identical heroes.[41] It is also noteworthy that it is a twin who is sent to Mani in the Manichaean text discussed by S. Dalley, a text resonating with themes from the *Gilgamesh Epic*.[42]

Psychological traits that characterize youth abound in the epic: competitiveness, aggressiveness, impetuosity, recklessness, risk-taking, to mention a few. Gilgamesh's behavior before his journey to Utnapishtim contrasts strikingly with what must have been expected of a mature adult. His immaturity is revealed in the dangerous battles against the monster Humbaba and the ferocious Bull of Heaven. The admonition of the elders is of no avail. His grieving mother addresses Shamash: "Why have you imposed— nay inflicted—a restless heart on my son Gilgamesh? Now you have touched him so he wants to travel" (III 46–47). Gilgamesh in his hubris challenges and insults the goddess Ishtar, rejecting her proposal of marriage.[43]

Several times the author likens Gilgamesh to a wild bull (*rīmu*) (I 29, 52, 66, 193, 210). Foster interprets this simile as a positive attribute belonging "to the conventional inventory of terms of praise for kings."[44] For Oppenheim its meaning is obscure. I think that M. G. Kovacs is on target, capturing the simile's import with its nuance of "youthful arrogance," when she translates a passage (I 193) describing Gilgamesh as one "who struts his power over the people like a wild bull."[45] The author, I think, is critical of Gilgamesh's wild and uncontrolled behavior, frequently characteristic of youth.

Gilgamesh is excessive in his emotions. Shamhat the harlot describes him insightfully to Enkidu when she says: "I show you Gilgamesh a man of extreme feelings" (I 215). As Kovacs comments, "the original means literally 'happy-woeful man'—a man of changing moods."[46] The harlot describes him then as temperamental, which is defined by *Merriam Webster's Collegiate Dictionary* as "marked by excessive sensitivity and impulsive changes of mood < a ~ child >." The Akkadian idiom aptly captures the emotional instability of the immature Gilgamesh at the very beginning of the story.

A principal way by which youths prove themselves cross-culturally is in the demonstration of physical skills. This is easily shown to be true of both Gilgamesh and Enkidu in their battles with Humbaba and the Bull of Heaven. Anthropologists have also observed that sexual capacity and sexual attractiveness are "attributes of youth."[47] The former is only hinted at about Gilgamesh (I 62, 74), but of course it is emphasized in Enkidu's sexual encounter with the harlot for six days and seven nights (I 174–175). However, Gilgamesh's sexual attractiveness is described several times:

> Beautiful, handsomest of men
> . . . perfect . . . (I 49–50)
> Look at him, gaze at his face—
> He is a handsome youth, with freshness (?)
> his entire body exudes voluptuousness. (I 216–218)

Princess Ishtar raised her eyes to the beauty of Gilgamesh.
(VI 6)
. . . animal skins have ruined his beautiful skin. (XI 244)

The harlot comments on Enkidu's beauty, "You are beautiful,
Enkidu, you are become like a god" (I 188).

The Akkadian terms used to describe Gilgamesh—*kuzbu, dumqu,
damqu, banû,* and *inbu*—I suggest, all have a sexual nuance. Especially relevant is the scene at the very beginning of Tablet VI in
which Gilgamesh, after his battle with Humbaba, is described as
grooming and dressing himself:

> He washed out his matted hair and cleaned up his
>   equipment (?),
> shaking out his locks down over his back,
> throwing off his dirty clothes and putting on clean ones.
> He wrapped himself in regal garments and fastened the
>   sash.
> When Gilgamesh placed his crown on his head,
> Princess Ishtar raised her eyes to the beauty of Gilgamesh.
>   (VI 1–6)

Ishtar as voyeur to these activities then proposes marriage. The
emphasis on hairdo and clothing suggests that they may have been
of special concern to the elite young blades of Mesopotamia, as they
were to those of ancient Rome.[48]

Dependence on adults is a feature of childhood that should
disappear with maturity. Noteworthy here is the much greater role
played by Gilgamesh's mother in the Standard Babylonian Version
than in the earlier version, especially in her interpreting of his
dreams. He shares his fears with Ninsun when he and Enkidu
decide to do battle with Humbaba (III 20–24). Gilgamesh is depicted
then as a kind of mama's boy.[49] (Significantly, perhaps, his father
plays no role at all in the epic.) Gilgamesh will have to distance
himself from her before he can attain maturity, though maternal

figures (as I discuss in chapter 7) continue to play a role throughout the epic.

As observed by Jacobsen, Gilgamesh before his quest for Utnapishtim is still a boy who has not yet crossed the threshold into maturity. He is too immature to recognize the importance of marriage and children. For the boy Gilgamesh, Venus does not hold sway. Rejecting Ishtar's proposal of marriage, he rejects mature sexuality. (Enkidu, I might add, remains the eternal boy—he will never marry, will never sire children, and dies young.)

Two additional points in the epic may cautiously be interpreted as signs of Gilgamesh's youthfulness.[50] First, I turn to the insight of modern psychologists, which can deepen our understanding of the *Gilgamesh Epic*. They have found "that the most difficult topic for adolescents to deal with is their fear of their own death."[51] This observation calls to mind Gilgamesh's words after Enkidu's death: "Am I not like him? Will I lie down never to get up again?" This passage is reiterated three times as Gilgamesh journeys to Utnapishtim (X 72, 146, 242). There is during this period of life "a strong death anxiety and a coping behavior based almost entirely on denial. Although at any age the death of a peer can force a confrontation with one's mortality, for a young person such a loss can be especially profound, due to the fragility of the youthful ego and the intense relationship adolescents often have with their friends."[52]

For the Mesopotamians, death was an ineluctable part of the human condition, but Gilgamesh as an immature youth was devoid as yet of the "real" experiences that characterize adulthood, until Enkidu dies and he embarks on his journey. The counseling on death that Gilgamesh receives from Utnapishtim leads to his acceptance that he too, like Enkidu, must die. Perhaps the psychologically sophisticated Sin-leqi-unnini deliberately linked the hero's youthfulness to the death motif, a central theme of the earlier versions.

Of importance too are the dream-episodes, which are frequent in all the versions of the *Gilgamesh Epic*, Sumerian and Akkadian. They have been studied at some length by others.[53] The "meat," as

Cooper puts it, of the dream interpretations of the Standard Babylonian Version is the "rescuing friend" motif.[54] A recent study on dreams in myths by K. Bulkley is of significance to the subject of Gilgamesh's youthfulness.[55] Citing recent research on nightmares, Bulkley observes that people with frequent nightmares have "thin" or "permeable boundaries": the formation of boundaries is part of a child's development of mental structures, and thin boundaries are characteristic of children. Bulkley thinks that such boundaries accurately characterize the personalities of both Gilgamesh and Enkidu, who suffer from "harrowing nightmares in the epic" (this is especially true of Gilgamesh). He presents a psychological assessment of the epic's dreams, going beyond the usual view of the dreams simply as literary devices used to further the plot. For Bulkley they are "highly accurate representations of genuine psychological experience."

My response to G. S. Kirk's questions, listed earlier, is that Gilgamesh's withdrawal from civilization and his subsequent journey to Utnapishtim is a metaphorical rite of passage that marks Gilgamesh's transition from childhood to adulthood.[56] As V. Turner has observed, "in liminality nature is stressed over culture."[57] Furthermore, "travel is the most common source of metaphors used to explain transformations and transitions of all sorts."[58] "The ancients," E. J. Leed observes, "valued travel as an explication of human fate and necessity."[59]

The classic study of the rituals and various elements of rites of passage is of course A. van Gennep's *Rites of Passage*. They have since been studied by numerous anthropologists and other social scientists, notably V. Turner and J. S. La Fontaine. La Fontaine has focused on initiatory rites.[60] Van Gennep observed that initiation rites ensure "a change of condition or passage from one magic-religious or secular group to another."[61] Involved are crossings of boundaries, changes in time and social status.[62] There are three stages in rites of passage: (1) the preliminal stage, which involves rites of separation (in Gilgamesh's case this would be separation from the world of childhood by leaving Uruk); (2) the liminal transitional stage, which is characterized by danger and ambiguity, by deprivation and ordeals (Gilgamesh's leaving Uruk, journeying to Utnapishtim, his stay with Utnapishtim); and (3) the aggregation or integration of the individual into a new state (Gilgamesh's return to Uruk as a mature adult). The initiatory theme of the Standard Babylonian Version is succinctly encapsulated in the addition to the prologue: "He went on a distant journey" (first stage), "pushing himself to exhaustion" (second stage), "but then was brought to peace" (third stage) (I 7–8).

For Gilgamesh his journey "is death to the indistinct and amorphous state of childhood . . . in order to be reborn into masculinity and personality."[63] I would add that Gilgamesh's rebirth is into the finest masculine adulthood, as viewed by the exorcist Sinleqi-unnini. "It is not a matter of physiological development but of social definition."[64]

Little space appears to be devoted to the preliminal stage— Gilgamesh's symbolic rite of passage, his separation from childhood, from his city and cultural group—although there are too many lacunae in the relevant passages to be certain of this. It is described in the following lines, blending into the rites of mourning for the dead Enkidu, which also contain features of a rite of passage:

> He (Gilgamesh) shears off his curls[65] and heaps them onto the ground,
> ripping off his finery and casting it away as an abomination . . .
> and after you [Enkidu] (died) I let a filthy mat of hair grow over my body,
> and donned the skin of a lion and roamed the wilderness.
> (VIII 51–52, 86–87)

Gilgamesh reverses the journey of his friend Enkidu, who had gone from nature to culture. He removes his clothing of civilization and dons animal skins; thereby he "uncultures" himself. He separates himself from society and journeys to regions far removed from ordinary human life. "Persons undergoing ritualized transitions do without status, privileges, material pleasures and often even clothing."[66] Not surprisingly the greatest space is devoted to the liminal stage, to the period betwixt and between. And it is this section of the *Gilgamesh Epic* that must have had the greatest appeal to the ancient readers and listeners, as it had for the author himself. In contrast to the Old Babylonian Version,[67] marriage and the begetting of children seem to have been of little interest to the author; for him, the acquisition of secret knowledge was foremost. The *limen* is the period of suffering and woe, characterized by fear. "I saw lions and I was terrified" (IX 7). When Gilgamesh comes to the place of the Scorpion-man and his wife,[68] composite creatures who confound the categories otherwise kept separate in nature, "trembling terror blanket[s] his face" (IX 56). "Though it be in sadness and pain" (IX 215), he persists in his journey.

Gilgamesh is involved with various crossings, gates, and thresholds on his way to Utnapishtim. At the gate of the Scorpion-beings he leaves behind familiar human space and reality, wandering into terra incognita, a never-never land inhabited by strange composite creatures who guard the passage through the mountain of the rising sun.[69] "He finds himself in a fabulous jeweled garden" (IX 280–322).[70] He crosses the sea, with its waters of Death (XI 102, 104). Becoming a mature, wise adult involves embarking on a dangerous, solitary journey, though this of course is never stated explicitly. Gilgamesh on leaving Uruk has stepped across the boundary of youth and will return to Uruk as an adult.

In the liminal state Gilgamesh is neither alive nor dead; rather he is betwixt and between. So too the creatures he meets are neither quite human nor gods. The geography of this liminal space is not of the human world or where the gods reside. It is a mythic geography, outlandish, an unfamiliar world. Utnapishtim lives "at the mouth of the Rivers, at the end of the earth."[71] Gilgamesh is surprised that Utnapishtim looks no different from himself (XI 2–3). But because Utnapishtim is immortal, he is not human; but neither does he dwell with the gods. Time in Utnapishtim's region appears to be human time, for the days of Gilgamesh's sleep are measured as human days (X 206). Sin-leqi-unnini with magnificent skill has introduced elements of mystery and paradox into the hero's liminal journey as *homo viator*. And as the addition to the prologue emphasizes, Gilgamesh's journey was arduous and exhausting, as he comments to Urshanabi the ferryman toward the end of his journey: "For whom have my arms labored, Urshanabi? / For whom has my heart's blood roiled?" (XI 302–303).

In the liminal stage Gilgamesh is deprived of all his "worldly goods." The alteration in his dress and appearance is so drastic that all who meet him comment on them. He wears a skin (X 6); his cheeks are emaciated (X 39) (perhaps as if he has been fasting). Gilgamesh has become a marginal person, frightening Siduri the tavernkeeper, who does not at first recognize the slayer of Humbaba and the Bull of Heaven (X 34ff.).

The experience of pain is common in rituals of maturity. Suffering is a necessary part of the rituals and perhaps a means of transforming the initiate.[72]

Gilgamesh undergoes the test of overcoming sleep during the *limen*, a test that he fails. But this failure can be described as part of the learning he must acquire. Indeed, Oppenheim has noted that Gilgamesh is offered additional opportunities to acquire immortality (motifs of "the nearly won means to conquer death"), but he misses all of them.[73] As an adult he cannot deny death but must accept its inevitability. Enkidu had achieved the status of becoming a civilized human being, but Gilgamesh's development entails the transformation into much more—a fully mature, sagacious adult.

Although women help Gilgamesh along the way (see chapter 7), it is a man—not his father but his ancestor Utnapishtim (IX 136)— who transmits to him the secret teachings from before the flood.

This knowledge is, so to speak, handed down through the generations as were the rites and practices of the exorcist. Although Kovacs maintains that the recounting of the flood story[74] "in no way advances the movement of the Epic" and was included "only for its narrative interest,"[75] I would differ with her and emphasize that it was an essential addition. The details of the flood are connected with esoteric knowledge from the mythical period "before the flood" (*lām abūbi*) (I 6).

Gilgamesh must undergo at least a symbolic rite of passage, just as an exorcist would have had to do, to receive the secret knowledge that was not accessible to just anyone but only to this paradigmatic hero, descendant of Utnapishtim, who was two-thirds divine and one-third human. "Gnosis, 'deep knowledge' is highly characteristic of liminality," and through the acquisition of esoteric knowledge the innermost being of the initiand is transformed.[76]

The beginning of the third stage of incorporation and integration[77] is clearly noted in Tablet XI (246–319):

> "Take him away, Urshanabi, bring him to the washing
>   place.
> Let him wash his matted hair. . . .
> Let him cast away his animal skin . . .
> let his body be moistened . . .
> let the wrap around his head be made new,
> let him wear royal robes worthy of him! . . .
> Gilgamesh and Urshanabi boarded the boat, . . .
> and sailed away."

Clothing serves as a boundary marker once more. Just as Gilgamesh had taken off his finery at the beginning of the initiatory journey and donned lion skins, so before his return and incorporation once again into human society he takes off the lion skins, throws them away, and puts on regal attire. Just as he crossed the waters to enter the liminal stage, so he crosses them on his return home. Washing too serves as a boundary marker. He was dirty and unkempt in the liminal period, "uncivilized" in other words; he washes thoroughly as he is about to return.

Finally the two arrive in Uruk-Haven. The journey away from Uruk was undertaken by Gilgamesh as an isolated, marginal man. On the return he is no longer alone. When Gilgamesh and Urshanabi come to Uruk, Gilgamesh says to the ferryman: "Go up, Urshanabi, onto the wall of Uruk and walk around" (XI 314). Though it is the visitor and not Gilgamesh who walks around, it is perhaps noteworthy that circumambulation is frequently associated with ritual acts.[78]

One last point needs to be made. One cannot know for certain if Tablet XII is to be attributed to the authorship of Sin-leqi-unnini. Kovacs, for one, rejects its belonging to the epic.[79] I argue in chapter 7 that Tablet XII is an integral part of the *Gilgamesh Epic*, stressing as it does the centrality of family and offspring. Its contents would certainly fit into the exorcist's view of mature adulthood, which included having a wife and children. Furthermore, the information Enkidu gives Gilgamesh here about the ways of the netherworld was secret knowledge, most important for the hero who was thought to be the king and judge of the netherworld.[80]

Indirectly we learn more about Sin-leqi-unnini's view regarding the prime of life for a man. It was neither youthfulness nor old age that was for him the most valued life stage, but rather the period in between the two. It was a view (as noted in chapter 1) perhaps shared by many, to judge from Mesopotamian art, in which rulers and others are usually depicted as neither very young nor very old.[81]

The Standard Babylonian Version perhaps contains a subliminal polemic against the millennia-old royal ideals of war and conquest and of military prowess. It has been noted that the battle scenes in the late version, compared with earlier versions of the *Gilgamesh Epic*, are surprisingly brief and "remarkably free of detail." Indeed, there is almost "an ellipsis of battle" in the epic.[82] Jacobsen has commented on the "climate of constant wars, riots, and disorders" in the early first millennium.[83] Long before this, Sin-leqi-unnini may have subtly polemicized against age-old military ambitions. It was particularly fitting then that he selected the paradigmatic warrior hero of eons before as the exemplar of the superiority of maturity and learning.

CHAPTER THREE

On Aging and the Elderly

The elderly did not have "a high profile" in Mesopotamia, as they did in ancient Greece and Rome. There seems to have been no special interest "in the final stages of life [that] is reflected across genres in the thematic importance of old age."[1] The dearth of data may stem from a desire to avoid dealing with an unpleasant subject or may instead indicate that the Mesopotamians had simply accepted its inevitability resignedly. No Mesopotamian Aristotle or Cicero[2] reflected on and wrote about the life cycle and old age. No diaries remain to inform us about the thoughts of men and women, young and old. We can only search about in a wide variety of texts looking for inferences and passing remarks. At present only a provisional sketch of aging—the quality of old people's lives, their responses to the inevitable decrepitudes, the attitudes of others toward them—is possible.[3] It is often difficult, if not impossible, to distinguish between individual reactions and perceptions and what were popular or prescribed. Little work has to date been done by Assyriologists on the subject of geriatrics,[4] so this analysis breaks new ground.[5]

The terminology used to describe the aged and the aging process is instructive. The common Akkadian words for "old man" and "old woman" are *šību* and *šībtu*, which literally means "gray/white hair."[6] The usual Sumerian term is *šu.gi*$_{(4)}$ with determinatives added to indicate whether the old person is male or female. There seems to be no particular meaning to the word (at least, none has yet been suggested, to my knowledge). Frequently in Sumerian *[lú].ab.ba* "father," the head of the family and therefore its oldest member, is used, as is *um.ma* "mother" for old woman.[7] The verb *šâbu* "to become old" (literally, "to become gray-haired") appears less frequently than *labāru* (to be discussed shortly) and more often in texts outside of Mesopotamia proper.[8] For the Mesopotamians, then, the appearance of gray hair was *the* distinguishing sign of old age as it is and has been for other societies. Like other Mediterranean peoples, most Mesopotamians were dark-haired. Indeed, a common poetic Akkadian expression for mankind is "the dark-haired" (*ṣalmat qaqqadi*).[9] So unpleasing was gray hair for the ancients, such as the Mesopotamians and Egyptians, that they sometimes dyed their hair. Recipes "to darken (prematurely) white hair" were apparently used in both societies.[10] It is surprising that even though neither was a youth-oriented society both seem to have shared an attitude prevalent in our own society. Perhaps this was so because ageism, devaluation of the old, was not uncommon. This attempt to look young is in marked contrast, for example, to colonial America, where it was common for people of all ages to powder their hair, as if it had been whitened by old age. At that time, too, men of all ages in their desire to mimic old age wore coats that made their spines appear to be bent by the weight of many years.[11] Interestingly, the two most characteristic markers of old age in Mesopotamia were gray/white hair and a bent or stooped posture. Precise age was irrelevant.

The common verb to describe aging is *labāru* "to last, to endure," which in its intensive form *lubburu* means "to last a long time, to live to an old age." The latter is used to describe both human beings and buildings; the adjective *labīru* "old" is used of buildings and ruins as well as of human beings. The idiom *labīrūtu alāku* "to become delapidated" is also used of buildings and human beings. *The Assyrian Dictionary* translates the phrase as "to reach old age" when applied to humans.[12] Perhaps a pejorative nuance is embedded

in the Akkadian *labāru* and its derivatives, with the same metaphorical implication found in seventeenth-century English literature,
where the metaphor of a decayed building describes old age.[13]
Another infrequent idiom for reaching old age is *amēlūtu alāku*.[14]
The verb *alāku*, usually meaning "to go, to travel," perhaps connotes
that life is a course or road to be travelled.

Other words, far less commonly used, also describe the old. One
is *puršumû* (feminine, *puršumtu*), also meaning "gray-haired."[15] It
occurs as a loanword in Sumerian, where a positive connotation is
attached to its use. A rare term, *šugû*, is a loanword from Sumerian.[16]
Two terms equated with *šību* in a scribal synonym list are
significant: *pisnuqu* and *kibrû*.[17] The former denotes helplessness
and powerlessness. It appears, for example, in *The Babylonian
Theodicy*, where Lambert translates it as "beggar."[18] It thus bespeaks
the poverty that many aged Mesopotamians must have faced. So
too *kibrû*, perhaps related to *kubartu* "old garment," may also
convey a pejorative view of the aged.[19] Finally there is a late rare
word, *littu*, related to the common term for extreme old age, *littūtu*.[20]
Not surprisingly, *šībūtu* is the common term for senectitude.[21] The
existence of both *šībūtu* and *littūtu* suggest that there may have been
age grading in Mesopotamia comparable to our young-old age and
old-old age. Of special interest is the unique text (usually referred
to as STT 400) somewhat inexactly classified by its publisher as "a
learned compendium of theological and other equivalences."[22] It is
a theoretical reflection on the various stages in later life, as described
in chapter 1.

The number of elderly in the population cannot, of course, be
estimated. There is little reason to believe that many lived beyond
their sixties. The age at death is rarely noted in the sources.[23] D. Snell
utilized king lists, enumerating the length of rulers' reigns, in an
attempt to discover whether cycles of infectious diseases affected
the dynasts' life expectancy.[24] His findings were negative.

L. Curchin cites data yielded by pathological examinations of
early skeletons found at various sites.[25] Overall, few of the people
had lived beyond their thirties. The ravages of warfare, disease and

other calamities, he notes, took their toll. It can be assumed that elite
men and women—depending on their constitution, nutrition, and
living conditions—might, more likely than others in the population,
survive beyond their thirties. This was the case for the *nadītu*
women, cloistered women dedicated to the god Shamash of Sippar
in the Old Babylonian period.[26] As celibates, they avoided the
dangers of childbirth, and living in a fairly segregated community,
the *gagû* (cloister), they escaped many of the deadly diseases of the
time. Several of them lived well beyond their sixties. M. Roth has
quite rightly questioned M. Dandamaev's conclusion, based on the
careers of ten scribes and five slaves, that life expectancy in first-
millennium Babylonia was "relatively high." She thinks that his
examples are the exception rather than the norm.[27]

The ancient Mesopotamians, at least in the written sources, seem
not to have been consumed with dread toward old age as was
characteristic, according to S. Humphreys, of the ancient Greeks in
the archaic period.[28] Nevertheless, they looked back longingly to a
time when, according to the Sumerian myth *Enki and Ninsikila/
Ninhursaga*:

> No old woman belonging to it said there (in Dilmun): I old
>   woman
> No old man belonging to it said there: I old man.[29]

The fervent desire to live long and grow old is voiced over and
over again, especially in letters from all times and places. A good
old age was usually viewed as reward for, and therefore proof of, a
virtuous life.[30] Sentiments abound in royal inscriptions and epistolary literature requesting that the gods grant long life to rulers and
ordinary people.[31] The ancient Mesopotamians wished not only for
long life but for a life accompanied by health of mind and body (*ṭûb
libbi, ḫûd libbi, ṭûb šēri*); for without this, longevity was a curse. In a
study of the colophons, inscriptions added at the end of Babylonian
and Assyrian texts, L. E. Pearce found that the tablets were votive
offerings to the gods for the good (*ana ṭûb*) of the scribe and to

ensure a long life (*arak umēšu/šattišu*).[32] One first-millennium copy of a Hammurabi inscription of centuries earlier was made for the long life and well-being of the copyist, and for the hearing of the copyist's prayer. (At times votives were offered for the well-being of the scribe's family and its continuity.)

The belief that the gods rewarded the pious and devout with longevity is widespread throughout the ancient Near East. It is explicitly expressed in the fictive autobiography of Adad-guppi, mother of Nabonidus, the last ruler of Babylonia (555–539 B.C.E.). Devotee of the moon god Sin and his coterie, faithful caretaker of the moon cult, she was granted incredible longevity—104 years— along with extraordinary good health. T. Longman believes that the primary purpose of this text was to encourage the worship of the gods, especially of Sin and his associates, as well as to glorify Nabonidus.[33]

With age and experience, it was thought, might come greater devotion: "In my youthfulness, I am inexperienced, I do not know whether I have committed a sin."[34] In a prayer to the god Nabu, an old man says, "Now that I am old my hands make petition to all the gods. I am breathless [from] prostration."[35] However, a moving and sorrowful prayer, also to the god Nabu, describes a quite different picture of an old man "wasted by suffering, as if I were not fearing your divinity." He closes his prayer by beseeching the god, "Let the dead man revive [by your] breeze. Let his squandered life become gain."[36]

Growing old was often an unattractive, painful process for the ancients, marred by physical and psychological decline, as well as a downgrading in status. Most must have experienced reductions in height and weight, wrinkling of the skin, loss of hair, stiffening of the joints, and alterations in posture, to mention some of the changes usually accompanying old age. But remarkably little is said about such infirmities.

The fascinating stele of Adad-guppi, a memorial formulated as autobiography, depicts ideal old age. What is here described is the outstanding physical and psychological well-being of an extraordinarily long lived woman, unaffected by the changes that to some degree more or less typify old age:

> In his love for me who (always) worshipped his godhead . . .
> Sin . . . did what he never did before, gave (to me) . . . many
> (lit.: long) days (and) years of full mental capacity. . . . For 104
> years . . . my eyesight was keen, my hearing excellent, my
> hands and feet in perfect condition, my diction well chosen,
> food and drink agreed with me; . . . I was in good spirits.[37]

Adad-guppi would be an exemplar of perfect old age at any time or place: her vision and hearing were excellent, her limbs pain-free, her speech eloquent, her digestion excellent, her spirits high. And on top of all this she lived to old–old age, living to see great-great-grandchildren. One might well ask whether she indeed lived to such an advanced age, in such incredibly good health, or whether this is a case of extreme hyperbole.[38] Perhaps Adad-guppi was simply an example of someone who had lived so very long that one lost track, so to speak, of her age. After all, Mesopotamia was a society, like other ancient societies, where chronological age was irrelevant (see chapter 4).

Adad-guppi's life as described in her stele was one-of-a-kind. A passage in a bilingual version from Emar of a Sumerian folktale, *Enlil and Namzitarra*, assesses the human reality of longevity in stark, harsh words: "One hundred twenty years (are) the years of mankind—verily *it is their bane* [my emphasis]. (This is so) from the day that humanity exists until today."[39]

Realistic and far from sanguine is the picture of old age depicted in a Sumerian folktale, which its publisher titled "The Old Man and the Young Girl."[40] Its basic motif is widespread in world literature: an old man marries a young girl to achieve rejuvenation. The story line, though many passages are missing, is as follows. An old man asks for advice regarding his physical problems. A wise *zikrum* (perhaps a cloistered woman and therefore to be read *sekrum*) counsels that he marry a young girl. He agrees, and the king orders

the girl to prepare for marriage. The aged man describes his
infirmities in vivid, unusual images:

> (I was) a youth, (but now) my luck, my strength, my
>   personal god, and my youthful vigour have left my loins
>   like an exhausted ass.
> My black mountain has produced white gypsum.
> My mother has brought in a man from the forest, he gave
>   me captivity.
> My mongoose which used to eat strong smelling things
>   does not stretch its neck towards beer and butter.
> My teeth which used to chew strong things can no more
>   chew strong things.
> My urine used to flow (?) in a strong torrent (but now) you
>   flee (?) from my wind.
> My child whom I used to feed with butter and milk, I can
>   no more support it,
> and I have (had to) sell (?) my little slave girl, an evil demon
>   makes me sick.
> The king paid attention to the words of an old man.
> The king spoke to the girl:
> After I have given him to you, he will lie in your lap like a
>   young man.[41]

That his "youthful vigour" has left him may well refer to his
impotence; the ass probably exemplifies high sexual prowess.[42] This
is followed by the image describing the whitening of his formerly
dark hair. The man from the forest is a metaphor for the cane or
crutches the old man must now use. His loss of appetite may be due
to the loss of most, if not all, of his teeth. He suffers from prostate
problems and flatulation. As to the child and slave girl, J. L.
Crenshaw suggests that they may refer to his wife and to his
concubine, whom he can no longer satisfy sexually.[43] He would
therefore conclude his list of problems as he had begun it, with
impotence. His sexual dysfunction, it is hoped, will be remedied by

marrying a young girl. Thus, described in this folktale are whitening of the hair, a decline in digestive and kidney functions, the inability to walk unaided and enjoy food, and especially the loss of sexual potency. Interestingly, the tale also adds that the young girl "will become a mature woman." She too is thought to gain from the age-disparate marriage, probably a not-uncommon occurrence, when not a few women died in childbirth.

The theme of rejuvenation was probably an important aspect of the festivals of the great goddess Ishtar.[44] Her celebrations were characterized by the carnivalesque, when normal, acceptable behavior was temporarily suspended. Remarkable was the possible participation by adults in children's games, reflecting the topsy-turvy nature of her festivals, their licit subversiveness and antiauthoritarianism (see chapter 10). They served as a safety valve to let off steam, while reaffirming the status quo.

Weakness and feebleness usually characterized old age. This is explicitly stated in an Old Babylonian letter from the Diyala region in which the names of both the writer (or more likely the one who dictated the letter) and the addressee are no longer preserved. The former had been close to a now-old man from Jamnunu for thirty years. The old man was subjected to various accusations that the letter sender believed to be untrue. Furthermore, he added that "the Jamnunite has grown old and has become feeble; they should not pester him."[45] The term translated as "has become feeble," *umtiq*, more basically means "to do things slowly, to delay."[46] In the next chapter I note that old men and feeble women (*muqqūti*) would be joined by a child, all to sit at the hearth warming themselves. When basket carriers were needed for the Old Babylonian labor force, the ancient Mesopotamians believed that "a single weak, or old man, or child should not be among them[,] . . . only strong young men."[47]

The marginalization of elderly men by being equated with children and women is discussed more fully in chapter 4. This marginalization no doubt can be accounted for by the decreasing economic contribution of elderly men compared to younger male adults. The ration system for the temple labor force in Sargonic and

Ur III periods clearly shows this. Old men, though they received more quarts of barley per month than women, received far less than younger men.[48]

In times of war, endemic in Mesopotamia especially in its later history, the marginalization of the aged would become even more aggravated. This condition is starkly portrayed in the myth of *Erra and Ishum*, in a graphic description of the horrific consequences of extreme violence. The seven gods try to arouse the fearsome Erra to do battle, saying:

> . . . up, do your duty!
> Why have you been sitting in the city like a feeble old man,
> Why sitting at home like a helpless child?
> Shall we eat womanfood, like non-combatants?
> Have we turned timorous and trembling, as if we can't fight?
> Going to the field for the young and vigorous is like to a very feast.[49]

Later in the myth describing the indiscriminate devastation wrought by Erra, Ishum includes among those who die, "The old men you killed in their bedrooms / The young maidens you killed in their beds."[50] Both age groups were viewed as helpless and vulnerable; the bedridden aged men were unable to escape.

As already noted above, physiological descriptions of the aged are rarely mentioned. But the bent posture, characteristic of the elderly, is referred to in a prayer: "(Not receiving a reply to my prayers) has bent me like an old man."[51] Perhaps it was a bent old man with cane in hand that ancient Mesopotamians saw when they looked at the constellation of Perseus and so named it "The Old Man."[52] The Greeks perceived it as the hero Perseus, son of Zeus, with sword upraised, holding the head of the slain Medusa in his outstretched hand.[53] For the ancient Egyptians, too, the stooped back was one of the characteristics of the old, as noted by L. Green.[54] Hearing and sight were, as mentioned earlier, often affected by aging. One man complains in his prayer: "I am not old, (yet) my hearing is heavy, my glance cross-eyed."[55]

The story entitled "The Old Man and the Young Girl" emphasized what must have been the common problem of impotency.[56] Medication and/or magic might be recommended for treatment. Young men were thought to be so afflicted because of witchcraft.[57] The term for impotence, *muṭṭû*, refers to a reduced appetite or capacity not only for sexual intercourse but also for eating, drinking, and seeing.[58]

Though, to my knowledge, wrinkles and wrinkled skin are not mentioned in the extant texts, a well-known episode in the *Gilgamesh Epic* is relevant to the subject. The dry skin of the aged is a universal "symptom of . . . general desiccation . . . hence the related notion of old age as a skin to be scraped or sloughed off."[59] In the epic, as a farewell gift to the hero, Utnapishtim, at the urging of his wife, tells him where he will find the plant "The-Old-Man-Becomes-Young," which lies in the freshwatery deep. Gilgamesh dives into the water and plucks the plant. He decides, because he is yet young, to try it out on the old men of Uruk when he returns home. On his way back, he goes bathing in a pool. "A snake smelled the fragrance of the plant, *silently* came up and carried off the plant. While going back it sloughed off its casing."[60]

Senectitude is regarded at times as a tragic human reality. B. R. Foster observes: "In prayers and other religious literature, old age and death can be tropes for penitents who have lost favor."[61]

Information on the psychological changes affected by aging is for the most part implicit and indirect. These changes are discussed more fully in chapters 4 and 5. Mesopotamian myths focus almost exclusively on the psychological differences between young and old. This is not surprising, because gods do not visibly age in Mesopotamia as they might in ancient Egypt.[62] In the confrontations between young and old gods, a shift has taken place in the aged gods from "active mastery" to "passive mastery," from "aggressive competitive behavior" to "apathy and immobility." These alterations would of course also be related in humans to physiological transformations.

Depression and anxieties all too often accompanied the aging process. An aging royal official in the late Old Babylonian period, in one official report, fears that other officials are negligent in carrying out King Ammisaduga's instructions. He complains "about the worries that befall him in old age."[63]

Ancient attitudes toward the imbibing of alcoholic beverages by the elderly may differ considerably from contemporary views.[64] Plato in his *Laws* enumerates rules for the drinking of wine. Prior to age eighteen, children are not to drink any wine. After this, up to age thirty, citizens may drink in moderation. From age forty on they may invoke "the presence of the other gods, and especially Dionysus . . . which he has bestowed on human beings as a drug that heals the austerity of old age. Its effect is that we are rejuvenated, and the soul, by forgetting its despondency of soul, has its disposition turned from harder to softer."[65] Implied here is that old age brings depression in its wake that can be countered by wine.

A remarkably similar outlook is found in the far earlier *Hittite Testament of Hattusili I*, recorded about 1620 B.C.E. The king advises his recently adopted son and heir Mursili to "eat (only) bread and drink (only) water. But when maturity is within you, you may eat twice, three times a day and treat yourself well. But when old age comes upon you, you may drink to the full and set aside the word of (your) father."[66] To my knowledge, no Mesopotamian text explictly attests to the alleviating effects of alcoholic drinks on the sorrows of old age. However, T. Jacobsen years ago observed that "important discussions originated when the gods were in their cups."[67] In *Enuma Elish*, tasty food and drink were important to the old gods, as noted in chapter 5.

The elderly gods are at times ridiculed in Mesopotamian myths. This is the case in the myth of *Erra and Ishum*. Jacobsen remarked that Erra managed "to fast-talk Marduk—depicted as an old fuddy-duddy—into leaving him in charge of the universe while Marduk went off to have his crown jewels cleaned and . . . Erra then settled down to stir things up."[68] The young and powerful god of *Enuma*

Elish is here represented as an old, unimaginative, old-fashioned person. J. Black and A. Green describe Marduk's portrayal in *Erra and Ishum* "as a bumbling and old incompetent whose insignia need repairing and cleaning."[69] Foster, by contrast, sees him depicted "as remote and all-wise; he knows Erra's plans even before Erra arrives at his temple. He speaks in sonorous, scholarly diction. There is never any doubt that he is king. Yet the poet is troubled that there can be disorder in the realm that could threaten even Marduk himself."[70] The different views about Marduk mirror, I think, the ambiguity that the myth's author held toward the aged—respect for their wisdom, coupled with antagonism toward and questioning of their high status. I also found here an emphasis on the tedious loquacity of the elderly Marduk as he talks about events that happened "once long ago," describing his past glories. Marduk even takes credit for causing the flood though no other text does so.[71]

Foster has insightfully called attention to the subtleties of the author(s) of *Enuma Elish* in the contrast between the speeches of the old gods and those of the young Marduk. Theirs are replete with lengthy repetitions "as opposed to the rapid, non-repetitive passages in which youthful Marduk takes charge."[72] It is perhaps the garrulousness of the old that is here mimicked.

W. L. Moran discerns the mocking of the great god Enlil in *Atrahasis*. "'The warrior Enlil,' an epithet he often enjoys; and yet when his house is besieged by the rebel gods, the only occasion he has to display his valor, he pleads with his attendant Nusku for protection and cowers behind him in fear. . . . Throughout the crisis he is singularly inept."[73] Not only is disdain for the aged revealed here, but what must have also been their desperate plight in wartime.

Utnapishtim, ancestor of Gilgamesh, who along with his wife alone of all human beings attained immortality, should also be included in the literary portrayal of an old man. His is a positive image of the wise, old sage. He reminisces, as the elderly often do, about their past,[74] recounting to the young hero the events before, during, and after the flood. Utnapishtim is the repository of ancient traditions, which he communicates to his descendant. He thus functions in the prestigious and significant role of a traditional elder. In a community where literacy was greatly limited, it was old men who linked the young with the past and its traditions. A goodly part of Utnapishtim's earliest speech to Gilgamesh is only partially intelligible, but as suggested by Kovacs, it may be derived from traditional wisdom literature.[75]

Artistic representations of the old are rare in Mesopotamia, in contrast to Egypt.[76] This may have been due to a negative attitude toward old age (see chapter 4). Curchin mentions in passing that "the subjects of Sumerian statuary are not uncommonly bearded elders."[77] They are, however, more likely to be mature bearded Semites rather than "elders." H. Frankfort in a discussion of Early Dynastic III sculpture remarks that in this period "a double chin adds to the material well-being and folds of fat are sometimes indicated between chest and stomach."[78] It is impossible to say if these details were included to render middle-age and/or prosperity as they did in ancient Egypt.[79]

R. D. Barnett describes a scene in one of the reliefs in the North Palace of Ashurbanipal as showing "a father, a son, and perhaps an adult (?) elderly male" (possibly three generations) who are urged forward by an armed Assyrian soldier brandishing a long stick; but no age distinctions are shown between the adults.[80] In an earlier Sennacherib relief, J. Reade points out that "a few old men and women are crouching out of sight on one of the boats built from bundles of reeds; others are slipping away along a backwater, while younger men shoot arrows from hiding-places."[81] It is their posture and situation, not the physical features of the men and women, that point up their age: "crouching out of sight" and "slipping away," rather than fighting. Fighting is left to the young men.

The advisory function of the old and their association with knowledge and wisdom is attested cross-culturally. Though attested to only sporadically in Mesopotamia, it can nevertheless be assumed to have been a given throughout Mesopotamian history. Utna-pishtim discussed above is prototypical. The *šībūtu* "elders," whether of a city or a country, are frequently mentioned in the texts.[82] A recent study by H. Reviv also treats this Mesopotamian institution.[83] He quite rightly emphasizes that a distinction must be drawn between the elders and old men (women to date have not been found to appear in this capacity). Not all elders were old men nor were all old men elders. Nor is it known whether there was any age requirement to become a member of the šībūtu. Rather, as I found to be the case in Old Babylonian Sippar, the šībūtu were "the heads of the most influential and wealthiest families of Sippar."[84] They would of course often be the oldest members of their extended families. Reviv has discussed the various legal and financial functions of "the elders."

It is in the sapiential literature of Mesopotamia, as in other ancient Near Eastern civilizations, that the old counsel the young, typically fathers their sons. Their expertise and knowledge, acquired through life experiences, are useful to others, and these qualities accorded prestige to the elderly (men and women alike) when their economic contribution to family and community had waned. As B. Alster has demonstrated, the corpus of proverbial teaching incorporated the cultural traditions to be transmitted from generation to generation. The behavior of the civilized (i.e., Mesopotamians) as opposed to the barbarians was particularly stressed: "Civilized people respect the ideal relations between parents and children, husband and wife, citizens and rulers."[85] Not that wisdom was considered the exclusive property of the old; nevertheless, its association is more strongly linked to this stage in the life course. So, for example, even though the god Marduk was born wise, he too had to be instructed by his father Ea in the performance of the correct magical rituals.[86] Wisdom teaching is found not only in proverbs, adages, and precepts, nor was it confined to intellectual circles, but as everywhere it was part of the folk tradition.[87]

One may assume that the most important criterion for being truly old was not gray hair, bent back, or wrinkles but the inability to continue working, whether in one of the bureaucracies (military, civil, and religious), in one's private enterprises, or in the servile labor force of either the palace or the temple—to cite, for example, the rich data available from Old Babylonian Sippar (1894–1595 B.C.E.). Many of the city, temple, and military offices were lifelong and hereditary.[88] From the earlier Ur III period, R. Zettler has demonstrated that for four generations one family held the lifelong office of chief administrator of the temple of Inanna.[89]

The old appear in numerous work lists throughout Mesopotamian history.[90] Their participation in the work force not only indicates that there was not an institutionalized retirement age, but also may suggest a fear of dependency, although ideally one looked to sons for support when working was no longer possible. P. Steinkeller includes the elderly in a "list of work-categories for 'soldiers/workers' arranged in descending order," ranking them second-last, followed by deceased workers.[91] In the hierarchy of workers, the head worker was the father; lower ranks were held by sons in order of seniority. "Upon the death or retirement of the head worker, his position was taken over by his oldest son, whereas the younger sons moved successively up the hierarchy until the sequence was restored. The same principle was in operation in case of the death of any of the lower ranking workers. . . . A worker generally continued to work there until his death or retirement."[92] These workers were prebenders performing forestry service to the state in return for grants of land. They worked for several months each year in specific forests.

Several hundred lists of forced laborers from much later in the fourteenth and fifteenth centuries B.C.E. have been studied by J. A. Brinkman.[93] Workers are "categorized as male or female and then assigned to one of five divisions by age: old ($\check{s}u.gi_{(4)}$), adult, adolescent, child/'weaned,' infant ('suckling')." Of special interest is Brinkman's observation on "the relative paucity of old people (and especially of old men)."[94] In these late personnel rosters, grouped by families, very rarely is an old man listed as family head,[95] reflecting presumably how few in number old men were.

The plight of childless old men and women must have been devastating. I. J. Gelb in his discussion of the Ur III *arua* institution observed that "the practice of giving human beings to the temple is a form of exposure. . . . It was a way of getting rid of unwanted people—children, old people, especially women, and others such as blind and deaf people, cripples."[96] But one can view this practice quite differently: as an act of beneficence by the temple, rescuing the marginalized in society from certain death, by offering shelter and food rations.[97] I. M. Diakonoff finds no explicit information "on the killing of old people in the numerous wars of Mesopotamia."[98] He adds that because old people and children were frequently deported, most would have died while being transferred.

An overriding concern of Mesopotamians was to be buried properly at death, to be lamented and remembered by survivors with prayers and rituals.[99] Tablet XII of the *Gilgamesh Epic* focuses on the necessity of progeny to ensure nourishment and thus vitality to the dead. The more progeny, the better the deceased's fate in the netherworld. Extant sources from early times down through the Neo-Babylonian period inform about the obligations of male survivors, especially heirs, to dead parents. Indeed, as A. Skaist has noted, the inheritance of property was accompanied by the duty of the heir(s) to perform the *kispu* funerary offering to the dead.[100]

Those who died and were left unburied were believed to turn into vicious, vengeful demons who tormented the living.[101] In a terrifying description of the havoc of war in *Erra and Ishum*, among other horrors mentioned is that of

> He who begot a son saying,
> "This is my son, when I have reared him he will requite my
>   pains,"
> I will put that son to death, his father must bury him,
> Afterwards I will put that father to death, but he will have
>   none to bury him.[102]

Poignant is the Old Babylonian letter a woman sent to her brother in which she says: "Now I have (aquired and) am raising a boy, telling myself: Let him grow up, so that there will be somebody to bury me."[103] The boy, a slave, is being claimed, she says, by the merchant who presumably sold him to her.

When there were no children or other family members to care for the aged, adoption was an alternative.[104] Frequently a man or woman would adopt a slave with the proviso that at the adoptive parent's death he/she would be free. In a recent analysis of the adoption texts of Old Babylonian Nippur, E. C. Stone discusses the different patterns of adoption, which varied from class to class. Most frequently a man adopted one or more sons. In this type of adoption the adoptee(s) would receive "an inheritance of property in exchange for a contribution toward his future support."[105] Thus, orphans were provided with parents and childless couples with children and heirs. Stone found that the alimentary amount given to adoptive parents was about 550 kg of wheat, equivalent per year to what has been calculated as the average subsistence level in Iraq in the 1950s. The adoptee would provide support and security in old age in exchange for real estate desired by the adopted son. Failure not only to provide maintenance but to show the proper attitude of respect and obedience would lead to punishment.[106]

Despite the infirmities, incapacities, and frequent powerlessness that attended old age, the Mesopotamians looked forward to enjoying longevity. Having "the satisfaction of growing very old, good health and happiness"[107] was a gift from the gods. But length of years might also be accompanied by the increasing acrimony of long-grown sons, impatient to claim their inheritance and finally live economically independent lives, free of paternal supervision and restraints.

CHAPTER FOUR

THE CONFLICT OF GENERATIONS IN ANCIENT MESOPOTAMIAN MYTHS

Recent years have brought a proliferation of studies on the family on such topics as household composition, marriage patterns, childbearing practices, and life-cycle transitions. Scholars in ancient Near Eastern studies have contributed mainly to the legal and economic aspects of family history.[1] Frequently the work done has centered on philological questions. The cuneiform data on the Mesopotamian family, accidental and all-too-often limited, are spread over a period of some three thousand years. Nevertheless it is time to broaden the focus, despite the inherent problems. In this chapter, I treat the question of the dynamics of Mesopotamian family life, more specifically intergenerational conflict, a topic barely touched upon by scholars in the field.[2]

Assessing the affective relations between members of the Mesopotamian family is no easy matter. Information on actual relations between parents and children, between old and young is not easily come by. No tracts on family relations, no diaries or memoirs from Mesopotamia exist to give insight into everyday familial life. But helpful and revealing scattered data, if all too often indirect, do exist. Especially relevant are literary sources, such as proverbs, myths and epics. But these cannot be taken at face value. Proverbial material often articulates the norms considered appropriate to ideal familial behavior. Epics and myths may incorporate

ideals and stereotypes far different from the realities of human life.
They must therefore be checked against other sources, such as legal
texts—which include inheritance, adoption, and lawsuits—more
likely to reflect real life situations. Most important for exploring
family dynamics are the epistolary materials, which, though
fraught with numerous problems, are nevertheless the most
revealing type of source.[3] As A. L. Oppenheim put it, letters " allow
insights into the Mesopotamian society of such an immediateness
as no other texts . . . are able to offer."[4] But such letters are very
thinly and unevenly distributed both chronologically and geo-
graphically. This form of documentation is mainly concerned with
the activities of the upper levels of urban society and only margin-
ally with other strata.

Undoubtedly spurred on by the protest-filled events of the 1960s,
generational relations has in recent years become of interest to
gerontological anthropologists. Most useful in suggesting new
ways of looking at the problem is N. Foner's study, *Ages in Conflict*,
which takes as its starting point the idea that "age is a basis of
structured inequality or social stratification."[5] Mesopotamian
society was structured not only on age but also on sexual and status
inequities.[6] Drawing on more than sixty ethnographic reports on
preindustrial societies, Foner posed questions, which she then
sought to answer. Despite the many differences between those
cultures and the highly bureaucratic urban-centered civilization of
Mesopotamia, her questions are relevant for us too, alerting us to
new directions in approaching the cuneiform texts. Do inequalities
between old and young inevitably lead to tensions? In what ways
are these tensions expressed? What factors reduce discord and
enhance solidarity? When do frustration and hostilities lead to overt
conflict? What are the sources of accommodations between the
generations? What are the societal and self-conceptions of old age?
What is the behavior of and toward the elderly?

Foner observes that potential conflicts are discernible in every
society. But the particular way in which individuals age and the
meanings attached to the various stages in the life cycle are not

universal; hence, modes of generational conflict will differ, for patterns of age inequalities vary cross-culturally and historically.[7] The forms of residence and the patterns of inheritance must be considered as factors in exacerbating or reducing generational strains. Whether households are nuclear or multigenerational and whether grown sons inherit before the death of the father or must wait until he dies are some of the critical issues affecting the degree of intergenerational hostility.[8]

In the agricultural society of Mesopotamia, social continuity rested upon inheritance.[9] Complex relationships including affection and exploitation must have been at the center of family life. There were basically two kinds of inheritance division in Mesopotamia: equal division, in which all male heirs divided the estate equally, and primogeniture, in which the eldest brother took a double share or received a preferential portion. The second form presumably made for fraternal tension. For the most part the father as the head of the family retained both possession of and control over land for life, but it was always possible, depending perhaps on individual preferences, for a son to receive an outright gift upon his marriage, independent of his future share of the inheritance, or even to receive his patrimony during his father's lifetime.[10] It was presumably also possible for one child to be favored above others regardless of birth order.

More problematic is establishing the various forms of residence found in Mesopotamia. For example, the extent to which the extended family can be considered a characteristic pattern is open to question. Although M. A. Powell assumes it was the norm throughout the third millennium, he observes that "if, however, we can establish the existence of the extended family, describing its structure is another matter."[11] Perhaps economic constraints largely determined household arrangements.

The inequality between young and old is embedded in the very nuances of the Akkadian terms for son and father. *Māru* "son" is also a form of address to a subordinate, just as *abu* "father" can be used as an honorific title expressing superordination.[12] This inequitable relationship is extended to the elder brother and the elder sister: "[The elder] brother is indeed a father, the elder sister is indeed a mother."[13]

Certain literary passages suggest that age-specific behavioral traits may have been a major source of tension between young and old—the cautiousness and restraint of the old against the impulsiveness and risk taking of the young. Episodes in Sumerian and Akkadian accounts of Gilgamesh's adventures come to mind. Especially illustrative is the admonition of the elders: "You are young, Gilgamesh, [and] your enthusiasm carries you away. You do not understand what you persist in doing."[14]

Roth concludes that in both Neo-Babylonian urban and Neo-Assyrian rural households "males marry relatively late in life and females considerably earlier. . . . By the time the overwhelming majority of men in first millennium B.C. Mesopotamia reached the age of thirty, even if they were first-born sons, they no longer had living fathers. The age at which a man would marry, therefore, effectively coincides with his realizing his patrimony. At his father's death, he becomes economically independent, and can set up his own household. It is at this point that he will seek a bride." The bride, Roth notes, is "typically in her early teens at her first marriage and her groom is at least in his mid twenties."[15]

Her observations are relevant for our topic. That a young man would usually receive his patrimony at marriage would, on one hand, make him independent when he became head of a household; but, on the other hand, a virile young man's tension and hostility may well have grown as he waited to marry and come into his own, perhaps resulting in frequent wishes for his father's death. The difference in the ages of the spouses probably made for distance between father and son, promoting greater closeness between mother and son; the mother frequently acted as mediator and buffer to reduce the intrafamilial tension.[16]

Actual parricide (or filicide) was undoubtedly rare in Mesopotamia. The age-old precepts of respect and obedience by the young toward their elders surely saw to this. But that it might occur can be seen from two intriguing cases. In one, the eldest son of the Inanna temple's chief administrator—a member of one of Nippur's most illustrious families, which held the highest secular and religious offices in the Ur III period (2112–2004 B.C.E.)—twice brought suit against his father, charging cultic violations that warranted the death penalty. The first time the father was pardoned. The second time, the accuser himself was put to death. Although we have no way of knowing for certain, this may have been an instance in which the eldest son, frustrated in his ambition to succeed his father, resorted to legal means to dispose of him.[17] In a much later case of political parricide, an older son tried to kill the renowned Assyrian king Sennacherib (704–681 B.C.E.) because he had passed over older sons to designate a younger son, Esarhaddon, as his successor.[18]

One must very carefully distinguish in our sources between appearance and reality, between ideal and actual behavior toward parents and elders. From adoption contracts especially we learn what was considered proper behavior toward parents: to show affection (*râmu*), to honor (*kubbutu*), to please (*libbam ṭubbu*), to revere (*palāḫu*), to be at one's parents' disposal (*wašābu maḫar* PN).[19] In short, a child was to obey and support his/her parents. But the prescriptions imply that the reverse was not uncommon. The desirable qualities in a son were humility and obedience. Their opposites were deplored: "A father gives a special blessing for a humble, obedient son, the begetter curses . . . a proud, disobedient son."[20]

The sapiential literature of Mesopotamia is replete with advice on proper generational behavior. And indeed as B. Alster emphasizes, one function of the proverbs was to indicate the way in which civilized people, in contrast to barbarians, were to "respect the ideal relations between parents and children" and between young and old.[21] "The instructions of an old man are precious, may you submit to them," the young were counselled. And a son was told to pay heed to his father's words as if they were the words of a god.[22] But children's rebelliousness and perversity were facts of life: "A perverse child—his mother should never have given birth to him."[23]

One man writing a letter sadly noted that "there is no son who does not give his father trouble."[24]

Gender differences are occasionally mentioned. "A mother is able to discipline her daughter but not her son."[25] "A rebellious male may be permitted a reconciliation. A rebellious female will be dragged in mud." E. I. Gordon suggests that the proverb implies that it was a male, but not a female, prerogative to rebel against the status quo.[26] A son's laziness and indolence as a source of generational conflict was probably all too common: "A father drags a boat along the canal, while his first born lies in bed."[27]

The *patria potestas* of Rome, the power of the male head of the family to determine the life and death of all members of the household, has no parallel in Mesopotamia.[28] From D. Marcus's discussion of the pertinent laws of the code of Hammurabi, it appears that children perhaps had some legal protection from absolute parental authority, even in cases where children assaulted parents.[29] The courts may have served then as a mechanism for reducing generational conflict by forestalling an immediate parental response to filial rebelliousness.

The increasing incapacities that often attend old age must have led to the erosion of the authority and influence of senior men. Old age was not a golden age in Mesopotamia. The last years of indigent elderly of the lowest socioeconomic strata were undoubtedly sad ones if they had no means of support, were unable to work, and had no family to provide for them, as discussed in chapter 3.[30]

Mesopotamian societal norms attempted to mitigate ageism, the devaluation of the elderly. But denigration and devaluation of the aged were realities. The equation of the elderly with the child occurs with some frequency.[31] "He is a child, we will make him serve as a doorkeeper with the old men and weak women."[32] "Why are you staying in town like a miserable old man? [Why] are you lingering at home like a weak child?"[33] Even more striking in its denigration of the elderly is an Old Babylonian treaty from Ishchali, enumerating the compensation to be paid for murder: "An old man or an old woman . . . [is] like one child in price."[34] The basis for the evaluation here and elsewhere seems to be an economic one: children and the elderly can do little if any work, hence their loss to society is substantially less than is that of a working adult.[35]

But this should not lead to the conclusion that the Mesopotamians did not care for and love their children and their aged parents. Poignant too are the cases in which the old, abandoned by members of their family, must seek others to take care of them. In one Neo-Babylonian contract, an ill man deserted by his son and brother turned in desperation to his daughter for assistance.[36] What was a filial or fraternal responsibility might in times of crisis be assumed by a daughter, who would be rewarded with a bequest.

When examining the Mesopotamian myths as a source of information on generational conflict, I avoid Freudian interpretation. Apart from lacking expertise in psychoanalytic theory and methodology, I question the applicability and viability of a view that is inextricably tied to a particular historical and cultural period.[37] Instead, like N. Foner, I assume that myths, like folk tales and songs, may "offer a way for the young to express hostility toward the old *indirectly* [my emphasis]."[38] Myths thus function as safety valves to reduce the pressures exerted by age inequalities. Moreover, as observed by R. Wagner, "Myths model and resolve certain recurrent interpersonal and kin tensions and relationships."[39]

In Mesopotamia, myths appear to mitigate generational tensions by countering the idealization of the elderly and old age, focusing instead on the injustices perpetrated by the old against the young. Myths frequently depict hostility as originating with the old and often caricature the old gods. The conflicts between Mesopotamian gods have usually been interpreted by Assyriologists as indicative of conflicts between the cities of these gods.[40] Given the multidimensional aspects of myths, this may well be true. But in my view, myths also mirror human tensions, which are thereby dissipated or at least reflected upon.[41]

The significance of *Enuma Elish*, the great so-called Babylonian creation myth, composed in all likelihood in the eleventh century B.C.E., has been the subject of much study. Most fruitful is T.

Jacobsen's illuminating analysis in *The Treasures of Darkness*,[42] although I will expand on and sharpen some of the points he makes. *Enuma Elish* is a political myth, a charter justifying and reinforcing the hegemony of Babylon and its god Marduk as the god of the realm. But it can also be understood as a justification for granting the young (namely Marduk) the possibility of assuming power. The generational conflict here between the young and old gods is not merely a minor theme but at the heart of the succession struggle. This myth emphasizes paternal (and maternal) hostility toward offspring, challenging the authority and wisdom of the old. Though the old may be wise (for example, Ea, Marduk's father), they are often weak and insecure.

The older gods are pictured as tired and passive, unable to tolerate the aggressive, boisterous behavior of the younger gods. The age-specific behavior of both old and young is underscored as the source of conflict: the old want to rest by day and sleep by night; the young want to dance and play.[43] The generational conflict in *Enuma Elish* leads to creative change,[44] establishing a new relationship between the young and the old based upon gratitude and the loyalty of the old gods to the young god Marduk. The myth concludes with a stunning image of the young god Marduk's power and glory. But at the same time the young have responsibilities for the care and maintenance of the old—Nudimmud (Ea) is "the champion of his fathers," a theme repeated with Marduk, Nudimmud's son, who is "the avenger of his ancestors."[45] Marduk, in his creation of the final stable order and structure of the universe, provides for the establishment of sanctuaries and offerings.[46] The old, therefore, instead of being a bastion of security for the young, come to rely on material and emotional forms of security provided by the young. They turn from a productive position toward a receptive one. Mutual accommodations are arrived at: the old must cede or at least share their privileges with the young; in return the young are to provide for and protect the old.

Kinship terminology abounds throughout *Enuma Elish*, usually of father and son but also of brother and mother. The first tablet emphasizes that each succeeding generation of gods is the equal of or superior to the preceding generation,[47] thus pointing up the pro-youth bias of the myth and laying the grounds for the generational conflict. There are images of the good father (Ea) and the bad father/progenitor (Apsu), of the good mother (Damkina) and the bad mother/progenitrix (Tiamat).[48] The amusing scene of the grandfather, Anu, giving his grandson, Marduk, the four winds as play-toys may reflect the easier, more relaxed relationship in Mesopotamia, as in many societies, between grandparents and grandchildren.[49]

Although myths are not historical documents, they at times do have a historical context. Jacobsen's view regarding this aspect of *Enuma Elish*'s parricide theme has merit. He says, "in warring with the Sealand, Babylon warred with the territory of ancient Sumer and all its renowned and venerable ancient cities and their gods. It waged an upstart's war with its own parent civilization."[50] Never-theless, deference and respect for the old gods remained. It is significant that on the fourth day of the *akītu* festival, the Baby-lonian New Year festival, when *Enuma Elish* was recited, that Anu's tiara and Enlil's seat were kept covered out of respect for these older gods, who had been replaced by Marduk.[51]

T. Jacobsen describes the *Harab* myth (or Theogony of Dunnu), composed early in the second millennium B.C.E., as showing " a gradual change from early barbarous indulgence in parricide and incest to somewhat more restrained conduct" and notes that it "is in that sense a history of cosmic morals. Briefly it may therefore be described as a genealogy of cosmic morals."[52] The *Harab* myth certainly seems to be the Oedipal story of Mesopotamia: the account of the son's rivalry with the father for the possession of the mother. But the elements of this conflict are totally muted. Indeed, the females—the mother, then the daughter and sister—are the aggressors at first and take the initiative, a kind of muffled myth of matriarchy justifying the rule of men over women.[53] The *Harab* myth is a condensation of Hesiod's *Theogony* (which is linked to it directly or indirectly) but entirely devoid, in the existing part, of the morally charged context of the *Theogony*. Unfortunately a substantial portion of the end of the myth is missing, and one can only guess at its content.

The myth, Jacobsen proposes, is the story of civilization's progress from chaos to order.[54] At first, close kin relationships represented in the extreme by incest with mother and then sister are overevaluated; the undervaluation of kin relationships is represented in the extreme by a sequence of parricides:

> [Harab], in the first [beginnings, took Earth to wife,]
> to [found] a family and [exercise] lordship. . . .
> [Earth] lifted [her] face to Sumuqan, his son,
> and said to him : "Come let me love thee !"
> Sumu[qan] took Earth, his mother, to wife, and
> Harab [his father] he killed, and
> in Dunnu, which he loved, he laid [him] to rest.[55]

The goals even in this early time of founding a family and exercising kinship are desirable, but neither is accomplished in a civilized fashion. Interestingly, even though the son murders the father, he fulfills the filial responsibility, in each instance, of proper burial. There is then a cessation of parricide and instead the imprisonment of the father—in short, a gradual but definite movement away from barbarism:

> [At New Year] he took over the lordship of his father, but
> he did [not k]ill him; al[ive]
> he seized him, and ordered his city to hold his father captive
> and he was put in cha[ins.][56]

Incest and patricide taboos are basic, therefore, to civilization. We may assume, without too much difficulty, that in the break were narrated the events that ultimately led to exogamy and to the legitimatization of succession by the assembly of gods who together select the ruler. The *Harab* myth thus encoded a message to sons: they should contain and restrain their hostilities and ambitions and wait to assume power and succession in accordance with civilized behavior and the laws of the land.

The generational conflict between young and old, a subsidiary motif in the *Atrahasis* myth (first composed in the Old Babylonian period), is a motif nonetheless. In the beginning the senior gods—Anu, Enlil, and Enki—are in charge and make all the decisions. The young gods perform services for their elders, doing the necessary hard work of digging rivers and canals, but after forty years they rebel, set fire to their tools, and decide to defy the authority of the old gods. Enlil is all for punishing them but is finally dissuaded from doing so by wise Ea's intervention. Enlil's vizier, Nusku, had earlier pleaded with him, twice saying:

> "O my lord, your face is [sallow as] tamarisk!
> Why do you fear your own sons?
> O Enlil, your face is [sallow as] tamarisk!
> Why do you fear your own sons?"[57]

The older god Anu agrees that "their work was indeed too hard, their trouble was too much."[58] Wise Ea advised that man be created to bear the yoke instead of the young gods.[59]

The latent tension and fear of the old toward the young is spelled out here; the vulnerability of the old, presumably in the face of the greater strength and aggressiveness of the young, is underlined; and the legitimate grievance of younger gods who do the dirty work is recognized. Here the young question the authority of their elders and meet with success. Sympathy is with the young. Again the usefulness of Foner's perspective is demonstrated: The myths "offer a way for the young to express their hostility indirectly."[60] In Mesopotamia, where positions of power and authority were usually in the hands of the older members of society,[61] younger citizens had much to complain about. *Atrahasis,* among other things,[62] may have functioned as a mechanism to reduce conflict.

The warrior god, Ninurta (sometimes known as Ningirsu), is the chief protagonist in several Akkadian and Sumerian myths. In each one he battles on behalf of his father, Enlil, and the other older gods. In the Akkadian *Anzu* myth,[63] he fights and finally kills the frightful bird, regaining the Tablet of Destiny stolen from Enlil. Again a young god, more powerful than his father and elders, comes to their aid.

The earlier Sumerian myth, *Angim*,[64] contains strong intimations of generational conflict. Here a triumphant Ninurta returning home from battle with an array of frightening trophies is admonished by Nusku to refrain from terrorizing his father, Enlil. "Do not frighten your father in his residence. Do not frighten Enlil in his residence."[65] As J. S. Cooper notes, "the ambivalence of this action is indicated by the awed perhaps frightened reaction of the gods. . . . The great mountain Enlil humbled himself. . . . The gods have become worried [and fled (?)] to the mountains. Like a swarm of birds they b[eat] their wings."[66] Promised rewards for fulfilling Nusku's request, Ninurta complies only partially. Yet he is received, as he wished, with respect by the old Anunnaki gods, his father, and his older brother Sin, by those who ordinarily are to be treated with deference and respect. His mother greets him with special warm praise.[67] *Angim* highlights the age-specific behavior of the young— arrogance and boastfulness—which though questionable is not punished. What is striking, as Cooper observes, is not the fear and deference of the Anunnaki gods but rather the rare fear of Enlil toward another god, in this case his son.[68]

In another Sumerian Ninurta myth, *Lugal-e*, probably composed at the time of Gudea (c. 2150 B.C.E.), generational relations are noted. Ninurta, whom his father has made greater than himself, also rivals his grandfather.[69] Here, too, the older gods are fearful and intimidated: "An shivered, sat down, wrung his hands over the heart. Enlil trembled, leaned against the wall, the Anunnaki hugged the wall, and mourned in the house like doves out of fear."[70] The father needs a son: "A son sits not where I [take my] rest, who is going to hold my hand?"[71] But the father is also important, for he comes to the son's rescue when he is needed. Thus reciprocity and mutuality between the generations are essential.

This brief examination of Mesopotamian myths strongly suggests that perhaps, if only on a subliminal level, generational conflict and discord were mitigated in human society by relegating youthful antagonism and revolt to the realm of the gods. Through their pro-youth bias, the potentially dysfunctional and disruptive competitiveness between the generations was allayed, thus protecting the authority of and control by the senior members of society.

CHAPTER FIVE

GENDERED OLD AGE IN
ENUMA ELISH

Enuma Elish was a "remarkable attempt to understand the universe, to come to terms with the human condition."[1] It is also a myth that can be probed for information and insight on the issue of aging and the old in ancient Mesopotamia: not only intergenerational conflict (as discussed in chapter 4) but also the little-known Mesopotamian attitude about the aging patterns of men and women—or more accurately, the views and attitudes held by the author(s) of the myth and perhaps of the *eduba*-trained elite. Certain assumptions made here should be noted before turning to an examination of the myth.

The old undoubtedly constituted only a small portion of society, and ageism (the devaluation of the elderly) was probably common, as it has been and continues to be in many societies, despite the ideal of respecting the old. I presume that myths reflect and refract the world the author(s) lived in, and perhaps their own life experiences. Myths tend to "generalize, symbolize and make the particular exemplary."[2] Stated somewhat differently, *Enuma Elish* depicts emblematic representations and prevailing stereotypes of old men and old women that incorporate the views and the biases of the ancient author(s).[3]

In recent years, cross-cultural gerontological studies have proliferated, providing helpful approaches and methodologies that can assist in eliciting data from *Enuma Elish* on aging and the aged.

Some may object to reading this ancient non-Western text "through the prism of modern methodology."[4] But gerontological research has produced significant information that appears less likely to be culture-specific and culture-bound than might be expected. There is therefore available a fresh angle from which to examine the myth, which reveals its complexity and profundity and thereby enriches our knowledge of an area as yet little explored by Assyriologists.

Especially useful in studying the issue of gendered old age has been the pioneering work of David Gutmann, a life-cycle developmental psychologist.[5] He draws on a variety of ethnographic studies that pay "some attention to the roles and behavior of older men and women." He finds that "the male endowment of aggression is not fixed over the entire life span . . . [but] declined with age." He notes moreover that "in later life women can become for men the embodiment of that eternal threat; they can present the aggressive visage that men come to deny in themselves." As for younger men, Gutmann observes, not only do they enjoy aggressiveness, but they also take pleasure "from being a source of security and provision to others, from the contentment and love of their dependents." Older men, by contrast, derive their pleasure "more and more directly on the productive efforts of others in their behalf, on the affections of others toward them, and on the satisfaction of their own appetites for tasty foods, pleasant sights, and soothing sounds. . . . [The older man] draws his psychological sustenance from his own receptors—mouth, eyes, skin, ears—as well as from outer sources of strength: the reliable providers of satisfaction and security who cater to his senses and to his wish for security."[6] One can perceive even from these few observations the insight they offer, especially into the myth's descriptions of the relationship between young Marduk and his elders.

One should not overlook the ongoing complaint by the old gods about their interrupted sleep and their need for rest.[7] For example, Apsu complains to Tiamat: "Their [the young gods'] behavior is noisome to me! By day I have no rest, at night I do not sleep!" (I 34–38). This should perhaps be viewed in light of the prevalence of insomnia, which modern researchers have found increases with age. Recent studies of sleep disorders have shown that sleep fragmentation characterizes many elderly people.[8] It appears to be a perennial problem of aging.

Enuma Elish is obviously biased in favor of the young Marduk. As noted by P. Michalowski, if *Enuma Elish* "is about anything at all [it] is about the exaltation of Marduk, the city god of Babylon, to the head of the pantheon.[9] The bias in favor of the young over the old is common in Sumerian and Akkadian myths (see chapter 4). It is therefore not surprising that ambivalence is expressed, if only subtly and indirectly, toward the old gods.

The wisdom of Marduk's father, Ea/Nudimmud, and his advice and assistance are important and helpful. These functions generally remain a significant contribution of the old to the young in traditional societies.[10] But what is emphasized in different ways over and over again are the incapacities of the old male gods, their dependency and loss of status, especially when faced with the challenge by Tiamat.

The recently published Tablet II vividly underlines these fears and inadequacies.[11] First Ea and then Anu attempt to confront Tiamat, but both return too terrified to act (*adurma rigmaša atura arkiš*).[12] It is the young Marduk who helps dispel fear and provides the needed security: "When Anshar saw him, (Marduk), his heart was filled with joyful feelings; he kissed his lips, he vanished his gloom." Earlier, Ea had calmed him: "When Anshar heard [Ea's soothing words, calming speech] it pleased him, he calmed down."[13] So important is the reassuring function of the young for the old that the nineteenth of Marduk's fifty names is the one "who dispels the benumbing fear from the elder gods" (VII 42).

The focus in the myth is on the psychological aspects of aging, rather than on the physiological changes.[14] The coping responses of the old gods are restricted and ineffective. Ea had been able to easily dispose of Apsu when he had been younger, before the birth of his son (I 60–69). But he cannot face Tiamat when he ages, any more than can his father, Anu. The older gods, having lost their youthful, competitive aggressiveness, allow Marduk to move into a position of ascendancy. They still have power, but it is inadequate to the task of aggressive action.

What is noteworthy in the myth is the importance of "orality" for the older gods, "a shift to the oral zone as a preferred site of pleasure."[15] Gutmann notes that orality appears to be a crucial dimension of the diurnal, waking experience of old men. Depression, he adds, is an emotional disorder that "is a frequent side effect of the oral character."

Depression many times in *Enuma Elish* describes the mood of the old gods:

> Anšar became despondent and looked down. (II 86)
> Painfully he (Ea) became faint, like one who lapses into silence he sat down. (II 26)
> [He (Anšar) smote his loins], and he bit his lips. (II 50)[16]

T. Jacobsen has commented on the banquets of the gods, observing that "important discussions originated when the gods were in their cups. Wine and beer were evidently necessary to lift the spirit out of the humdrum existence of everyday cares to original thought and perspective."[17] I find another dimension in the vivid lines describing one of the gods' feasts:

> They kissed one another in the assembly. They conversed (and then) they sat down for the banquet. Let them eat grain, drink fine beer. They poured the sweet liquor down their throats. Drinking beer, feeling good, they became quite carefree, their mood was high. (III 133–137)

We have here described the satisfaction and pleasure of the appetite for tasty food and drink, the oral pleasures, which replaced the joy of battle and violence. Fighting was no holiday for the old as it was for young men as the Poem of Erra put it.[18]

The depiction of Tiamat is far more interesting, detailed, and complex. Jacobsen notes the ambiguous attitude expressed toward her.[19] He observes that at first her motherliness is emphasized and later she is treated as the archenemy. I would account for this ambiguity by suggesting that Tiamat is first encountered as a young woman in her childbearing years. At this time, tolerant and forgiving, she is totally opposed to decimation of the young gods, her offspring. The younger Tiamat resigns herself to her spouse's death for the sake of the children. In the earlier period, the positive image of the goddess is underlined by her epithet *elletu* "pure" (I 36).

But later the older Tiamat does an about-face. She is now ready to avenge Apsu's killing. In the portrayal of the old(er) Tiamat we find the ubiquitous stereotype of the old woman as crone and witch. This emblematic representation, I suspect, not only mirrors the view of the ancient author(s), but as other sources suggest probably reflects the larger cultural misogynistic attitude of male Mesopotamians (see chapter 6). Positive images of older women are found in Mesopotamian literature, where maternal (both literally and figuratively) older women act as mediators and intercessors on behalf of men, especially their sons (see chapter 7). The goddess Damkina, the only other female mentioned in *Enuma Elish*, is the ideal mother, focused on her son, passively remaining in the background. She is as a mother ought to be, dependent and restrained.

Tiamat is a prime example of the negative stereotype. The increased assertiveness and independence of older women (especially of widows) make for their association in many societies with witchcraft and other nefarious practices.[20] Elderly women frequently have to contend with the double whammy of ageism and sexism.

Gutmann found ample evidence in ethnographic studies that "women do not replicate but instead reverse the order of male aging. . . . Across cultures, and with age, they [older women] seem to become more authoritative, more effective, and less willing to trade submission for security." Gutmann describes "the essence of the healthy, capable older woman: adventurous, expansive, self-asserting. By contrast old men stress their self-control, their friendly adaptability, and even their passivity. . . . [O]lder men seek to control their spontaneous urges, older women appear to seek out opportunities for vigorous action . . . older men strive for quiescence and comfort. Their psychological defences do not facilitate overt action but replace it with inhibitions." He later adds that "it may be that the older woman . . . realizes two fantasies in later life—the dream of union with the oedipal lover and the dream of being made whole, both feminine and masculine."[21] Gutmann's description of the older woman is a remarkable fit for Tiamat.

The old male gods of *Enuma Elish* are characterized by passivity and timidity, whereas the old(er) Tiamat is a virago. When she springs into action, as Michalowski notes, she is Mother Hubur, mother noise: "The metaphor of noise establishes a privileged position for the concept of creation, activity, independence."[22] Tiamat becomes a monster mother who creates monster war machines to destroy her children and descendants. And many lines (I 131–146), repeated several times, are devoted to her terrifying creations. It is noteworthy that in the descriptions of the monsters she creates is mentioned the phrase "instead of blood she filled their bodies with venom."[23] Tiamat is the prototypical "venomous woman" who is "an image of fear of female power to deceive and destroy men."[24] Not only her creations but Tiamat herself is full of venom.[25]

Tiamat, a far more formidable opponent than was Apsu, asserts her authority in masculine fashion:

> She installed him (Kingu) on a *karru*-throne. (I 152; II 38; III 100)
> She prepared for battle against the gods, her (tet: his)[26] (own) offspring. (II 2)
> She called an assembly. (II 12)
> He who was not fitting you established for office. (IV 82)

Fighting battles is a sex-specific skill and activity in Mesopotamia, yet Tiamat engages in it. She instigates the revolt against the gods (IV 77–84). When Kingu's nerve fails him on seeing Marduk, Tiamat does not waver or turn back (IV 71: *ul utâri kišadsa*). The vituperation and vehemence directed toward Tiamat are remarkably strong. In her one-on-one confrontation with the young Marduk she is derided: "She has become like an ecstatic (*maḫḫutiš*), she has lost her reason (*ušannî ṭenša*)" (IV 88). Reference is made to her ferocity and fury:[27] "She rages furiously" (II 12; III 16, 74) and "(Tiamat) who was fuming with rage" (IV 60). In addition, her proclivity toward evil and deceit is noted:

> *ina šaptiša lullâ ukal sarrati*[28] (IV 72)
> She conceived an evil plan. (I 44)
> You have fully established your evil plan against the gods my
>   fathers. (IV 84)

Yet Tiamat's power is recognized, as the recently published Tablet II found in the Neo-Babylonian Shamash temple clearly indicates: "Her might is enormous, she is imbued with terror; she is altogether mighty, none can go against her."[29]

Anu and Ea both turn back from confronting Tiamat. Both try to belittle her strength, for a woman is not as strong as a man (*emuqša sinništi lu dunnuna ul mala zikri*.)[30] But only the young, energetic Marduk will be able to defeat the aggressive, old goddess.

Her battle with Marduk can of course have only one outcome. Her powerful "masculinity" threatens male control, which is intolerable. It is not surprising that there is special emphasis on her repulsiveness and a strong need to dehumanize her, for thereby she is reduced in status. E. Cassin has remarked that Marduk combats Tiamat with a net (*saparru*) (IV 41), and she is thus seen "as a wild animal to be hunted, rather than as an equal."[31] Far more lines (IV 95–103, 129–132) are devoted to her killing than to that of her husband, Apsu. And there is a particular vehemence in the words describing her slaying: "Go out and cut the throat of Tiamat" (IV 31) and "Let him (Marduk) subdue Tiamat, constrict and choke her" (VII 132). After killing Tiamat, Marduk inspects her body to cut "the monstrous form" (*UZU kūbu*). The term *kūbu* has here the thrust of an invective.[32] Marduk splits her corpse "into two parts like a fish (split) for drying."³³ The primal mother becomes the raw material for the formation of the universe. The male god decides the form; the goddess contributes the matter, thereby losing her form (and her individuality).

Once Tiamat has been disposed of, the initiative earlier attributed to her (IV 77–84) is transferred to Kingu: "He caused Tiamat to rebel and set up the battle array," (VI 23f.) and so he is punished.

Enuma Elish is a male myth, exalting male order, male rule, male relationships,³⁴ male power and creativity. There was no place for a powerful, assertive, old goddess.

The very one-sided, misogynistic depiction of the old goddess Tiamat relates to her "masculine" behavior, which threatened partriarchal norms. But a far more balanced perspective of the roles and status of older women emerges from the evidence of a variety of other sources.

CHAPTER SIX

OLD(ER) WOMEN

That historical treatments of old age all too often overlook the experiences of women's aging has been noted by scholars in recent years.[1] Older women have been conspicuous by their absence in such analyses. This deficiency is now being addressed in numerous studies. For example, several classicists have focused on elderly women in the Greco-Roman period.[2] Given the paucity generally of studies on old age in ancient Mesopotamia, it is not surprising that barely any writing on this topic exists.[3]

The age at which a woman would be considered old in this long-dead society can only be speculated upon, for chronological age was of no interest to it.[4] But J. Henderson's definition, in my view, would be as applicable to Mesopotamia as it is to ancient Greece: "A woman was old when she was no longer defined in terms of procreative or erotic sexuality, when she stopped bearing children and so ceased to be a source of anxiety for men of the household."[5]

The Akkadian term for a postmenopausal woman is *sinništu paristu*, literally "a woman (whose blood) has stopped flowing."[6] The Sumerian equivalent *mud.da.gi₄* may mean "her blood has stopped" or "she has stopped giving birth." In an article of some twenty-five years ago, two biologists, utilizing classical sources, estimated that in the ancient world menopause took place anywhere from the age of forty to fifty, with a maximum of sixty years.[7]

Interestingly, the rare mention of chronological age, appearing in a thirteenth-century B.C.E. letter from Rameses II of Egypt to the Hittite king Hattusili III, links age to the reproductive cycle: "(I) your brother the king know 'Matanazi my brother's sister. (You say) she is fifty years old—but no, she is sixty years old! Now see here, a woman of fifty—let alone a woman of sixty—one cannot prepare medicinal herbs for her to enable her to conceive."[8] This text, far earlier than the classical sources, seems to confirm the estimated age noted above for the cessation of menstruation.

But recent research questions the "assumption of universality in the menstrual patterns familiar to contemporary industrialized societies. . . . There is evidence for later menarche, and *earlier menopause* [my emphasis] . . . than that to which we are now accustomed."[9] Given the Mesopotamian indifference to chronological age, the onset of menopause may well have made for a conundrum as to when menopause really began, as was the case so much later in medieval Europe.[10] There is no reason, however, to assume that Mesopotamians regarded menopause as "the final stage of death," as it apparently was millennia later in Victorian England.[11] Nor would it be surprising if Mesopotamians believed, as did later Europeans, that women aged earlier than men, although no data exist to prove this.[12] This undoubtedly would be so if women's aging was defined in sexual reproductive terms and men's in social, functional categories.

Mesopotamian textual and material remains yield only limited and problematical glimpses into the lives of older women over a period of some three thousand years. What can be extrapolated is based all too often only on indirect and implicit evidence.

As M. T. Roth has commented, "not even the most basic questions about life expectancy can be readily answered."[13] Apart from the incredible lifespan of Adad-guppi—mother of the last native ruler of Babylonia (Nabonidus [556–539 B.C.E.]), who lived until she was 104 or 102, no age at death of a male or female is recorded.[14] Pathological studies of skeletal remains, for example, from the north Babylonian city of Kish have disclosed that on the whole, women died earlier than men and often in childbirth. Yet women were healthier than men.[15]

Of relevance to the question of women's life expectancy are the life spans of the sequestered *nadītu* women of Sippar. These mostly elite women entered the cloister (*gagû*) of Sippar probably in their teens, at an age when a girl normally married, and were expected to remain there until their death. Living as celibates, they were occupied not only in cultic ceremonies and prayers devoted to their deity, Shamash, and his consort Aya, but also with various business and legal transactions.[16] Most of these texts are dated and thus inform about the duration of their activities. A considerable number of them were involved for twenty-five years and more. Several are attested to for more than fifty years.[17] It is reasonable to assume that their longevity was due to their celibacy and childlessness. Undoubtedly, too, their living in the cloister, fairly isolated and cut off from the general population, protected them from the hazards of epidemics that affected the general population.

Similarly, the estimation by W. W. Hallo that the earlier attested celibate *entu*, high priestesses of the moon god at Ur, beginning with the preeminent princess Enheduanna, daughter of Sargon of Akkad (2334–2279 B.C.E.), "held office for an average of 35 to 40 years. They functioned during the nearly half-millennium of their continuous attestation (ca. 2280–1800)."[18] Like the later *nadītus*, these women too escaped the perils of giving birth. Furthermore, some data indicate that women might, if they survived beyond the childbearing years, live longer than men.[19]

Like old men, and probably more often, aged women were marginalized members of society, especially if they belonged to its lower strata. Economically, their worth was measured in terms of their productivity. Thus in early ration texts down through the Ur III period most old women receive the same allowances of wool, oil, and barley as do children. This is in contrast to younger women, who receive considerably more, though usually half again of what grown men receive.[20] K. Maekawa assumes that old women (age is of course never given) along with prepubescent children were not

required to work, for "old women [were] . . . regarded as useless
for actual labor. Hence they receive[d] the same rations as non-
grownups."[21] But H. Waetzoldt disagrees, observing that old
women and children from about the age of five or six were required
to work. However, elderly women—some being grandmothers in
the same workforce as their daughter and grandchildren—were
designated as workers "with half labor" (or "half wage"), probably
able to perform only half the work of a younger, healthy adult
woman.[22] Nevertheless, there are instances where old women were
allotted the same rations as fully able-bodied men and women,
presumably because their work was equivalent.[23]

An old slave woman was likely to be sold for considerably less
than a young slave-girl. In one such case, the former fetched
fourteen shekels; the average rate for the latter was about fifty
shekels.[24] The young woman's sexual and reproductive functions
obviously made for her greater value to her owner.

In wartime, old women (like old men, young women, and
children) were particularly vulnerable. In one Ur III record of ration
distributions to prisoners of war, 167 old women are included, of
whom 46 are dead and 23 ill![25] Like that of an elderly man, an old
woman's worth, if she was murdered, was equivalent to that of a
child, according to an Old Babylonian treaty, the oldest of its kind
in Akkadian.[26]

The terminology for an old woman is discussed in chapter 3. But
one Sumerian term, *buršuma*, an early loanword from the Akkadian
puršumtu "gray-haired," deserves special mention. It is used as an
epithet of some goddesses (never of male gods) and "denotes
elderly women of stately dignity who have charge of domestic
affairs. It is therefore a complimentary term in Sumerian, empha-
sizing the greater responsibility and status that women might attain
with time rather than age per se."[27] This term for the elderly, like
the English "hoary," connotes both gray-haired and distinction.[28]
Presumably, elderly women, like old men, were not only characterized by gray hair, but this was *the* marker of senectitude in
Mesopotamia.

To what extent ordinary old women enjoyed a greater margin of freedom than they had in their youth is not easily answered.[29] The textual evidence from all periods underlines that Mesopotamian women generally, like ancient Egyptian women, participated in all kinds of business activities—buying, selling, lending, initiating lawsuits, and so on—without the restrictions to which Greek and Roman women were subject.[30] Well-to-do widows, especially when their children were grown, certainly enjoyed more freedom than when their husbands were alive. It appears that the cessation of menstruation probably brought about a positive change in later life.

For one thing, the relief from pain and/or discomfort should be considered. Akkadian medical texts (written by male scribes) metaphorically describe a menstruating women as "wounded by a weapon."[31]

More cogent to the potentially greater freedom of a post-menopausal woman are the purity/impurity rules of Mesopo-tamian tradition. Menstruation causes impurity; mother and child also become impure in the birth process. Even the incantation priest who assisted in the delivery was not to be seen again for thirty days. Presumably the pollution caused by childbirth lasted this long. However, the exact nature of the mother's uncleanness and the taboos associated with it are to date not known. It did not apparently include abstinence from sexual relations.[32] Nor were men free from impurity; constant ejaculation could make for it.[33] As for older women, R. D. Biggs observes that there are "examples in rituals where certain actions are to be performed by a woman who is menopausal." He suggests that this may be because she was free from menstrual impurity and so would not be "vulnerable to contrary works of magic to render her infertile. . . . She would not cause defilement and at the same time she would not be subject to harm."[34]

A prototypical negative view of older women is drawn of the old goddess Tiamat, as discussed in chapter 5. She is, in my view, emblematic of the misogynistic attitude toward aging women. In a role reversal with the old male deities, it is she who becomes active and assertive, giving battle to the young, vigorous Marduk. Her assumption of what were considered masculine traits was repugnant. Little wonder that a Neo-Assyrian literary text refers to Marduk defeating the goddess with his penis![35] But apart from this literary representation of a horrific hag, I know of no other explicit association of old women and ugliness, a theme commonly found in Greco-Roman writings.[36] It is significant that although the ancient Mesopotamians believed that a plethora of female demons plagued human beings at all stages of life, none was considered to be old.[37]

As with men, so too women are almost invariably depicted as mature and assured individuals in Mesopotamian art.[38] One does not find here the stereotypical youthful, elegant creatures of Egyptian art, especially of the New Kingdom period.[39] The one exception, a statue of an elderly woman, dates from the Early Dynastic period.[40] D. P. Hansen considers her old because "her hair is so plain and dull in contrast to the generally very elaborate hair-do's of so many Sumerian women." He believes that this was done to indicate "a very specific type." Furthermore, her sunken cheeks add to the impression of age.[41] To my knowledge, no evidence from Mesopotamia indicates that changes in dress and hair-do correlate with different life stages.[42] A Neo-Assyrian relief showing two women and a child fleeing from the city, perhaps representing an older woman, her grown daughter, and her grandchild, does not distinguish in any way between the appearance of the mother and daughter.[43]

B. D. Starr observes, "If ageism typifies the history of attitudes toward the elderly, then nowhere is this prejudice more apparent than in the area of sexuality."[44] Mesopotamian sources reveal little about the attitudes toward elderly males' sexuality but are somewhat more forthcoming regarding male views toward the sexuality of older women.[45] Age-disparate marriage between an old man and a young woman was acceptable, probably in contrast to one between an older woman and a younger man.[46] This biased attitude is understandable given the underlying assumptions of Tablet 104 of the omen collection *Šumma Ālu*. In a seminal analysis of this intriguing series, A. K. Guinan found to be central the view that the male must always be the dominant, active sexual partner. This was far less likely to be the case if an older, assertive woman was involved (see chapter 8). Moreover, such a relationship would separate sex and reproduction, intolerable in the male-female relationship. Mesopotamian males would not have agreed, I think, with Pseudo-Demosthenes (fourth century B.C.E.): "We have mistresses for our enjoyment, concubines to serve our person, and wives for the bearing of legitimate offspring."[47]

A bilingual proverb describes an old prostitute defending her ability to continue her profession: "My vagina is fine (yet) among my people it is said of me: 'It is finished with you.'"[48] Interesting is the protasis of Tablet 104 of *Šumma Ālu*: "If a man has sexual relations with an old woman (*šībtum*), he will quarrel daily." This is an unfavorable prognostication. A. Guinan in a personal communication suggests that this is so because "the old woman has lost her sexual currency"; she is no longer fertile or sexually attractive. Another possibility, according to Guinan, which I find convincing, is that a man who enters such a relationship does so because the woman had "non-sexual power" over him. This is then a case of a man who is not in control.[49]

In a medical treatment, perhaps for paralysis, the practitioner is instructed to wrap his finger in a piece of linen and to rub the patient's anus with salt, then put in a pubic hair from an old woman (*šībtum*). In another case, hair from a young woman (maiden) and a young man who has not known a woman is prescribed. What all three—old woman, maiden, and young man—have in common is freedom from impurity, because none has engaged in the sexual act, which causes impurity. Their pubic hair may, therefore, have been thought to have healing power.

Seemingly neutral is a late Babylonian ritual text that advises the patient to present a votive offering and kiss the face of an old woman.[50] But the kiss too may have curative benefits.

One must take note before leaving the subject of old women and sexuality of an unusual Sumerian text that appears on the surface to be greetings sent by a son to his mother via an unnamed courier.[51] The son, living some distance from his mother, is concerned that she is worried about him, unable to sleep, and constantly asking visitors to Nippur about his well-being. The messenger, not knowing the mother, is given signs to help identify her. As M. Çig and S. N. Kramer note: "Actually none of the signs are specific and detailed enough to have served their purpose." They think the author used lyrical, hyperbolic words and phrases "to portray the ideal Sumerian mother."[52] Curiously, the mother's unmatched beauty and charm are dwelt on in terminology that more recently has been shown to belong to the metaphorical language of love poetry.[53] In one simile the mother is likened to "a garden of delight, full of joy," also used to describe a "maiden-harlot," a devotee of the goddess Inanna.[54] How is one to account for the blatant sexual language used by a son to his mother? One possibility is suggested by the Greek parallel of the more intense, even libidinal, relationship between mother and children, especially sons, because of their greater age proximity than between fathers and sons.[55] The recent suggestion by G. Leick that the "mother" (*ama*) is perhaps a pun on *ama* ᵈInanna, who is "listed among persons connected with sexuality"[56] and therefore is really a courtesan. There is, in my opinion, much merit to this alternative interpretation.

The association of witchcraft with elderly women, especially poor women, has long been made at various times and in numerous places.[57] This linkage may very well stem, as J. Henderson has observed, from the fact that cross-culturally as women age "they seem to become more domineering, more agentic, less willing to trade submission for security." He suggests that witches are "an imaginary personification of the social power of older women in its negative aspects."[58] The stereotypical "adult witch is an independent adult woman who does not conform to the male idea of proper female behavior."[59] I would further add that perhaps older women's experiences with birth, disease, and death, locating them in dangerous liminal arenas, may make them particularly objects of fear.

Witchcraft was part and parcel of Mesopotamian life. Practitioners seem more often to have been women than men.[60] One of the chief sources of information on Mesopotamian witchcraft in general and in Assyria in particular is the series *Maqlu*, which means "burning."[61] It consists of nine tablets; the first eight are incantations, and the ninth provides directions for performing the magical actions needed to render the incantations effective. Although men are referred to as sorcerers in *Maqlu*, it is primarily women, especially foreign women, who are thus designated. As noted by Rollins, there exist no documents from either Assyria or Babylonia that concern explicit accusations of witchcraft. Nor is there much evidence that witches were elderly women.[62]

However, in the Sumerian narrative poem *Enmerkar and Enšuḫkešdanna*, one episode focuses on the competition between the old woman (*um.ma*) Sagburru, who is a witch, and an unnamed sorcerer.[63] Five times they contend to determine who has the greater powers. Each throws an object into the river and produces an animal. Her animals overcome his every time, and she is the victor. She accuses him of performing forbidden things in the primeval city of Uruk without her consent, and though he pleads for his life, she kills him.

Five Old Babylonian letters published by S. D. Walters also yield relevant information.[64] They concern the tension between a father and son. Indirectly it is learned that the father has accused his son's wife and her mother of witchcraft. The son also accuses his father of using a witch, who is unnamed. The father had given his son barley seed to plant in a field. The son did not follow his father's wishes but instead disposed of the seed and leased out the field to a tenant farmer. The father brings the matter before the mayor, believing that his son had acted contrary to his wishes under the influence of his wife and mother-in-law, whom he describes as witches (*kaššaptum*). In a second letter addressed, in Walters' view, to the mayor, the father accuses the mayor of siding with the women. The five letters are linked by the repeated mention of the father's name with references to the judges, the mayor, and Adad-dumqi. The last addressee in three of the letters is the mother-in-law, Adad-dumqi. Walters suggests that this woman was in charge of stocks and supplies and had also been involved in some questionable dealings with a woman; she participated in wool transactions and supervised females taken as pledges. He opines that because "Adad-dumqi was an aggressive and opportunistic administrator, it would be easy to suggest that the father's accusation against her was an expression of the general uneasiness in the village about a woman playing a role which [she] had come to play."[65] Adad-dumqi was then an agentic, assertive, and influential older woman (her daughter was married) who challenged the traditional norms. Little wonder that her son-in-law's father harbored hostility toward her.

The depiction of the old goddess Tiamat, creator of monsters, is also that of a powerful witch with formidable magical powers. This may be relevant in assessing her negative portrayal (see chapter 5).

Perhaps one may also infer from the following passage that witches might be old, though not described as such explicitly, from the descriptions of their victims:

> She (the witch) robbed the fine man of his vigor
> She took away the attractiveness of the fine young woman
> With malignant stare she took away her charms
> She looked at the young man and took away his vigor
> She looked at the young woman and took away her
>   attractiveness.[66]

The victims are young and attractive. What is apparently described here is the "loss of libido," the inability of the young man to achieve satisfying intercourse; the young woman becomes sexually unattractive and perhaps therefore unable to find a sexual partner. It is the old woman, past her prime, no longer enjoying a sexual life herself, who might have been especially suspect in causing impotency and sexual dysfunction.[67] Similarly, Lamashtu, the demon par excellence who caused infant mortality, was regarded as a frustrated mother who snatched infants belonging to others.[68]

Finally, mention should be made of the well-known Hittite Old Women (*mí.šu.gi*), who belonged to a special class of ritual practitioners, even though they functioned outside of Mesopotamia. They would be considered "good" witches. So influential were they that an Old Kingdom edict of King Hattusili I sought to curtail their influence on the women of the palace. The names of thirteen Old Women are known. Along with other women, they were "authors" of magical rituals. Surprisingly, several of them were slaves, able to transcend their lowly status.[69] So firmly linked were magic and old women among the Hittites that this was their title.

Women, especially older women, serve as mediators and intercessors, not as creators of culture (see chapter 7).[70] D. Herlihy's observation about women in medieval households is also applicable to Mesopotamia: "The mother [is] . . . ideally placed to serve as intermediary between the often conflicting generations. She remained much nearer in years to her children, was easier to approach and emotionally more committed to their welfare."[71] This description best applies to elite and royal women, and especially to goddesses. But although intercession, the entreaty by a woman on behalf of someone else, is considered a preeminent feminine role, it is not surprising that in this traditional patriarchal society the common idiom for intercession is *āḫiz/ṣābit abbūti*, literally "to assume a *fatherly* [my emphasis] attitude on behalf of someone."[72] Undoubtedly women's mediation relates to their quality of compassion, regarded as a primarily feminine attribute, for in both Sumerian and Akkadian the terms for "womb" and "compassion" are one and the same.[73] Women intercede on behalf of those with lesser power to those with greater power than themselves.

This special function of women is especially prominent in mythology, where goddesses, emblematic of human beings, serve as exemplars for women's roles and behavior.[74] In the Sumerian myth *Enki and Ninmah*, for example, the younger gods complain bitterly about their workload: "They poured their tears before (the goddess) Nammu. She brought them to her boy (Enki)."[75] Furthermore,

Nammu advises her son on how to deal with the labor problems, by creating man to work instead of the young gods, and he heeds her. In an episode in the ongoing conflict between the god Ninurta and the monster Anzu, Ninurta acts against the older god Enki and is rescued from the god's punishment by his mother.[76]

In a Neo-Sumerian letter prayer addressed by a scribe to the god Enki, the scribe laments his sorry plight. He pleads that Enki's "beloved first wife [Damgalnunna] may she bring it (his lament) to you like a mother, may she introduce my lament before you." This follows with a male god doing the same.[77]

Especially important as intercessor is Gula, the goddess of healing par excellence. "Patients sometimes ask her to entreat other gods to relieve their anger against the suppliant. . . . [Her] intermediary role in healing is directly related to the Mesopotamian medical theology"[78] that among the various causes of illness is the wrath of a deity.

The intercession of human women, especially older women, was thought to be especially efficacious. This may be linked to the view that women tend to be more pious than men and hence the gods will be more favorably disposed toward their requests.[79] So one Sumerian proverb has a man saying: "(Since) my wife is at the outdoor shrine (and) my mother is at the river (shrine), I shall die of hunger."[80]

Noteworthy is the example of Addu-duri, probably mother of Zimri-Lim, ruler of Mari. Her letters are replete with omens and cultic minutiae. Her son's letters to her also focus on religious observances.[81] Of interest too is the letter of Ashurbanipal to his father, Esarhaddon, where he notes that the gods Ashur and Shamash chose him as crown prince because of his mother's righteousness.[82] Nor should the piety of Nabonidus' mother, Adad-guppi, be overlooked. All are queens or of the royal family.

Although crying and tears were not a "gendered category" in ancient Mesopotamia as they were, for example, in Greece, nevertheless lamentation and keening were usually associated with women.[83] They were related to the maternal emotion, compassion.[84]

"May the pasture land shriek in mourning as if it were a mother," laments Gilgamesh over the dead Enkidu.[85] As T. Frymer-Kensky observes, "the self-laceration and frenzy" in the description of lamenting goddesses "is almost certainly a reflection of mourning behavior on the human scene."[86] Particularly vivid is the description of the goddess Nammu, mother of Enki, abandoning her city: "Her hands have become heavy through wailing. She cries bitter tears. She beats her chest like a holy drum. She cries bitter tears."[87]

Mainly old women probably made up the ranks of professional mourners at funerals of nonrelatives, though there is little evidence to prove this conclusively. Five wailing old women (*umma.ír*) appear in a pre-Sargonic Lagash text, alongside the lamentation priests (*gala*) who play the *balag* instrument.[88] However, public congregational laments were performed by male singers called *kalû* (Sumerian *gala*) and not by women.[89] But they sang the women's parts in a Sumerian dialect known as *eme sal* "the thin tongue," which suggests they may have sung these parts "in a special thin falsetto voice."[90]

There exist several terms for wailing women, who may or may not have been professional keeners, notably, *lallarītu* and *ama'irakku* (or *ama'erakku*), a loanword from the Sumerian meaning literally "mother of mourning."[91] A recently published Old Babylonian tag catalogue was once attached to a basket of thirty-nine tablets, containing seven compositions used by professional female mourners and wailers in the cult of the goddess Belet-ili.[92]

A significant aspect of the positive view toward older women relates to their wisdom, their ability to advise and guide male and female members of their society. Thus, terms relating to advisory ability and knowledge—*maliktu*, *mudû*, *nēmequ*, among others—describe not only male gods but also goddesses.[93] And although most examples of wise females are goddesses, they mirror the realities of the human sphere.[94]

One Neo-Assyrian letter warns the men to keep quiet to avoid imparting men's secrets to women: "Anyone who opens his mouth will have ruined us by his wife's cunning (*ina nēmeqi ša sinnissišu*)."[95] It was assumed that women, like men, learned from life experiences. As *The Curse of Agade* put it: "She (the goddess Inanna) endowed its (Agade's) old women with advice / She endowed its old men with counsel."[96]

In a hymn to Enlil, his wife Ninlil is described: "In advising she finds the perfect word."[97] In a hymn to the goddess Nanshe it is said, "With her who makes the experts' words come right, the lady and woman sage of settled Lagash, Gatumdug, she advised and to Nanshe, she spoke most fair words."[98] When young Ninlil's mother warns her not to bathe in the river lest she be raped by Enlil, the daughter ignores her advice:

> At that time, the mother that bore her gave advice to the
> young woman,
> Nunbarshegunu gave advice to Ninlil. . . .
> In giving this advice, she offered wisdom to her.[99]

In one version of *Enki and Ninhursaga*, the grandmother counsels Nintur not to give in to Enki when he wants to sleep with her. In another version it is the great-grandmother Ninhursaga who warns Nintur. But Enki is successful in seducing her.[100] In all three instances, the girl is naive and foolish: ignoring an older woman's cautions leads to grief.

Mothers advise married daughters on how to behave toward in-laws:

> ɯ
> Verily [you are] his [spou]se, he is your spouse . . .
> Verily your father is (now) a stranger only
> Verily your mother is (now) a stranger only.
> *His* mother you will respect as were she *your* mother!
> *His* father you will respect as were he *your* father![101] ⁄⁄

In the myth *Enlil and Ninlil*, the recently married Sud is counseled on how "to keep her man": "Never forget charms and pleasure, make them last a long time."[102] When the god Martu wants to marry he asks his mother to find him a wife. She responds:

> Oh . . . [instruction] I would give you . . .
> [Take] a wife wheresoever you raise (your) eyes
> [Take] a wife wherever your heart leads you.[103]

S. N. Kramer suggests that Martu's mother may have given him very specific instructions in the fragmentary and difficult lines that follow.[104]

Frequently cited in discussion of the *Gilgamesh Epic* is the advice of Siduri in the Old Babylonian version of the epic. She speaks as a worldly-wise woman and so can be considered emblematic of an older woman. She advises the weary hero to give up his fruitless quest for immortality and instead enjoy the diurnal pleasures of life: eating, partying, dancing, wearing clean clothes, washing himself, attending to the little one who holds his hand, delighting in his wife's embrace.[105] Gilgamesh's mother, the goddess Ninsun, described as "the wise, all knowing," also plays a most important role in her son's life, assisting him on his way to maturity.

Curious is the example of one mother goddess, appearing with different names, who advises her son Ningirsu (also called Ninurta) on strategy in battling the monster Anzu. In both the Old Babylonian and Late versions of the myth she "instructs" her son in the detailed specifics of the attack.[106] He listens to her advice and succeeds in overcoming his enemy.

An early example of a human *femme sage* is found in the Sumerian epic *Enmerkar and the Lord of Aratta*. Here Enmerkar, ruler of Uruk, goes to the city of Aratta, being besieged by his soldiers, to acquire its precious stones and metal for the building and embellishment of temples. The female sage approaches him to give advice:

> She came out to him like a maiden when her days are over (i.e., her monthly period), on her eyes she had painted kohl, was wrapped in a white [garment]. . . . She gives advice about bartering food for precious metals saying "My master come! Let me advise you, and may you take my advice, let me say a word to you and may you heed it."[107]

He takes her advice for negotiation, and an amicable settlement is reached between the two rulers.

In the somewhat fragmentary Sumerian myth of *Inanna and Bilulu*, the latter—who appears nowhere else in mythology—is a wise old woman. She is described as *buršuma nin.ní.te.na.ka* "an old woman who is her own mistress," an independent person. There is some ambiguity as to whether or not she and her son were responsible for the death of Dumuzi, Inanna's spouse. But she is cursed and transformed into a waterskin.[108]

Perhaps there were, though few in number, professional wise women at least in the Sumerian period, similar to such women in ancient Israel, to judge from the occurrences mentioned above.[109] A lament for the city of Ur refers to the goddess Gatumdug, sometimes pictured as an old woman: "Lagash's woman sage was abandoning it (Lagash) and her sheepfold to the winds."[110] A late Kassite incantation addressed to Uttu, the goddess of weaving, also links an old woman to special knowledge. It mentions a cord or rope used in the ordination of a priest of Enlil:

Uttu placed a cord in his (the candidate's) hand.
Inanna having prepared the cord,
A skillful woman having served his genitals,
A knowledgeable old woman having prepared it.[111]

Very much part of the human world as evidenced by textual sources are the writings of two princesses: Enheduanna, daughter of Sargon of Akkad; and more than four centuries later, Ninshatapada, daughter of Sin-kashid, founder of a dynasty at Uruk. Much has been written about the former: her three Sumerian hymns have been published, the little that is known about her personal life examined. She has been characterized "as a kind of systematic theologian, whose works must have served as a model for much subsequent hymnography."[112] Foster describes these religious compositions as bearing "all the hallmarks of highly cultivated genius and deep feeling."[113]

The "letter-prayer" composed by Ninshatapada in 1800 or 1799 B.C.E. was addressed to King Rim-Sin (1822–1763 B.C.E.) of Larsa after his capture of her city, Uruk. She has been exiled from Durum, where she served as high priestess to the twin gods of the nether-world, and pleads with the king to permit her to return. Her composition—and it is surely hers, for she refers to herself as a scribe (*mí.dub.sar* in line 16)—is a masterful piece with vivid, moving imagery, complimentary to the king, whom she addresses as the young protector (line 2). She describes her pitiful circum-stances in exile:

> Though vigorous, I am abandoned in old age like a day
> which has ended, I am scattered (from) my chamber
> Like a bird caught in a trap whose fledglings have fled from
> their nest.[114]

Hallo notes that "the fact that her letter-prayer was incorporated in the royal correspondence of Larsa makes it appear likely that her plea was granted."[115]

These are examples of learned old priestesses and princesses, of whom there were few. There may have been more such women, of whom nothing is known from remaining sources.[116]

The names of other authoresses have been suggested. Il-ummiya, a "tapstress," Jacobsen believes was the composer of many "rather outspoken love songs to Shu-Suen, king of Ur, which became part of the Isin-Larsa school curriculum."[117] T. Frymer-Kensky thinks that Kubatum, the king's wife, authored these love songs. It has been suggested that the poignant lament over the premature death of king Ur-Nammu was composed by his wife Watartum; and a lullaby may have been composed by Shulgi's wife.[118] But, in my view, one must be very cautious in making such assumptions regarding the *vox feminae* presumed in these Ur III compositions. More study must be done on style and imagery, and investigation of female rhetoric is required, if indeed it is to be found in the written sources (see also chapters 7 and 8).[119] Though love songs and laments cross-culturally belong to women's oral traditions, as do work songs and lullabies, we cannot automatically assume that women authored the written love songs, laments, and lullabies that remain.[120]

The tasks of women, old and young, were primarily in the household: cooking, cloth making, and beer brewing, to mention a few. Frymer-Kensky observes that women were "in charge of household management and administration. This was the job of adult but *not aged* [my emphasis] women, typically the married daughter-in-law."[121] Her assertion assumes that an old woman (presumably widowed) would live with her son and his family. But I suggest that, depending on her relationship with her son and on her personality, the old woman might very well lord it over the younger woman. It is noteworthy that the professional cooks in the royal kitchen were usually male.[122]

One can assume that whatever work women did, like men's, it extended over their lifetime; only death or illness terminated labor. But the activities of women are rarely mentioned in the written sources, for "control of writing in ancient Mesopotamia was directly related to the hierarchies of power in society." Although some women, "particularly those of high birth, were active in economic and political affairs, the majority of women from the middle levels of society were defined by the roles of their husbands, fathers and brothers."[123] Thus women's names are frequently omitted and only their relational connections with men noted. Women from the lower strata remain nameless, with few exceptions, hidden from view as individuals.

Some scholars have studied the range of women's work and activities.[124] But when examining the occupations, particularly of older women, we are at a disadvantage, for rarely are age categories included in the literature, and only speculative conclusions regarding them can be drawn.

Perhaps it is best to begin with the question of what enterprises or professions might be expected to be pursued by women at this stage of life, whose experiences made them "naturals" for these activities. Here would belong the position of professional mourners and keeners, discussed above. One hymnic reference also links an elderly woman to the serving of beer:

> Lord, enter not the alehouse, smite not the old woman
>   (*puršumtum*) who sits beside the beer (to serve it)
> Lord, enter not the tavern (*aštammu*), smite not its old man
>   wise in lore (?)[125]

In the *Lugalbanda* epic, Ninurta's mother, Ninkasi, an older woman, is depicted as a dispenser of beer.[126] Frymer-Kensky observes that women did much of the brewing in breweries and certainly at home.[127] The occupation of female brewer disappeared in the Old Babylonian period, but significantly the deities of brewing and alcoholic beverages—Sirish and Ninkasi—remained feminine.

Another arena linked to older women by only meager data is the realm of the cultic and mantic. But such women probably played a much more prominent role than is attested to in the texts. A. L. Oppenheim discusses women's special talent for dream interpretation. Gatumdug, the goddess of Lagash—the divine dream interpreter—is sometimes depicted as an old woman. Nanshe, referred to as the "mother" of Gudea, is the gods' oneiromancer.[128] Women, especially mothers, function as dream interpreters in the epical literature, suggesting that women gained in expertise as they aged.

The female diviner (*šā'iltu*) appears in Old Assyrian texts in connection with inquiries to a deity having to do with everyday problems.[129] In one instance she is actually described as elderly (*šībtum*). One letter mentions more than one *šā'iltu*, as well as other female professional diviners (*bārītu*) and the spirits of the dead, who are approached with inquiries.[130] The plurality of *šā'iltu*s led Oppenheim to believe that they lived in groups. This too suggests that these women were no longer part of conventional households but perhaps widowed and independent. There is also a single reference to *šabrâtu,* a group of female dream interpreters, who functioned "mainly outside and below the domain of official temple-centered religious life."[131] Perhaps because women far more frequently than men experienced symbolic dreams, women required the services of these female oneiromancers.

An Ur III wool document lists expenditures for "the cult needs of the old woman (*šibtum*) of the temple (of) Ganuhum." But her priestly office is not indicated. She holds "a singular but unidentified position in the temple."[132]

Especially in the sphere of healing and caretaking, one expects to find older women, and particularly in the area of midwifery.[133] The Mesopotamians would have agreed with Plato that "no woman practices midwifery while she is still of an age to get pregnant and give birth herself. It's only those who are past child-bearing."[134] The midwife, the *šabsūtu* (borrowed from the Sumerian *mí.šà.zu* "the woman who knows the inside"), would not only assist in birthing but might also be called upon when a question of paternity, and thus of inheritance, arose at a later time (see below).[135]

In an Ur III Sumerian royal love song, the queen mother Abisimti, wife of Shulgi and mother of Shu-Suen, acts as "birth-helper" when his first child, a son, is born to his wife Kubatum.[136] Elderly women without children or with grown children might work as child caretakers (*tarîtu, tarbîtu*) for the well-to-do as they did in ancient Greece.[137]

Older women surely played a significant role in herbal healing. Theirs would be a tradition transmitted outside of the scribal schools, relying on folklore handed down the generations. They treated the aches and pains of ordinary folk. They undoubtedly helped in caring for the chronically ill of private households, because Mesopotamian temples did not serve, as did medieval nunneries, as large-scale infirmaries. The home would of course have been the locus of care for the elderly themselves. The early *arua* institution discussed by I. J. Gelb may have served as a collecting center for orphans, widows, or old and/or disabled people, but it was not a sanitarium.[138] The physician (*asû*) and the exorcist (*āšipu*) treated the illnesses, both physical and psychological, of the court and the elite.

Finally, older experienced women must have held managerial and administrative positions in the various areas of the palace. Of these, one of the highest offices available to women was that of *šakintu*. She was in charge of the queen's household in the Neo-Assyrian period.[139]

In considering older women, widows merit special attention.[140] Of course there is no way of knowing what proportion of women lived on after their husband's death. But given the fact that elite women at least were considerably younger at marriage than their spouses, it follows that widows may well have been a visible element in the population. M. Golden cites an estimate that in ancient Greece, where there was a similar disparity in age between husband and wife, there were twenty percent more widows than widowers.[141] Widowhood was, as in other times and places, for the most part a difficult situation for women. The ambiguity of the status of widowhood is illustrated by the comments in *The Assyrian Dictionary*: "The term *almattu*, although usually covered by the modern term 'widow,' does not denote simply a woman whose husband has died but a married woman who has no financial support from a male member of her family—and who thus, on the one hand, may be free to dispose of herself either by contracting a second marriage or by embracing a profession."[142] The very fact that there is no masculine equivalent for "widower" in Akkadian high-lights the gender difference. Men were far more likely to remarry.

For royal and upper-class women, widowhood might provide a greater margin of freedom to act and more options from which to choose than any other stage in a woman's life. But for the vast majority, and especially for those who were childless, widowhood led to poverty and want. As one Sumerian concisely put it: "Help-lessness (?) is a widow's lot."[143] Nor was there any guarantee that even if she had many sons a widow would be looked after: "The mother who has given birth to seven grown sons lies languishing in poverty," exclaims another proverb.[144]

Indeed, only rulers and gods might be relied on to come to the aid of unfortunate widows and orphans, the most vulnerable members of society. As King Hammurapi proclaims in the prologue to his laws, he was named ruler by the gods "to make justice prevail in the land, to abolish the wicked and the evil, to prevent the strong from oppressing the weak."[145] But ultimately only the gods could be directly appealed to for help by helpless widows. Often it was Shamash, judge of heaven and earth, concerned with the plight of the poor and wronged, who was addressed:

> Utu (his Sumerian name), you are their mother
> Utu, you are their father . . .
> Utu, for the widow you are like her mother bringing her
>   again into custody.[146]

Popular too in aiding the widow was the goddess Nanshe, also guardian of social justice and ethical behavior: "For the widow she had not helped remarry Nanshe was supporting, like a beam, a proper house." The goddess would punish "the married man whose wife came to him out of the widows, and on a day when he was angry he ridiculed, or jeered at her in the days of her infirmity."[147]

Many of the Mesopotamian law collections, from earliest to latest times, include clauses concerning the widow's rights to her deceased husband's property. Much would depend on whether or not the property had been assigned to her during his lifetime. Of special concern for the widow was her domicile, where she might live for the rest of her life. It was assumed that her children, in particular her son(s) if she had any, would take care of her. If a widow remarried, the question of which properties she might take into this marriage and which belonged to the children of her first marriage had to be adjudicated; the inheritance rights of these children had to be protected.[148] Of all the law collections, the Middle Assyrian Laws appear to have granted the widow the greatest margin of freedom: "If her husband and her father-in-law are both dead, and she has no son, she is indeed a widow (*almattu*); she shall go wherever she pleases.[149]

In all periods, it seems likely that a widow might be the head of her family,[150] a prestigious position if it was a well-to-do family. But for those without family or kin, life would be difficult and bitter. The concern would be not only for allotments of food, drink, and clothing, but also for proper burial with the accompanying rituals, as well as regular funerary offerings. One recourse for such a person was adoption; this was frequently followed by the childless *nadītu* when she aged and could not depend on the cloister administration for support.[151] In a poignant Old Babylonian letter a woman "writes" to her brother, "Now I have (acquired and) am raising a boy, telling myself: Let him grow up, so that there will be somebody to bury me."[152]

Private legal documents remain recording various arrangements made for the support of a widow. Marriage contracts would be drawn up in the Old Babylonian period for the express purpose of stipulating that the widowed mother of the bride was to be supported by her daughter or her daughter's husband after the marriage.[153]

The flexibility of the arrangements for the care of widows is illustrated by an Old Babylonian text from Ur in which two men are entrusted by a husband to support his wife for life.[154] After his death, in return they are his heirs. But fourteen years later one of them assigns a slave for her care in his stead. When she dies the slave returns to him. (Note how much longer she has already outlived her husband.) A Neo-Babylonian text records a childless couple adopting the wife's grandson from a previous marriage.[155] A Middle Babylonian adoption text from Nippur records the adoption of a girl by a woman who can be presumed to be an elderly widow, preparing for the time when she will be unable to care for herself. As W. G. Lambert observes, "She was one of the no doubt many widows who acted as legally independent people."[156] The adopted daughter is either to be given in marriage or she may work as a prostitute. The young woman's husband, if she marries, is to maintain the widow, or her income as prostitute will. If the adoptive mother makes her a slave she is to return to her father's house. If she were enslaved, she would be deprived of her rights of inheritance to her father's estate.

Noteworthy is the concern expressed in a letter of the Assyrian king Sargon II (721–705 B.C.E.) for the support of the widows of fallen soldiers. The king orders the addressee, whose name is no longer preserved, to

> [enqui]re and investigate [and write down] and dispatch to me [the names] of the [sol]diers killed and their [sons and d]aughters. Perhaps there is a man who has subjugated a widow as his slave girl, or has subjugated a son or daughter to servitude. Enquire and investigate and bring (him/them) forth. Perhaps there is a son who has gone into conscription in place of his father; this alone do not write down. But be sure to enquire and find out all the widows, write them down, define (their status) and send them to me.[157]

The rest of the letter is poorly preserved but continues with the king's concern about the widows (*mí.almattu*).

Roth discusses at length the plight of various widows, which led them to bring "lawsuits in order to secure their rightful properties." Figuring prominently in some of these instances are the rights to a domicile.[158]

Just as the temple in far earlier times served as a haven for the elderly, especially women,[159] so too in the Late Babylonian period the Shamash temple cared for widows; in exchange widows gave garments to the temple. Roth considers the rather mysterious *bīt mār banî*, a place offering physical shelter, a kind of asylum to widows, orphans, divorcées, or other people deprived of legal, social, and economic security.[160]

Obviously, remarriage was the most viable alternative for a widow, especially if she had young children.[161] And there seems to have been no opprobrium attached to such remarriages in Mesopotamia proper.[162] Roth estimates, albeit on the basis of limited sources, that there was a very high remarriage rate. The Roman ideal of *univira*, a woman who married only once in her lifetime,[163] was not a Mesopotamian ideal.

Among widows, the dowager queen or queen mother (in Akkadian she was referred to as "mother of the king") deserves separate consideration. Unfortunately, though not surprisingly, rarely is the identity of the king's mother known. Had it been it might have helped in "a better understanding of foreign diplomacy, and the principles of succession. If the mother of a new king had entered the royal household as the result of a diplomatic marriage (whether as first wife or not), she would naturally be a foreigner and this could radically affect the attitudes of the king and hence foreign policy. As for succession, it seems that the throne was not automatically passed from father to son."[164] The property and possessions of royal women through marriage and inheritance were the bases of their power. Intrigues surrounding succession to the throne might provide them with important roles during their husband's lifetime and afterward. "The position of queen [and I would add of queen mothers] was whatever these women could make of it."[165] In the examples of dowagers who did achieve sufficient power to influence the succession to the throne of a younger son, it can be assumed that it was due to their own considerable skills and ambition.[166]

Strong bonds must have developed between royal women and their sons that enabled some queens, albeit rarely, to act as regents for minor sons when their husband died.[167] But far more often dowagers must have served primarily as advisors and counselors. In circumstances where rulers might be suspicious of other men, a female member of their family, and especially their mother, might well assume these roles, knowledgeable, as the most astute of them must have been, about palace politics and intrigues. The dowager could, as N. Andreason suggests, provide a buffer between king and subjects. Male relatives were loyal up to a point, but mothers (and sisters) were far more reliable and dependable.[168] As for the queen mother, likely an older woman past the age of child-bearing, she vicariously through her son expressed her active mastery and received emotional gratification from her influence.

The high status of the queen of Mesopotamia down the ages has been treated by other scholars.[169] These queens engaged in multifarious activities and managed their own private estates, aided by their own administrative staffs. They might manage not only agricultural properties but also commercial establishments. Queens would be buried with great pomp and ceremony.[170] Power and prestige probably continued for many of them when they were widowed, although few sources remain to inform us about this.

For some of the queen mothers, much information is available. Abi-simti (wife of the Ur III ruler Shulgi and mother of his successor, Shu-Suen) probably administered Uruk, the ancestral home of this dynasty, after her son or the crown prince had done so. This dowager was long-lived, as is attested to throughout the forty-nine years of her husband's reign and nine years of her son's rule. Her administrative functions were integrated into the larger structure of Puzrish-Dagan.[171] The unifying theme of one of the Bal-Bal-e dialogues, according to T. Jacobsen, is Shu-Suen's praise of both mother and grandmother.[172] Lamassatum, mother of Lipit-Ishtar, ruler of the First Dynasty of Isin (1934–1924 B.C.E.), dedicated a storehouse to her personal goddess, Inanna of Murtum, "for the life of her son and for her own life."[173]

The many and varied activities of Addu-duri of Mari have been studied for years.[174] It is obvious that she was a woman of great influence and prestige who served in some kind of official capacity in the palace of King Zimri-Lim. It had been assumed that she was perhaps an elderly relative of the king. Only recently have scholars suggested that she was probably his mother.[175] She died in the ninth year of her son's reign. Only then did his primary queen, Shiptu, assume a preeminent role, often deputizing for her husband. We have here a not-uncommon situation in which the mother-in-law was the dominant female until her death.[176]

Addu-duri's jurisdiction was not limited to the palace and to temples but also included the whole of the capital city. Most touching is one letter in which palace servants appealed to her on behalf of an elderly slave. He had served the palace since his youth and was about to be callously given away to someone else as a gift, even though he was now an old man.[177] Who better than Addu-duri, herself aged, would be well acquainted with this slave and his loyal service to the royal family?

Most significant are the frequent prophetic messages mediated to the king by his mother, and other women as well. While away he was kept informed by letters about her ominous dreams and about matters concerning the official cult, such as the planning for sacrifices and the construction of a throne for the goddess Annunitum. In her letters she communicates her anxiety for her son, so often away on military expeditions, as well as concern for the welfare of the kingdom.[178]

Addu-duri also had palace administrative functions: she was in charge of supplies, such as wool. She was involved in legal matters, investigating disputes about property. She had some hand in the matter of horses and was concerned about runaway palace slaves. In one letter Zimri-Lim advises her to act forcefully so escapes would not become common.[179] Unquestionably Zimri-Lim relied heavily on his mother's trustworthiness, competence, and ability.

More names of queen mothers are known from the Assyrian period. A. L. Oppenheim believed that the influence of the king's spouse and mother, "politically important at times," was a "Western" custom, best attested in the Hebrew Bible and in Hittite sources.[180] The most famous of these was Sammuramat, wife of Shamshi-Adad V (823–811 B.C.E.) and mother of Adad-nirari III (801–783 B.C.E.); she is identified with the Semiramis of classical fame.[181] Sammuramat helped her son become ruler, even though he was a younger son. Herodotus considered her one of the great personalities of ancient Mesopotamia. One inscription relates that she crossed the Euphrates River in 805 B.C.E. and was closely associated with Shamshi-ilu, one of the highest ranking Assyrian officials in the first half of the eighth century.[182] J. Reade views her as "matriarch and possible regent" for her son for four years after her husband's death, exercising "a range of choices that were normally the prerogative of men."[183]

The new governor of Kalah (Nimrud), Bel-tarsi-ilumma, dedicated two inscribed statues at the entrance of a new temple to the Babylonian god Nabu, for the life of the king, Adad-nirari III, and his mother.[184] The cult of Nabu may have been introduced at this time at her instigation. She is described in her own stela from Assur as the wife of Shamshi-Adad V, mother of Adad-nirari III, and daughter-in-law of Shalmanesser III (858–824).[185] This dowager held real power, making dedications in her own name, which is even placed before her son's. The Hanging Gardens, one of the seven wonders of the world, was wrongly attributed to her by classical tradition. Her enormous influence in the realm gave rise to the classical tradition that this in turn correlated with the kingdom's weakness under her son Adad-nirari, a negative view indeed of an assertive, agentic older woman. The fame of this remarkable woman lived on long after her death. G. van Driel's comment is apropos: "The royal family is one of the important Assyrian institutions about which we have hardly any information during the 9th and 8th century: One can only notice the revolt of Aššurdanninpal and Sammuramat's obvious influence."[186]

The last powerful Assyrian queen mother was Naqi'a-Zakutu; Naqi'a, her West Semitic name, means "pure," and Zakutu is its Akkadian equivalent. She was the favorite wife of Sennacherib (704–681 B.C.E.), mother of Esarhaddon (680–669 B.C.E.), and grandmother of Ashurbanipal (668–627 B.C.E.).[187] Twice she was instrumental in choosing the successor to the throne: her only son, Esarhaddon (despite his being the youngest son of Sennacherib), and her grandson Ashurbanipal, despite his having an older brother, Shamash-shum-ukin. Her son and grandson, in contrast to her husband, were friendly to Babylon. However, in the case of the one grandson, it was the older brother's extreme pro-Babylonianism that made for his losing out to his younger brother. Naqi'a-Zakutu made use of the oracle of Ishtar of Arbela to legitimate the ascension of her son, Esarhaddon, to the throne.[188]

In a note on "An Inscribed Bead of Zakûtu," M. van de Mieroop concludes that the inscription on the bead of the necklace, "probably donated to a statue of an as-yet-unknown god of a temple, reinforces the image of Zakûtu as an active dowager queen, with a special affection for her son[,] Esarhaddon."[189] It is probably Naqi'a-Zakutu, J. Reade suggests, who is shown on an embossed fragment of bronze, behind the king. She "holds in her left hand the mirror of femininity, but in her right hand, she too [like the king] has the ritual object: she is fully involved in the ceremony."[190]

Finally, Adad-guppi's name should be added to the list of influential queen mothers.[191] She was in all likelihood instrumental in her son Nabonidus' rise to kingship. The fact that the date and place of her death were recorded in the Babylonian Chronicle strongly suggests that "she wielded considerable influence during the reign of her son. She died while accompanying the Babylonian army led by her grandson, the crown prince, Belshazzar."[192]

S. B. Pomeroy's comment on queenship is descriptive, too, of the position of the Mesopotamian dowager: it "was not a public office and therefore cannot be defined except as a private role. Private roles were flexible and depended upon individual personalities; there was no 'typical' queen,"[193] and, I would add, there was no typical queen mother.

The plight of dowagers, especially if they were of foreign origin, may at times have been a difficult one, if one can judge from the circumstances of widowed Hittite queens. As S. R. Bin-Nun has noted, "Whenever a Hittite queen remained in office [as Tawan-anna] after the death of her husband[,] trouble began in her relation with the new king."[194]

Insight into the relationship between younger and older women, particularly between mother-in-law and daughter-in-law, is difficult to come by. The advice of the goddess to her daughter noted above is instructive: ideally one's in-laws should be treated like one's real parents. But it is not unreasonable to assume that tensions in such relationships existed in Mesopotamia, as they usually have cross-culturally.[195]

In one Old Babylonian letter, the sender says to the addressee: "Your daughter-in-law dislikes you (*izêrkima*) and (so) did not give me anything."[196] The incantation series *Shurpu*, the compendium for exorcists, contains a conjuration against family estrangements.[197] After those between immediate family members are mentioned tensions between mother-in-law and daughter-in-law. An unpublished wisdom text warns: "What you, daughter-in-law, do to (your) mother-in-law, they (your daughters-in-law) will do to you."[198] Such generational conflicts were seen as ongoing and self-perpetuating. In a revealing passage of an Old Babylonian letter a woman says to her son-in-law: "If you are my son-in-law and I am your *mother* [my emphasis] I should be in your thoughts. Do not make me unhappy. . . . Stop my tears."[199] So mother-in-law and son-in-law conflicts were also to be found in ancient Mesopotamia. Of the relations between the multiple generations working side by side in the labor force, we know nothing.[200]

It is fitting to conclude with what was probably the most important role of older women—that of grandmother. Given that there were probably more old women than old men that lived on, a good many of them may have lived with son(s) and their families after husbands died. Grandmothers would have helped with child care and household chores.

It is, however, not surprising that little can be gleaned from remaining sources about the lives of grandmothers. It is a grandfather's response to a grandson's birth that is described in the sources, not a grandmother's (see chapter 4): "When Anu his grandfather saw him (Marduk) / He was happy, he beamed, his heart was filled with joy." It is a grandfather, not a grandmother, who gifts the child (Marduk) with a toy: "Anu formed and produced the four winds, / He put them in his hand, 'Let my son play!'"[201]

Not unexpectedly, grandmothers probably frequently participated in the birth of their grandchildren. As noted earlier, Abisimti, mother of King Shu-Suen, was most likely a "birth-helper" at the birth of her grandson. Far more detailed and somewhat more revealing than a mere glance into the difficult realities of everyday life is an old Babylonian legal text from Nippur.[202] It concerns the paternity of a man born after his father's death. His father had abandoned his pregnant wife "because she was always falling ill." When he grew up, probably after his mother's death, his paternal uncles contested his paternity, laying claim to his inheritance. Fortunately, when his mother had gone into labor her mother-in-law, the baby's grandmother, "sent for a midwife and informed two officials who sent a representative to witness the birth." The grandmother, a member of an important family and a prudent woman as well, "knew exactly which officials to notify." The grandmother probably foresaw what eventually did happen and took the necessary precautions to safeguard her grandson's legal rights to his father's estate. The child was looked after by his paternal grandmother and one of his father's servants. The testimony of the grandmother thus validated her grandson's right to his patrimony.

Older women, whether royal, elite, or poor, thus served and contributed to their families, and at times to their communities, in various important capacities. Like aged women elsewhere they functioned almost entirely in the private domain. Many may well have derived satisfaction and power from relationships that left no traces in the records and so remain hidden from view.

CHAPTER SEVEN

IMAGES OF WOMEN IN THE
GILGAMESH EPIC

Several years ago W. L. Moran urged Assyriologists to adopt "the more comprehensive critical strategies of the contemporary literary criticism" and to adapt "to new methods" in studying Mesopotamian texts.[1] This essay is such an attempt, tentative and programmatic, and at this juncture in no way definitive. The complex and multidimensional quality of the *Gilgamesh Epic* is too well known to require documentation. Like all classics that "frame human experience in enduring and universally meaningful forms," it cannot be encompassed in one final interpretation.[2] The many versions of the *Gilgamesh Epic* in ancient languages and the growing number of contemporary studies and translations attest to its enormous, abiding appeal.

Despite the many articles devoted to the *Gilgamesh Epic*, one area—images of women—has received no more than a passing comment or an occasional footnote. For the purposes of this study I will treat the epic as a coherent text, bypassing the many problems of composition and evolution (not that these are irrelevant to the topic). Elucidation of certain issues that pertain to composition and evolution might shed light on changing attitudes, if such there were, toward the roles of women in Mesopotamian society and on differences, if any, between this culture and those others whose scribes translated (and modified) the *Gilgamesh Epic* into their native languages. For example, J. Tigay has noted the different terms used for "wife": *sinništu*, *ḫirītu*, *aššatu*, and *marḫītu*, differences in terminology that relate to the evolution of the epic.[3] Of significance, perhaps, is the expanded role of Ninsun in the Late Version, in the scene preceding Gilgamesh's departure with Enkidu to do battle with Humbaba.[4]

What must be emphasized at the very outset, for it touches on all that follows, is the assumption that the *Gilgamesh Epic*, in whatever version, was composed by men for the edification and entertainment of a presumably male audience who read or to whom the epic was read. The *Gilgamesh Epic* is like the medieval *chanson de geste*, which was "written for a male audience, *to male taste* [my emphasis]."[5] Therefore, what we find in the epic are essentially male attitudes toward women, both human and divine. Central to the *Gilgamesh Epic* are the concerns and activities of men, with women functioning as supporting and subsidiary characters in the cast.[6] It must, moreover, be underscored that the correlation between the epic's images of women and actual women will not be "a simple unambiguous one of direct reflection or representation. . . . Images can also embody fears, fantasies and wishes."[7] The importance of women in the epic relates to their relationship with Gilgamesh. Their images incorporate the anxieties, longings, fears, and wishes of men, grounded in the realities of human life.[8] These images also reflect the diversity and ambiguity that characterized the lives of real women.

Women are regarded positively only when they assist Gilgamesh (and Enkidu) in those heroes' activities, when they nurture and advise in maternal fashion. The adventures of the heroes preclude a primary role for women. Though Mesopotamians did not live in a sexually dimorphic society like that of ancient Greece, women's domain, nevertheless, did not partake of the political and military arenas that were the masculine domain.

A crucial element in the epic, which I believe is linked to its images of women, is the frequent use of symbolic inversion, especially status and role reversal, in the depiction of women. As

B. Babcock notes, "Symbolic inversion may be broadly defined as any act of expressive behavior which inverts, contradicts, abrogates, or in some fashion presents an alternative to commonly held cultural codes, values and norms be they linguistic or artistic, religious or social and political." The term "derives from and conflates several existing discipline-specific uses."[9] Inversion serves more than one function in the *Gilgamesh Epic*; however, in this chapter I focus on "the comic switching of expected roles."[10] The reversal of the expected roles of certain women in the *Gilgamesh Epic* is, in my opinion, an essential feature of the epic's humor and comedy, which must have held great appeal for the ancients.

We now turn to the supporting cast in the *Gilgamesh Epic*, that is, to the women. Though they are not principal actors they are, nevertheless, significant in moving the plot along.

Ninsun, the divine mother of Gilgamesh, is all that a mother should be: caring, nurturing, and assisting her son in his quest, anxious though she is about it. Her name or epithet, Rimat-Ninsun "Wild-Cow Ninsun," incorporates the ubiquitous non-erotic metaphor used to describe tender, loving mother goddesses in Mesopotamia and elsewhere.[11] The all-knowing (*mūdât kalâma*) mother is expert, as are other Mesopotamian women, human and divine, in interpreting dreams (see chapter 6).[12] Addressed tenderly by Gilgamesh when he speaks to her, she is the only female with whom there is a loving male/female relationship in the *Gilgamesh Epic*.[13] She laments his restless heart (*libbi la ṣālila*) and pleads with Shamash to assist him. In a difficult passage in the Late Version (III iv 21), Ninsun seems to adopt Enkidu as her son, brother then to Gilgamesh. If this is so, then she, like Siduri, affirms the centrality of family and kin to human life, the importance of the private sphere to men who dominate the public sphere. Ninsun is the only real mother (that is, biological mother) in the epic, but "motherly" also characterizes the other females, except for Ishtar.

The prostitute Shamhat is an intriguing woman.[14] She and Siduri, the tavernkeeper, are working women who support themselves. Shamhat belongs to a class with low repute in society. Siduri is associated with a place of low repute. And Ishtar, not incidentally, is associated with both, as she is in the following hymnic passage: "When I sit at the entrance of the tavern, I am a loving prostitute."[15]

Both prostitute and tavernkeeper belong to the extradomestic domain; both were important in the leisure activities of Mesopotamian men. Though the real-life Mesopotamian prostitute had a bad reputation and was seen as a threat to the stability of the family,[16] her representation in the *Gilgamesh Epic* is quite the reverse. She is depicted, through her actions and words, as a maternal, beneficent, wise woman and not as a deceitful, lustful seductress. And significantly, like Siduri, and unlike Utnapishtim's wife, she is named, given individuality and personhood. The *ḫarimtu* is thus a prime example of role and status inversion: the lowly, marginal *ḫarimtu* is elevated to the central kin role of "mother."

The classicist P. Friedrich suggests "the connection between artful, or sophisticated, sensuousness and civilization" in understanding the role of Shamhat.[17] But the issue is far more complex. The intermediary role of the prostitute in transforming Enkidu from one at home with nature and wild animals into a human being (*awēliš īwe*) is crucial. Also pertinent is the Mesopotamian view that among the *me*s, which constitute the norms of civilized life, are included sexual intercourse and prostitution.[18] Relevant too is the fact that the prostitute in Mesopotamia, like the prostitute in ancient Israel, was a prime representative of urban life.[19] Of special value in appreciating the mediating role of the *ḫarimtu* are S. Ortner's comments, for she provides a frame of reference in understanding this function. Shamhat serves, as do women in other places and times, as "one of culture's crucial agencies for the conversion of nature into culture, especially with reference to the socialization of children." Shamhat is the primary facilitator of Enkidu's socialization. What she teaches Enkidu puts "her squarely in the category of culture," and "on the basis of her socializing functions alone, she could not be more a representative of culture."[20] Thus by profession an urban representative and by role (really a role reversed) the domesticator of Enkidu, Shamhat is indeed a fitting intermediary.

Enkidu's break with his former life among wild animals is first achieved through sexual relations and is completed through learning the way of civilized life. Shamhat's is a dual role, as a sexual creature[21] and as a maternal figure. The first is explicitly spelled out by the hunter: "Show him, the *lullû*-man (your) feminine wiles" (*epšišumma lullâ šipir sinništi* [I iv 13, 19]). The second is more implicit. Enkidu is untaught (*la lummud*), and Shamhat teaches him the basics that every child must learn: eating, drinking, dressing himself.[22] The predominant image is that of mother, her relationship with Enkidu that of mother and child.[23] That this is to be the prostitute's function is perhaps already intimated by the hunter even before she meets Enkidu, when he says to her: "Release your hold" (*rummî kirimmiki* [I iv 8]); the term *kirimmu* is described as "a characteristic and functional position of a mother's arm assumed in order to hold a child safely."[24] Shamhat later shares her clothing (*ištīnam ulabbissu*) with the naked Enkidu. She takes "hold of him as the gods do" and leads him away from nature to the hut of the shepherds.[25] Enkidu's dependence on the *ḫarimtu* is emphasized.

One final point should be noted—one that is, I suggest, an aspect of role reversal—Shamhat speaks in proverbial language and as a woman of wise counsel (*mil[k]um ša sinništum imtaqut ana libbišu* [P. ii 25]).[26] She thus emulates the wise Ninsun.

Siduri, the divinized tavernkeeper, is also depicted in ways that are very unlike the actual tavernkeeper.[27] Apart from Ishtar's association with taverns (as noted earlier), Siduri is linked to Ishtar in a problematic way.[28] Like Shamhat, Siduri has a name and is self-employed. Her name has been interpreted as perhaps having a Hurrian origin, meaning "young girl."[29] Yet unlike Shamhat, the *ḫarimtu* who undresses, Siduri is concealed by a veil (*kutummi kuttumatma* [X i 4]), as the modest wife of later Assyrian times would be: she is covered, as the *sābītu* in real life was surely not.[30] Here too is an example of status and role reversal. She too is represented as a supportive figure who assists Gilgamesh in his dangerous journey to find Utnapishtim, after proffering him words of advice. What she has to say deserves special attention: her discourses can be described more accurately, I think, as pragmatic and realistic than as hedonistic or as recommending carpe diem.[31] She speaks practically, and to everyday living.

> Now you, Gilgamesh, let your belly be full!
> Be happy day and night,
> of each day make a party, . . .
> Let your clothes be sparkling clean,
> let your head be clean, wash yourself with water!
> Attend to the little one who holds onto your hand,
> let a wife delight in your embrace.[32]

In contrast to Shamash, she stresses the goodness of food, clean clothing, washing, and bathing, which all belong to woman's domain. She stresses the importance of wife and child and thus of relationship. Siduri, then, like Shamhat, voices and upholds the social norms of Mesopotamian society. She too is depicted as a wise woman, speaking in proverbial language.

The two married women in the *Gilgamesh Epic*—Utnapishtim's wife and Scorpion-man's wife—are unnamed, anonymous creatures.[33] Their position is like that of Mesopotamian wives generally: relational, given definition as wife or daughter. Utnapishtim's wife remains entirely in the background of the flood story. She is passive, acted upon: Enlil brings her aboard the boat and has her kneel beside her husband (*ušteli uštakmis sinniši ina idiya* [XI 191]). But she speaks and acts on behalf of Gilgamesh. Hers is an intercessary role, a not-uncommon feminine and maternal role in Mesopotamian literary texts.[34] She beseeches her husband not to let Gilgamesh die when he falls asleep (XI 208). Begrudgingly he accedes, adding the jaundiced proverb, "Man is wicked, he will treat you wickedly" (*raggat amēlūtu iraggiki* [XI 210]).[35] He has her bake breads to prove to Gilgamesh that he has slept for days. When Gilgamesh has failed the sleep test and prepares to return to Uruk, it is she who, mindful of society's rules of hospitality and sensitive to his enormous efforts (*illika īnaḫa išūta*), sees to it that he does not leave empty-handed.

Unfortunately the passage about the Scorpion-man and his wife is poorly preserved. What may be noteworthy is the specificity of her response when her husband comments that "he who has come to us is of divine flesh" (*ša illikannâški šēr ilī zumuršu* [IX ii 14]). She corrects this: "(Only) two thirds of him are divine, one third is human." Whether this specificity was an aspect of real women's rhetoric cannot be ascertained without further study.[36] I would suggest that, in keeping with the pattern described above, the Scorpion-man's wife may have been instrumental in having her husband assist Gilgamesh on his way.[37]

Before turning to Ishtar, the most intriguing and complex of the females in the *Gilgamesh Epic*, note should be taken of the very minor roles of other women characters. Aruru, the mother goddess, is told to create a replica of Gilgamesh (*eninna binî zikiršu* [I ii 31]), and she follows those instructions. The mediating role of the women of Uruk, whose complaints against Gilgamesh are heeded by the gods, should also be noted.[38] As a result, the gods take action, which leads to the creation of Enkidu. Finally, attention should be given to Ninsun's suggesting to Shamash that Aya remind him of Gilgamesh lest he forget him (*Aya kallat liḫassiska* [III ii 20]).[39]

All of the above-mentioned women (both divine and human) are assisting, nurturing, caring persons. Ishtar alone departs from the paradigmatic feminine role in the *Gilgamesh Epic*. She alone does not fit the mold. (For a discussion of the paradoxes in Ishtar's personality see chapter 10.) And yet even she is depicted as "motherly" in the flood story related to Gilgamesh by Utnapishtim, when she cries out "like a woman giving birth" (*kīma ālitti* [XI ll6]) at the terrible destruction wrought upon mankind by the flood.[40] But her representation in the episode where she proposes to Gilgamesh and he rejects her (VI 1–79) is ruthlessly negative. What is to be made of this?

T. Jacobsen, in his sensitive analysis of Inanna-Ishtar, justly describes her as "in some respects the most intriguing of all the figures in the pantheon."[41] Although the Ishtar-Gilgamesh episode is open to various interpretations,[42] I suggest that a key to understanding it, if only in part, is the factor of inversion—the reversal of expected roles (see chapter 10).[43] One does not expect a mortal (even one who is two-thirds divine) to reject a goddess. And yet Gilgamesh does so, detailing his refusal at length with the sordid features of Ishtar's many love affairs and her previous marriage. He castigates her with a series of metaphors,[44] several of which may provide clues to the reason for his rejection of her: she has behaved like a man in proposing marriage and in offering him gifts. She has thus assumed an active, aggressive posture, an unacceptable role for a female. In the many-faceted and paradoxical aspects of her personality, Ishtar is often depicted as warrior and hence as one who participates in the public domain of males.[45] But in the *Gilgamesh Epic* this aspect of her is rejected. Gilgamesh mocks and scoffs at her, as if she were a man. Enkidu humiliates her later in an unbelievable way (Gilg. VI 161ff.). And like a man, she retaliates.

Gilgamesh, in describing Ishtar's many affairs, is illustrating graphically the negative view toward the prostitute, as one with "countless husbands" (*ḫarimtu ša šāri mutūša*).[46] Ishtar—the prostitute par excellence in religious texts, the patroness of prostitutes—is repulsed by Gilgamesh because she has assumed an intolerable role for a female. Shamhat and Siduri are depicted positively because they act "motherly." There are, then, two inversions in the case of Ishtar: the status inversion, in which a mortal mocks a goddess; and the role (or category) inversion, in which a female behaves like a male.

Scholars have interpreted Ishtar's rejection as having its roots in theological, political, or historical factors. I propose a different interpretive direction, which I borrow from W. D. O'Flaherty: she writes that "the gods are often imagined to *be* men, to *be like* men in character; and here they appear not on the top but rather at the very *bottom* [my emphasis] of the continuum, as ludicrous."[47] In the episode with Gilgamesh, Ishtar too is at the bottom, not on the top as one would expect a goddess to be. This is an accurate description of status inversion.

Related to the question of images of women in the *Gilgamesh Epic* is the nature of the relationship between Gilgamesh and Enkidu. Apart from his closeness to his mother, Gilgamesh's only other intimate relationship—demonstrated by kissing, embracing, and the holding of hands—is with Enkidu.[48] As Jacobsen has so aptly put it, "throughout the epic the relationship with Enkidu competes with, and replaces marriage."[49] I think that on a subliminal level, if not overtly, the composers of the epic were critical of so intense a relationship between men.[50] A. Kilmer has suggested that the word plays *haṣṣinnu : assinnu* and *kiṣru : kezru*, as well as the sexual symbolism of *pukku* and *mekku*, point to what may well have been a homosexual relationship between Gilgamesh and Enkidu.[51] She calls attention to what I would more precisely describe as reverse sexual similes and metaphors: Enkidu's hair is like a woman's (I ii 36), and Gilgamesh veils his dead friend like a bride (VIII ii 17), to mention a few. Several times in his early dreams, Gilgamesh makes love to Enkidu's symbol "some kind of meteorite (?) of Anu, as a wife" (*kīma aššate*).[52] The relationship between them is not simply that of male and female but that of husband and wife. Theirs, then, was a reversal of normal societal relations, which potentially undermined the continuity and stability of the family. It is an example of category inversion—male acts like female.

In view of this, one aspect of Tablet XII needs to be underlined. Along with others, I would contend that Tablet XII is an integral part of the *Gilgamesh Epic*.[53] Central to its theme is the importance of family, the necessity of offspring to mourn the deceased and provide the *kispu* offering.[54] Enkidu, who has been treated like a woman and wife, voices this view implicitly, if not explicitly. The nonbiological immortality that Gilgamesh sought so mightily is rejected by the author(s) of the epic: the importance of family and kin to a meaningful life is upheld.

Inversion, then, is one of the keys to understanding the *Gilgamesh Epic*. The reversals of the norms detected in the epic (of the *ḫarimtu*, of the *sābītu*, of Ishtar, of Gilgamesh and Enkidu) and thus the inversion of the social pyramid and of expected roles and categories must have made for humor and comedy, which would have had great appeal to ancient audiences. What has been said about inversions in carnival-like festivals may well be applicable to Mesopotamian society. Through inversion "a society with an acute sense of the necessity of everyday social distinctions [might experience] an apparently 'ideal' state of anarchy which it had no wish to bring permanently into being."[55]

Before concluding, we should give brief consideration to the paradigmatic image of "mother" in the *Gilgamesh Epic*. I suspect that this is a common image in other myths and epics in Sumerian and Akkadian. For example, in *Enuma Elish*, Tiamat is the mother regarded negatively (*Tiamat ālittani izirrannâši* [III 15, 73]). She, like Ishtar, breaks the boundary between male and female, setting up an assembly and doing battle with Marduk, thus participating in male spheres. Damkina, by contrast, like Ninsun, acts as a mother should (*ālittašu ušālilšu* [V 81]). When Marduk is raised to kingship, her gift to him is singled out (V 81–83).

What is the significance of this mother image? One might suggest that its prevalence in the *Gilgamesh Epic* reflects the wish for the intimacy of the mother-child relationship in infancy, for a time of deep security and ignorance of death and thus distance from the reality of human mortality.

One should also ask whether this pervasive image tells us something about intrafamilial relations in ancient Mesopotamia. Was the mother the significant female in a man's life even after he had grown up and married, as was and is the case in India and China?[56] Was there an "ascending scale of affection"[57] of wife, sister, and mother, with mother first in importance? Definitive responses to what must at this time remain questions require close and sensitive study of the sources reflecting everyday life: legal and economic texts and especially letters. Perhaps related to the issue is the parricide motif found in Mesopotamian myths such as *Enuma Elish* and the Theogony of Dunnu.

CHAPTER EIGHT

GENDER AND SEXUALITY IN THE MYTH OF *NERGAL AND ERESHKIGAL*

The myth of *Nergal and Ereshkigal* (polysemous like other myths) reflects, expresses, and embodies views about human sexuality and the relationship between men and women. The goddess and god, I believe, are emblematic, possessing what the ancients considered to be feminine and masculine human traits and characteristics.

Two different versions of the myth of *Nergal and Ereshkigal* are extant. The earlier one, found at Tell el-Amarna in Egypt and dating from the fifteenth or fourteenth century B.C.E., is a very abbreviated and probably incomplete story of some 90 lines. The much later seventh-century B.C.E. Late Assyrian version from Sultantepe is much longer, perhaps consisting of some 750 lines.[1] A later Neo-Babylonian fragment from Uruk restores some of the passages missing in this account. Both versions have many lacunae and present, therefore, numerous problems: at many important junctures in the story, the breaks leave one guessing. Nevertheless, the basic outline of the story and its themes and motifs are fairly clear.[2]

The celestial gods decide to have a banquet. According to cosmic regulations, the gods of heaven cannot descend to the netherworld, nor can chthonic deities ascend to the heavens. So a message is sent to Ereshkigal, "Mistress of the Great Land," to send a messenger to receive her "food portion."[3] Her envoy ascends "the long stairway to heaven" to do so. The celestial gods respectfully stand to greet

him, as befits the messenger of the great goddess—that is, all stand
except for Nergal.[4] Nergal must then make amends for his insult.

In the earlier account, he is apparently summoned to be punished
by execution. But the cunning god Ea comes to Nergal's rescue by
giving him seven demons, personifications of plagues, to accom-
pany him for his defense. With their help he is able to reach
Ereshkigal, and he overpowers her and becomes her husband.

In the later version, far more elaborate and in some crucial
passages very different, Nergal makes two visits to the netherworld.
It is unclear whether on the first visit he is to receive a pardon from
the goddess or whether he attempts to defy her. Here too the wily
Ea comes to his aid. For the first occasion, Ea has him make a throne
or chair of many different woods, perhaps as a compensatory gift.[5]
Ea also instructs him not to accept the hospitality he will be offered
as a guest—not to sit on a chair, not to eat bread or meat, not to
drink beer, and not to wash his feet—and also tells him,

> (When) she (Ereshkigal) has been to the bath
> And dressed herself in a fine dress,
> Allowing you to glimpse her body . . .
> You must not [do that which] men and women [do.] (p. 168)

On the first visit, of which many lines are missing, Nergal
apparently heeds Ea's advice. But after a break in the text the
goddess is found stripping for her bath. This time

> He [gave in to] his heart's [desire to do what] men and
>   women [do]
> The two embraced each other
> And went passionately to bed. (p. 171)

After six days of love-making Nergal is eager to return to heaven.
He tricks Ereshkigal and then the gatekeeper of the netherworld
and returns home. Once again Ereshkigal's messenger, Namtar, is
sent to heaven to bring Nergal back to her, and after one failure he

succeeds in finding Nergal. After a long break in the text, Nergal returns. He again sleeps with Ereshkigal and becomes king of the netherworld forever.

Most Assyriologists view both accounts as etiological, explaining how Nergal, a celestial god, became the ruler of the netherworld.[6] However, S. Dalley, quite rightly in my view, questions whether the myth simply relates "the transition of rule in the underworld from a solitary deity to a pair . . . for Nergal is called 'the Ellil of the Netherworld' in a composition from the late third or early second millennium, so it may be preferable to ascribe to the myth a different purpose, such as harmonizing two separate traditions. No Sumerian version of the story is known."[7]

As to the chief difference between the two versions, the French Assyriologist J. Bottéro succinctly remarks that in the Amarna story Nergal becomes ruler via violence, whereas in the later account the conflict between god and goddess leads to a love affair.[8] In the earlier text, Ereshkigal demands that Nergal, who had offended her, be sent to her to be killed (*ana mūti*). Instead she ends up making him her husband (*ana muti*). As Bottéro notes, "In a world where names and words had such objective value this is not merely an amusing pun, but the ruse perpetrated by Ea by playing upon the homophony of the two terms. The later version suggests a more subtle and psychological interplay" than the earlier one.

A quite different approach is taken by T. Frymer-Kensky, who interprets the myth as part of the general trend "towards total marginalization and privatization of goddesses" after Sumerian times.[9] Ereshkigal is "demoted" to the position of spouse of Nergal, who then becomes "the true ruler of the netherworld." She believes that the Akkadian myth was written to account for this takeover.

Some attention has been paid to the "love-story" aspect of the myth by E. Reiner and T. Jacobsen.[10] The latter has described it "as a tale of sexual attraction, of the adolescent gambit of attracting attention . . . of the thin line between the wish to kill and passionate surrender. . . . As a myth, the savage courtship it tells of seems somehow right for the forbidding powers of death." Especially insightful is the analysis by M. Hutter, who focuses on the nuances and subtleties of its language and motifs in discussing the erotic component of food and drink, the motif of seductive bathing, and the sexual relationship between the deities, among other topics.[11]

But what, to my knowledge, has not been explored in the myth is the issue of gender and sexuality and the information on those areas that a close examination of *Nergal and Ereshkigal* yields.[12] I suggest that this myth can be considered as a reflexive discourse on gender relations and male/female sexuality in late ancient Mesopotamia. Borrowing from S. Crane, I would define gender as "the exterior, social interpretation of sexual practices, specific to a particular society. Sexuality, broadly understood as the generation, expression, and organization of desire, is the ongoing behavior that informs gendered identities."[13] Moreover, "from the perspective of gender differences, masculinity is a composite of traits that contrast [with] feminine ones."[14]

I am well aware of the problematics of utilizing the genre of myth for recovering the attitudes, views, and experiences of ordinary men and women of a long–dead civilization.[15] The observation by B. Alster, who has done much seminal research on Mesopotamian literature, is relevant: "The common tendency in ancient literatures is not to describe ordinary people directly but only indirectly in the guise of deities."[16] He adds, however, that this cannot be verified in Mesopotamia. I contend that those parts of both versions in which god and goddess confront one another, despite their important differences, inform us about the definitions of maleness and femaleness from a masculine perspective. And if the myth does not reflect how gender relations were actually structured in Mesopotamia, it reveals how gender relations ought to have been structured, according to the androcentric perspective of Mesopotamian literature.

Passages pertinent to our topic appear in both accounts and warrant a closer examination. In the Amarna version, Nergal—

accompanied by the seven demons, who take up positions at each of the seven netherworld gates—makes a rush to kill Ereshkigal:

> Inside the house, he seized Ereshkigal
> By her hair, pulled her from the throne
> To the ground, intending to cut off her head.
>   'Don't kill me, my brother![17] Let me tell you something.'
> Nergal listened to her and relaxed his grip, [She!] (text: He)
>   wept and was overcome (when she said),
>   'You can be my husband, and I can be your wife.
>   I will let you seize
> Kingship over the wide Earth! I will put the tablet
> Of wisdom in your hand! You can be master,
>   I can be mistress.' Nergal listened to this speech of hers,
> And seized her and kissed her. He wiped away her tears.
>   'What have you asked of me? After so many months,
>   It shall certainly be so!'[18] (pp. 180–181)

Three times in this passage the verb *ṣabātu* "to seize" is used: he seized her by her hair, she offers to let him seize kingship, and he seized and kissed her. In the first and third instances Nergal is the active agent; in the second, Ereshkigal, still with some power, will permit him to act. In the first occurrence, Nergal acts in cave-man fashion. The iterative term is thus a key word underlining the power struggle between male and female, with the male emerging victorious.[19] Its use highlights the aggressiveness of Nergal, though the aggression is mitigated by his kissing the goddess and then tenderly wiping away her tears. A. L. Oppenheim suggests that Ereshkigal's offer of the kingship "is made in order to give Nergal the appearance of a legitimate ruler and not a usurper."[20] Yet the use of *ṣabātu* could only remind the reader/listener of the idiom *kussâm ṣabātu* " to usurp the throne." Nergal's actions against Ereshkigal graphically describe her humiliation and subjection. The verb *quddudu*, here translated "pulled," literally means "he bends (her) down, makes (her) fall prostrate." Nergal unequivocally renders

Ereshkigal submissive, in a posture associated with both the conquered and the old.[21]

Translators differ in their opinion as to who "wept and was overcome" after Nergal listened to Ereshkigal "and relaxed his grip." Dalley is in the minority in assuming it is Nergal. Although men cried in Mesopotamia when overcome with emotion, it is much more likely, in keeping with the spirit of the Amarna text and the evidence of the later one, that it is Ereshkigal who is so distressed. Nergal says little in this passage, in contrast to Ereshkigal, whose loquaciousness as a female trait is perhaps implied. Though Nergal's violence is emphasized, he does stop to listen to her. His potential for consideration is carefully noted in his relaxing his grip on her, kissing her, and wiping away her tears. His brief words at the end, though incomplete, imply that he would long before have complied with her wishes if only he had known what they were.

To sum up, if one can assume that we have in the story a picture of how relations between men and women ought to have been, the following picture emerges. A significant binary opposition existed between the two: active male as against passive female. The man, if necessary, could use aggressiveness to subdue the woman, but the aggression should have been restrained and even mitigated once the goal of domination was achieved. Concern and tenderness were components in a good relationship between the sexes. Nergal's readiness to listen to what Ereshkigal has to say may well mirror the regard men often had for women's understanding and prudence (see chapters 6 and 9).

Far more detailed and informative are the details of the later version, which is replete with subtleties and psychological insights. B. R. Foster proposes that the "expansion and revision of the story developed its motif of sexuality, and in fact makes this the cause of Nergal's triumph rather than his derring-do."[22] But the matter is far more complex than Foster's suggestion implies.

On Nergal's first visit to the Land of No Return, "he knelt down, kissed the ground in front of her" (p. 170), in deference to her position as ruler of the netherworld. He thus acknowledges her superior status at this point in the story.

On Nergal's second visit (after a break of some thirteen lines, according to Dalley), "The two embraced each other / And went passionately to bed." The wording of those two lines is significant: the use of *aḫameš* "each other" implies a mutual and egalitarian sexual relationship between the two gods. The term *šitmuriš* "passionately" comes from the verb *šamāru* "to surge, to become spirited, excited, to rage" and is frequently used to describe water, horses, lions, storms, and warfare.[23] It denotes the intensity and high pitch of the gods' encounter. The details of their sexual intimacy are few; more is conveyed indirectly than explicitly. For six days the two lay in bed. Each time Ereshkigal is named, she is referred to as queen (*šarrat*); significantly, no epithet precedes Nergal's name, but he is referred to by his other name, Erra. In the following poorly preserved lines, Nergal on the seventh day asks Ereshkigal to permit him to return home, promising to return later. She becomes enraged (literally, "her lips become as dark as the edge of a bowl"). But he manages to leave without her knowledge. He succeeds in deceiving the gatekeeper, saying that he is acting as messenger for Ereshkigal. In the morning the goddess "rises in a leisurely way, enjoys a bath, and calls that the rooms be freshened and breakfast served."[24] She assumes Nergal is somewhere about. Namtar then informs her of Nergal's disappearance.

> Ereshkigal cried out aloud, grievously,
> Fell from the throne to the ground,
> Then straightened up from the ground.
> Her tears flowed down her cheeks.
>   'Erra, the lover of my delight—
>   I did not have enough delight with him before he left!
>   Erra, the lover of my delight—
>   I did not have enough delight with him before he left.'
> Namtar made his voice heard and spoke, addressed his
>   words to Ereshkigal,

'Send me to Anu, your father, and let me arrest that god!
[Let me take him to you,] that he may kiss you again!' (p.
172)

Highly charged, vivid language describes Ereshkigal's response to
Nergal's desertion. In the Amarna version Nergal pulls her down
from the throne; here she falls down, symbolically foreshadowing
what will take place later.

Foster differs somewhat in his translation of the first four lines.
His heightens the picture of Ereshkigal's utter devastation:

> [Eresh]kigal was crushed and let out a wail,
> She fell [fr]om her chair to the ground,
> [She got] up [from] the ground, her eyes raining tears,
> Her tears ran down the sides of her nose.[25]

Hutter has pointed out the semantic relationship between eating
and sexual relationship in the text's use of the verb šebû "to become
sated, to be satisfied."[26] Though Nergal may not have been able to
resist Ereshkigal's charms, he was sexually satisfied after six days.
Ereshkigal obviously was not. The very repetition of her lament
underlines her ongoing craving for the god. What may well be
expressed here is the view that women have voracious appetites for
sex, a not-uncommon view about women.[27]

Namtar responds to her cries and plaint, prepared to forc-
ibly return Nergal to her. But she first carefully tells him what
to say:

> 'Go, Namtar, [you must speak to Anu, Ellil, and Ea!]
> Set your face towards the gate of Anu, Ellil, and Ea,
> To say, ever since I was a child and a daughter,
> I have not known the playing of other girls,
> I have not known the romping of children.
> That god whom you sent to me and who has impregnated
>   me—let him sleep with me again!

> Send that god to us, and let him spend the night with me as
>   my lover!
> I am unclean, and I am not pure enough to perform the
>   judging of the great gods,
> The great gods who dwell within Erkalla.
> If you do not send that god to me
> According to the rites of Erkalla and the great Earth
> I shall raise up the dead, and they will eat the living.
> I shall make the dead outnumber the living!' (p. 173)

Her speech, in my view, may well reveal the masculine view of female discourse. But before proceeding, note should be taken of a recent different and preferable suggested reading of the line "I am unclean, and I am not pure enough to perform the judging of the great gods." Instead read: "Or else I (Ereshkigal) will not decree death at all. I will not pass judgement for the great gods."[28] Much has been written about Ereshkigal's impurity here, which raised many questions that may now be resolved with the new reading. The goddess's instructions to Namtar consist of two parts—an appeal for pity and two threats.

First she bewails her lonely childhood, mentioning her status as daughter, thus calling on kinship ties to strengthen her appeal for a favorable response. (Foster's translation, "he had intercourse with me" is more accurate than Dalley's "who has impregnated me.")[29] She asks for only one more night with the god. She also puts the onus of responsibility for her plight on the gods by saying that they sent Nergal to her.

Erishkigal, in the revised reading, then threatens to withhold the death sentences for humans in accordance with cosmic norms. And more terrifying still, and identical to Ishtar's threat in *The Descent of Ishtar*,[30] she will raise the dead, who will eat the living. The importance of this speech by the imperious goddess is underlined by its verbatim repetition by Namtar to the gods. He is told to find the wrongdoer and take him. But Namtar fails to recognize the disguised Nergal. He returns to the underworld and tells his mistress, "My lady, there was only one god who sat bareheaded, blinking and cringing" (p. 174).[31] Ereshkigal, much shrewder than her messenger, immediately realizes that this is Nergal. She orders Namtar to return heavenward again and bring him back. He does, but only after Ea again instructs Nergal not to sit on a chair. Once more, Nergal descends "the long stairway of heaven." At each of the seven gates he strikes down its gatekeeper. Nergal enters Ereshkigal's wide courtyard:

> And went up to her and laughed.
> He seized her by her hairdo,
> And [pull]ed (?) her from [the throne].
> He seized her by her tresses
> [   ].
> The two embraced each other
> And went passionately to bed.
> They lay there, queen Ereshkigal and Erra, for a first day
>   and a second day.
> They lay there, queen Ereshkigal and Erra, for a third day.
> They lay there, queen Ereshkigal and Erra, for a fourth day.
> They lay there, queen Ereshkigal and Erra, for a fifth day.
> They lay there, queen Ereshkigal and Erra, for a sixth day.
> When the seventh day arrived,
> Anu made his voice heard and spoke,
> Addressed his words to Kakka, his vizier,
>   'Kakka, I shall send you to Kurnugi,
>   To the home of Ereshkigal who dwells within Erkalla,
>   To say, "That god, whom I sent you,
>   Forever [   ]
>   Those above [   ]
>   Those below [   ].' (p. 176)
>   (break, about 20–25 lines missing to end)

Nergal enters laughing. As Hutter has noted, the term ṣaḫû "to laugh" has a sexual connotation, thus intimating what is soon to come.[32] In language somewhat similar to that of the Amarna account, Nergal once again seizes (*ṣabātu*) Ereshkigal by the hair, pulling her down from the throne. The retention of this action, though the Akkadian differs, highlights in my view its significance in understanding a central theme of both versions: the proper hierarchical relationship between male and female; the male must aggressively subdue the female.

Their sexual encounter is phrased exactly as it was on the first occasion. When the seventh day comes, Anu speaks to his vizier, giving him a message to be relayed, presumably to both Ereshkigal and Nergal. Though very little is preserved of what follows, we are cued into the heart of its contents in the word "forever" ([*ana ūmē*] *darûti*). Nergal is to remain forever in the Land of No Return to rule over it with Ereshkigal beside him.

Thus, in the myth *Nergal and Ereshkigal* the male is characterized as aggressive and violent and, despite constraints, doing by and large as he pleases. Men were to stick together and support one another, as Ea does in instructing Nergal how to face the dangers of the nether-world (and probably disguising him in the later story so he would escape detection). Although males may have been able to resist certain appetites for necessities such as food and drink, the hunger for sex was seen as far more powerful and ultimately irresistible. The male voyeur was easily titillated by nudity. This observation is substantiated by a curious inscription on the back of a nude woman's torso made of stone (found at Nineveh) in which the Assyrian ruler Ashur-bel-kala claims to have mass-produced such figures and set them up throughout his realm "for titillation."[33] Despite the inherent aggressiveness of the masculine personality, tenderness might and perhaps should have been an aspect of his personhood as well. This is demonstrated in the Amarna account when Nergal wipes away Ereshkigal's tears, a sign of her submissiveness.

Nergal and Ereshkigal highlights perhaps *the* essential desirable characteristic of males, that of mastery and dominance. As A. K.

Guinan comments, "masculine aggressiveness is a prized trait."[34] She describes "the concept of male dominance" as "a vivid behavioral pattern." Sheer aggressiveness makes a man "foremost among his brothers and colleagues." Significant too is her conclusion that "a sexually aggressive woman represents surrender of power by the male." It is questionable whether Ereshkigal can be described as a "sexually aggressive woman," because the two versions of *Nergal and Ereshkigal* describe an egalitarian sexual relationship. Until she is compelled to share hegemony of the netherworld, the goddess is depicted as a powerful and autonomous woman. However, Ereshkigal as queen with sole power is intolerable and unacceptable. She must, because she is a woman, cede the throne to Nergal, or at any rate share it with him. Similarly, in the central myth of *Enuma Elish* (dating mainly from the first millennium and later) Tiamat, wife and then widow of Apsu, must not rule. She marries Kingu and appoints him as ruler; it is he who then leads the army, though unsuccessfully, against Marduk (see chapter 5). As Oppenheim has suggested, Ereshkigal offers Nergal "unconditional surrender and her hand in marriage";[35] the two go hand in hand.

Although the wives and daughters of rulers and high officials in Mesopotamia were important in various administrative and economic activities, no woman, with one exception, ruled in Mesopotamia.[36] The only woman who ruled was Ku-Bau of Kish, a barmaid, who in Early Dynastic times, according to late legend, "became king and ruled one hundred years."[37] Not surprisingly, her reign was viewed as an ominous anomaly that did not augur well for Mesopotamia: "If an anomaly has (both) penis and vulva—omen of Ku-Bau who ruled the land; the land of the king will become waste."[38] Interestingly, she is also described as having seized the throne, in short, a usurper. Indeed one might say that Ereshkigal's last act of dominion is handing over the tablet of wisdom (in the Amarna version) to Nergal, after first proposing marriage, a masculine act. In the *Gilgamesh Epic*, the hero rejects the goddess Ishtar's proposal of marriage, which would have compromised his masculinity (see chapter 7). A woman sitting on the throne was behavior unbecoming for a woman, just as a bearded woman was an unnatural phenomenon.[39] But a man usurping the throne was neither uncommon nor a heinous event in Mesopotamian history.[40]

Mastery was thus seen as a masculine aptitude, dependent on an ideological differentiation between gender roles. Once Ereshkigal begins to love Nergal she becomes emotionally dependent on him for her happiness, and she loses her capacity to rule. There was probably a general concern about men spending too much time with women. In one Mari letter sent by Shamshi-Adad, the great ruler of Shubat-Enlil, to his son Yasmah-Adad, he chides the latter for dallying with the women and thus being deflected from matters of state.[41] In short, Yasmah-Adad demonstrates an excessive interest in sexual pleasure. As Guinan notes, "any excessive, uncontrollable act or incidents of excessive sexual indulgence was an augury of misfortune. . . . By its very nature sexuality involves surrender of control[, and] . . . sexual expression must be subject to restraints."[42] Nergal, in contrast to Ereshkigal, has his full of sexual congress after six days. His love-them-and-leave-them attitude has him in control and in charge of the situation. As already noted, few details describe the sexual encounter between god and goddess: "The two embraced each other / And went passionately to bed." There is no description of the body or of sexual intimacies. It is reminiscent of an Old Babylonian love text discussed by M. Held in which, similarly, the woman is the faithful lover; the young man whom she loves, passionately, "has no regard for true love."[43] But there is mutuality in the relationship, a matter to which I return below.

What is especially striking about the later account of *Nergal and Ereshkigal* is its focus on feminine psychology as seen from an androcentric perspective. One might say that the last part of this version has as its main topos the issue of female desire. Described graphically and in detail are the goddess's reactions, words, and actions in response to Nergal's leaving her. In contrast, not a single word describes Nergal's response to their encounter. Ereshkigal, like women generally, places high value on relationship and bonding. Nergal, characteristic of men, values carnal passion, a short-term emotion, and the need for autonomy. For women love is not divorced from sexuality, as it frequently is for men. J. S. Cooper in a stimulating essay states that Sumerian "love poetry was an expression of female sexuality, and that the activities described therein have to do more with recreation than procreation."[44] He found that "sexual intercourse is hardly ever mentioned by name, nor is the male organ." In contrast, the Sumerian myths of the god Enki refer to his sexual exploits and his sexuality in terms that are "raw, often violent, phallocentric and . . . reproductive on both the metaphoric and concrete level." Cooper believes that "the explanation for these contrasting sexualities is to be sought . . . in the 'woman's voice' that pervades the Inana-Dumuzi material."

The study of Mesopotamian sexuality is barely in its infancy, so my comments are perhaps premature. (Then, too, there is the question of possible change from Sumerian to Akkadian historical periods.) But the observations by Guinan cited above are relevant here. Mastery and domination characterized ideal masculine behavior whether Sumerian or Akkadian. More difficult is the issue of a woman's voice in Sumerian love poetry, where the focus is on women's sexuality. That women composed love poetry in ancient Egypt is attested.[45] But was it so in Mesopotamia? To my knowledge no such evidence has been found. Do we have then in Sumerian love poetry what I suggest is the case for *Nergal and Ereshkigal*: female sexuality as viewed from a male perspective? Is not the emphasis on "unabashed sexuality" perhaps more revealing of a masculine view of (or fantasy about) female concupiscence and voracious insatiability?[46]

When the story opens, in both versions, Ereshkigal is depicted as neither lover nor wife nor mother, but rather as a ruler with power. Both accounts end with Ereshkigal as wife, or about to be wife, submissive and subordinate to Nergal, with whom she will share a far lesser role as consort. Love transforms her into a needy, dependent female. And yet as it was for the heroine of Jane Austen's *Pride and Prejudice*, so for Ereshkigal marriage is represented "as the capstone of success. . . . After constructing gender by demarcating the rules of behavior for the male and the female, the romance plot unites the sexes. . . . The reward for proper differentiation is marriage."[47] Full autonomy was not an option for women.[48]

Although wives were ideally to be submissive, prepared to be mastered by their husbands, Mesopotamian men hoped for a passionate response from their wives. To quote one Sumerian proverb:

> May (the goddess) Inanna cause a hot-limbed wife to lie
>   down for you
> May she bestow upon you broad-armed sons
> May she seek out for you a place of happiness.[49]

Both versions of *Nergal and Ereshkigal* end in marriage. Ereshkigal in both gives up her dominant sole rule of the netherworld. Their joint passion lays the foundation for a faithful marriage, based on mutuality. Ereshkigal "domesticates" Nergal.

In Mesopotamian marriage, the husband was the master (*bēlum*) of his wife.[50] This is articulated very clearly in a bilingual (Sumerian and Akkadian) proverb: "A house without an owner (is like) a woman without a husband."[51] But his rights were restricted and subject to the control of the courts. In a case of adultery, for example, which was always brought only against a wife and never against a husband, the husband had to prove his charge before punishment was meted out. Though *Nergal and Ereshkigal* appears to condone, indeed even presuppose, the right to control women through their sexuality, violence is unacceptable. This myth is a far cry from the Sumerian myths in which Enki is the "incestuous abuser of his daughters"[52] and from Greek myths, which are rampant with violence and rape.[53]

The myth also is in sharp contrast with what is found in ancient Greek and Roman poetry, in which "there is . . . a near total absence of conjugal passion [and there are] pervasive differences in status between lover and beloved. . . . Sexual passion for one's wife was

Figure 2. Sculpted seated couple made of stone, from the temple of Inanna in Nippur. Courtesy of the Oriental Institute of the University of Chicago.

not the norm in ancient Greece." Indeed, "interest in sex on a wife's part was considered potentially dangerous and, thus, [was] discouraged."[54] In Mesopotamia, a woman's erotic feelings were regarded as the basis for strong nuptial ties. There was an acceptance of desire, but at the same time there existed a highly developed sense of sexual propriety.

The mutuality and love between husband and wife resonates in a moving elegy, from which unfortunately the beginning lines are missing. E. Reiner observes that it "represents a specifically Assyrian sensitivity,"[55] which I suggest is perhaps also found in the later story of *Nergal and Ereshkigal.* This is the lament of a woman who has died in childbirth, a not-uncommon occurrence. The story is told as if she were herself narrating it.

> The day I bore the fruit, how happy I was
> happy was I, happy my husband . . .
> [My husband, who loved me], uttered a cry
> [Why do you take from me] the wife in whom I rejoice? . . .
> [All] those [many] days I was with my husband,
> I lived with him who was my lover.[56]

It is noteworthy that the term *lalû* "delight" found in this lament (fourth line) also appears in Ereshkigal's description of Nergal as "the lover of my *delight* [my emphasis]." It has a strong sexual nuance.[57] So too does the word *ḫā'iru*, found above for both husband and lover, appear in the very same phrase of Ereshkigal's.[58] Husband and lover mesh together; the two are one and the same person.

Although extramarital liaisons, in the case of some husbands at least, were a fact of life at all times, there is evidence that public authorities might have intervened to restrain such relationships when, R. Westbrook suggests, they were *contra bonos mores.*[59] He examines three cuneiform sources from different periods to prove his view. Moreover, Mesopotamian men, like men in other patriarchal societies, were ambivalent toward marriage, a view that found expression in the proverbial literature: "Who has not supported a wife or child has not borne a leash," or "For his pleasure— marriage; on his thinking it over—divorce."[60] This ambiguity is strongly put in the so-called Dialogue of Pessimism:

> I am going to love a woman . . .
> The man who loves a woman forgets sorrow and fear . . .

Woman is a pitfall—a pitfall, a hole, a ditch,
Woman is a sharp iron dagger that cuts a man's throat.[61]

For the ancient Mesopotamians the body was not regarded with
disgust; nor was it the source of sin, but rather the locus of erotic
desire for both men and women. The love lyrics of the Sumerians
and Akkadians, whether cultic (Inanna-Dumuzi), royal, or secular,
amply attest to this. At the same time, they saw differences between
men and women as desiring subjects—women being more
dependent on desire than were men. Asymmetry, the domination
of women by men (an almost universal phenomenon), also
characterized ancient Mesopotamia. But a careful examination of
Nergal and Ereshkigal affords a more sensitively nuanced understanding of gender and sexuality of that time and place.

CHAPTER NINE

THE FEMALE "SAGE" IN MESOPOTAMIAN LITERATURE

Mesopotamia was a traditional patriarchal culture whose traditions are chiefly known through the writings of male authors and male-oriented visual materials. The evidence suggests that in Mesopotamia home, family, and domestic life were central and crucial to women.[1] The arenas for male status and public prestige—palace, military, and priestly offices—were largely, if not entirely, closed to women. Inasmuch as education was a significant avenue to power and status, lack of educational opportunities was then, as it always has been, a way of curtailing female influence and authority.

Although neither ancient Mesopotamian nor Egyptian women lived the sexually dimorphic or circumscribed lives such as those lived by women in classical Athens, "real women, like other muted groups, are not to be found so much in the explicit text of the historical record as in its gaps and silences."[2] This absence of direct accessibility produced, as M. B. Skinner has put it, "a circumstance that requires the application of research methods based largely upon controlled inference.[3] Additionally exacerbating the problem of the researcher is a factor noted by A. L. Oppenheim, namely, the "remoteness from the realities of everyday life" that characterizes the cuneiform material.[4] Given the limitations of male dominance and remoteness of the sources, I here draw together a few preliminary observations based on my own research and that of others.

I say "preliminary," for the subject of roles played by Near Eastern women in history is only now beginning to receive the scholarly attention it merits.[5]

The term "sage" when preceded by the adjective "female" must be put in quotation marks, for it is highly questionable whether women in the ancient Near East were ever considered to be culture creators, or whether any mirrored "in themselves the ideals of wisdom" or were "folk heroes of the wisdom tradition."[6] The usual term in Akkadian for "sage" is *apkallu*, but apart from its application to goddesses such as Gula and Damkina, *apkallatu* "wise women" does not occur.[7] Does the ancient view that a goddess might be an *apkallatu* imply, even if there is no such example to date attested, that a mortal woman might also have been regarded as an *apkallatu*? One must be very cautious and not infer, as others have done, that the world of goddesses is a direct reflection of everyday life.[8] Indeed, "female" and "sage" were contradictions in terms in the ancient Near Eastern world.

A more fruitful and probably the only viable approach to the topic for now is by way of the rich vocabulary for wisdom and its derivatives, as it was actually used or might be inferred in reference to women and their activities.[9] One of the key terms, *nēmequ*, is defined as "knowledge, experience, wisdom (referring to the body of experiences, knowledge, skills, and traditions which are the basis of a craft or occupation, or form the basis of civilization as a whole), skill, cunning." The adjective *emqu* is translated as "experienced, skilled, educated, wise, wily."[10] Other derivatives of *emqu* also have meanings that fall within the range of skill and experience. It is significant that terms for housekeeper, such as *ēmiqtu* and *emuqtu*, imply that the woman who manages a household is a prudent woman.

The Greek *mētis* is close in its range of meanings to *nēmequ*, for it "implies a complex but very coherent body of mental attitudes and intellectual behavior which combine flair, wisdom, forethought, subtlety of mind, deception, resourcefulness, vigilance, opportunism, various skills and experience acquired over the years."[11] So too does the Hebrew *ḥokmâ* incorporate a similar diversity of meanings.[12]

It is therefore within the parameters of the multifold connotations of the vocabulary for *wise/wisdom* that the activities of the female "sage" are accessible to us in varying degrees. Included here are women as scribes and composers of written and oral literature, as healers, as musicians (vocal and instrumental), as mantics, and lastly as advisors in informal settings.

FEMALE SCRIBE AS BUREAUCRAT

Oppenheim in a seminal article notes the many problems inherent in the study of Mesopotamian scholarship, learning, and the art (and science) of writing.[13] He provides a useful framework for examining the female as scribe: the scribe as bureaucrat, the scribe as poet, and the scribe as scholar. The bureaucrat is usually connected with the two "great organizations"—the palace and the temple. The complex and lengthy training required to master reading and writing of necessity precluded most men and almost all women, who very early on (first as children and then as adults) took on the responsibilities of household tasks. It is therefore intriguing that it was a goddess Nisaba (Nidaba was her Sumerian name) who was for many centuries the patron goddess of scribes and the scribal art.[14] And yet only rarely could women read or write. Nisaba is "the lady with cunning intelligence" who provided the scribe "with wisdom and intelligence."[15] Goddesses sometimes take the role of scribe, especially of the netherworld.[16]

Only sporadically and meagerly, though for centuries, is the existence of the female bureaucrat scribe attested to. The one reference in an Ur III text to a female scribe receiving rations suggests that she was perhaps a slave-girl belonging to the temple force.[17] Much better evidenced are the *nadītu* women of the cloister (*gagû*) of Sippar who served as scribes.[18] Several of these had Sumerian names and were the daughters of scribes.[19] These female scribes acted as recorders of and witnesses to the transactions of *nadītu* women only. They are referred to only for the earlier part of the Old Babylonian period and then disappeared from the scene at some time in the reign of King Samsuiluna. At that time *nadītu*s also served in other official capacities in the cloister administration. They and the female scribes apparently disappeared with the growing concentration of property and power in the hands of a few male administrators.[20] The cloister administration, which handled the affairs of its residents—the *nadītu* women, celibate devotees in Sippar of the god Shamash and his consort Aya—was itself under the jurisdiction of the administrators of the Shamash temple, Ebabbar, the "great organization" of Sippar. With the *nadītu* scribe we have therefore a situation in which women served other women. There is no evidence that they functioned outside of the confines of the *gagû*.

The extensive "correspondance féminine" of Mari is well known. Published in *Archives royales de Mari* 10, it served as the basis for the excellent study by B. F. Batto.[21] These letters are nowhere said to have been written by their senders. They were for the most part probably dictated, as was generally the case in Mesopotamia. However, there is now evidence that at least ten women did serve as scribes in the Mari texts. One list mentions nine who received rations alongside others who worked in the harem; they were therefore slaves or at least of low status.[22] Nothing is known about the training they received. At times a Mari princess leaving her natal home to marry a ruler of another town might be given a slave-girl trained as a scribe as part of her dowry.[23] It would seem, therefore, that slave-girls might be specially trained to serve the correspondence needs of the harem women and princesses leaving Mari. They would thereby perform the important function of curtailing harem women's contacts with non-kin males, namely male scribes.

We learn no more about female bureaucrat scribes. In a study of Neo-Babylonian scribes by the Russian Assyriologist M. A. Dandamaev, not a single female scribe occurs among the more than three thousand known scribes![24]

FEMALE SCRIBE AS POETESS

The female scribe as poetess is also rarely attested to in the texts. But it is in this category that Enheduanna, high priestess of the moon god Nanna and the remarkable daughter of the Akkadian ruler Sargon, belongs. The Sumerologists A. Falkenstein, W. W. Hallo, and A. W. Sjoberg all believe that she wrote and compiled a collection of Sumerian hymns to temples. Hallo has described her "as a kind of systematic theologian, well-versed in the subtleties of a—perhaps already traditional—set of Sumerian beliefs, and capable of adapting them to a new point of view."[25] In a line of her magnificent *nin-me-šar-ra* hymn to the goddess Inanna, Enheduanna refers all too briefly to the process of her creativity as "I have given birth."[26] Her creative agony is compared to labor pains, a fitting metaphor for a poetess.[27]

More than four centuries later another princess, priestess, and poetess, also the daughter of a founder of a dynasty, appears on the scene—Ninshatapada, daughter of Sin-kashid (ca. 1865 B.C.E.), founder of the Old Babylonian dynasty of Uruk. The letter-prayer that she composed and wrote to Rim-Sin of Larsa, conqueror of the city in which she had served and from which she was exiled, became part of the scribal curriculum. Hallo notes that this document adds new historical information: "She thus stands in a long tradition of princely women of Sumer who enriched Sumerian literature with their creative talents."[28]

In an informative article, Hallo calls attention to a moving lament to Ur-Nammu, who died in battle; the lament, Hallo suggests, may have been composed by his widow.[29] S. N. Kramer considers the wife of King Shulgi of Ur the possible authoress of a lullaby to her son, the future king. He attributes a love song to the *lukur* Kubatum, the concubine of Shu-Sin, son of Shulgi.[30] Indeed, a very good case could be made for the female authorship of lullabies and love songs. Along with work songs, stories, and proverbs,[31] they fit into the types of oral literature that have traditionally and cross-culturally belonged in the domain of women. The question remains, however, whether women would have been able to write down any of their compositions.

FEMALE SCRIBE AS SCHOLAR

There is to my knowledge one single tantalizing piece of evidence concerning a Mesopotamian female scribe. A fragment of the vocabulary text Proto Aa is known from its colophon to have been written by a female scribe named Beli-remenni. She is assumed to have been a *nadītu* of the Sippar cloister mainly because "the existence of female scribes during the Old Babylonian period is attested [to] only in Sippar."[32] The same scribe probably wrote an extant literary tablet. Whether the woman who "wrote" the partly preserved requests for an oracle from the god Lahar on behalf of King Ashurbanipal was a scribe is unknown. She says, "Disregard that it is a (mere) woman who has written and submitted (this) to you."[33]

It is certainly within the realm of possibility that the *nadītu* scribes not only served the needs of their sister *nadītus* but that they and other celibates such as the *entu* priestesses, Enheduanna and Ninshatapada, living outside of the embroilment of wifely and motherly demands, had the leisure (motivation and capacity) to devote themselves to learning and scholarship, as did many a medieval nun.[34]

FEMALE PERFORMING ARTISTS

Another area that should be noted if only in passing is women's participation in the performing arts—in dance and music (vocal and instrumental). King Shulgi of the Ur III period considered the playing of complex musical instruments and the composing of songs to be as much a part of learning as was the learning of the scribal art.[35] One must be careful to separate the performers from

Figure 3. Alabaster disk of Enhuduanna, from Ur. Courtesy of the University of Pennsylvania Museum, neg. no. S4-139330.

the musicologists. It is doubtful whether singers and songstresses could read or write. It was rather the male *galmāḫu*, chief singer of temple dirges, who was trained in the scribal school.[36]

Very little is known about the training of men and women as singers. There may have been a kind of music academy for upper-class girls (and boys), to judge from a few references.[37] But what, if any, were the differences in training for free individuals and slaves, for men and women? It seems likely that royal and upper-class women (and men) received instruction in singing and the playing of musical instruments as part of their education (which in Meso-potamia did not usually include reading and writing).

WOMEN AS HEALERS

Healing is an area frequently "assumed to be a mere extension of wifely functions and so female practitioners are often taken for granted." Female healers are "more likely to define themselves as informal practitioners, to operate within the home and not fit the model of medical knowledge, practice, and advancement."[38]

For Oppenheim, "Mesopotamian medicine is shown to be a typical folk medicine . . . [and] the *materia medica* consists mainly of native herbs of many kinds."[39] He points out that the two medical traditions and schools of Mesopotamia can be divided into the "scientific" and the "practical."[40] Women may safely be assigned only to the latter; the former presupposes a modicum of literacy. But once again we are at the mercy of the anonymity and the elusiveness of the women we seek.

There is the rare reference to a female physician (*asâtu*): one appears in the palace at Larsa in the Old Babylonian period.[41] In a Mari letter a secondary wife is in charge of an unnamed female physician who is remiss in her job of caring for the women of the harem.[42] Perhaps she too, like the female scribes of Mari, functioned to curtail the access of male non-kin to women of the harem and did not serve male members of the court.

Oppenheim has insisted that the goddess Gula, who was associated with healing, is "a deity of death and healing . . . and has no function as a patron deity."[43] He perhaps overstates the case. Goddesses and women cross-culturally have been regarded ambivalently (by men), linked with both healing illness and causing illness.[44]

The status and training of the female practitioner who was undoubtedly important throughout Mesopotamian history—the midwife (*šabsūtu*)—are little known.[45] Her techniques were not part of the written medical traditions of ancient Mesopotamia. It is likely that, as was the case with the Hittites, so too with the Mesopotamians the midwife was "the wise woman."[46] In a late Babylonian poem to the greatness of Marduk and his city, mention is made of "the *nadītu* women who with skill [*nēmequ*] save the foetus."[47] It is unknown whether the *nadītu*s ever functioned as midwives during their heyday. More likely it was their contemporaries, the *qadištu* women, who did.[48] Although little can be said about Mesopotamian midwives, I would suggest that theirs was a profession that may well have covered the services of a modern gynecologist, obstetrician, and pediatrician. Perhaps they also served to advise and help with family problems. Their knowledge was presumably taught by mothers to daughters and other relatives.

WOMEN AS MANTICS

The penultimate area to be considered under the rubric of female "sage" is the mantic. For men, divination and the profession of the diviner (*bārû*) were central. The diviner's lore, the wisdom (*nēmequ*) of the gods Shamash and Adad,[49] was closed to women. The goddess Gula might be addressed as "a wise women, a diviner, an exorcist."[50] But there is to date only one Old Assyrian reference to a group of female diviners (*bārāitu*) who are consulted, significantly by a woman, along with female dream interpreters and spirits of the dead, to learn whether the god Ashur continues to care for her.[51] On the basis of this one reference nothing can really be said about female diviners except that the Old Assyrian letter may represent an atypical situation.

It is rather in the realm of dream interpretation that we find women. The *šā'iltu*, the oneiromancer, apparently functioned mainly outside and below the domain of the official, temple-centered religious life.[52] Oppenheim has surveyed the role of female dream interpreters such as Ninsun, divine mother of Gilgamesh, in the epical literature. Dream interpretation in this genre is an aspect of maternal concern for men, as well as being illustrative of women's advisory functions (see chapters 5 and 7). Oppenheim stresses that the methods of the dream interpreter "were interpretive rather than technical."[53] So again, years of scribal training were not required. It is noteworthy that *entu* priestesses, such as Enheduanna, were dream interpreters.[54] Not surprisingly, it is a goddess, Nanshe, who was the patroness of dream interpretation.[55]

I bypass the Mari phenomenon of prophetesses, which has been extensively studied by B. F. Batto.[56] That phenomenon and the occurrences of "the Assyrian prophetesses of the goddess Istar (of Arbela and even of Assur)" were "deeply alien to the eastern, Mesopotamian, attitude toward the god-man relationship."[57]

Attention, however, should be called to the belief, especially evidenced for the late Assyrian period, that women might have had a far greater propensity for sorcery than did men. A rich vocabulary exists for witches and sorceresses, who were thought to possess great power and esoteric knowledge. The compendia utilized by the exorcist priest, the *āšipu—Shurpu* and *Maqlu—*abound in terms for women who were regarded as powerful, disruptive elements in the social order, enemies of the order and well-being of the community (see chapter 5).[58] It must be emphasized that no witch was designated as such by name. Women remained outside the ranks of the exorcists (*āšipu*), who required lengthy training in difficult texts.

WOMEN AS COUNSELORS

Last, and most important for our topic, is the role played by women of intelligence and cunning in advising and assisting men in their activities and enterprises (see chapter 5). Despite the oft-expressed ambivalence toward women, the literary and epistolary materials particularly can reveal much.[59] There appears to have been, as Camp has demonstrated for ancient Israel,[60] the literary topos of wise women, especially of the wise *old* woman, in ancient Sumerian literature (see chapter 5).

But capable, even remarkable, women are found at all times, especially and not surprisingly from the royal and upper class but not confined to it, as is evidenced perhaps most clearly in Siduri, the tavernkeeper who advises Gilgamesh on how to cope with the realities of death. The women of Mari have already received well-deserved attention. The case of Kiru the princess giving advice to her father on political matters might be noted as well. In a letter to her father she reminds him that he had previously disregarded her advice. This time he ought to pay attention to her "even if she is only a woman."[61] Is this self-deprecation her own view of herself, the male view generally of women, or a way of appealing subtly to male prejudice to achieve her goal?

Unfortunately, these tantalizing hints as to Mesopotamian women's cultural contributions are too meager to permit one to draw any conclusions regarding women's intellectual achievement. Except for celibate priestesses, women's roles were essentially maternal and domestic.

CHAPTER TEN

INANNA-ISHTAR AS PARADOX AND A COINCIDENCE OF OPPOSITES

Inanna-Ishtar frequently has been described by scholars of the ancient Near East as a complex, multifaceted goddess.[1] T. Jacobsen concludes his sensitive discussion of the goddess by saying that Inanna has "become truly all woman and of infinite variety."[2] S. N. Kramer has taken note of "the contrasting strands in Inanna's multifaceted character."[3] A. L. Oppenheim was of the view that Ishtar possessed "divine qualities which are extremely difficult to characterize."[4] In his thorough article on Inanna-Ishtar, C. Wilcke comments that, although all possible epithets are attributed to the goddess, little within the scope of human life falls within her domain.[5] That Inanna "represents the irrational notions within Sumerian society" is the suggestion of B. Alster.[6]

More recently, the French Assyriologist J. Bottéro has emphasized the bipolarity and marginality of the goddess that he believes derived from her association with the prostitute.[7] Of special interest too is the stimulating article by H. L. J. Vanstiphout in which he stresses the goddess's "variety of features, her constant movement, her unabating struggle for domination." He concludes that the Mesopotamians "so to speak eliminated strife as an abstract principle by incorporating it into the psychology of Inanna."[8]

These scholars and others all touch on a highly elusive yet essential aspect of the goddess's configuration. This baffling yet basic quality of the goddess was at the core of her awesomeness and was the source of the abiding fascination felt for her by the Mesopotamians and their neighbors.[9] Inanna-Ishtar was a paradox; that is, she embodied within herself polarities and contraries, and thereby she transcended them. She was, to put it somewhat differently, a deity who incorporated fundamental and irreducible paradoxes. She represented both order and disorder, structure and antistructure. In her psychological traits and behavior she confounded and confused normative categories and boundaries and thereby defined and protected the norms and underlying structure of Mesopotamian civilization.

Prayers, hymns, myths, festivals, and cultic personnel reveal the contours of this distinctive aspect of the goddess who was far more than simply the goddess of fertility, of love and war, and of the morning and evening star. I might add that in Mesopotamia it could only be a goddess and not a god who would incorporate anomalies and antinomies. As S. Ortner suggests, it is the female who is usually assigned "completely polarized and apparently contradictory meanings, since extremes, as we say, meet."[10]

Although the oxymoronic aspect of Inanna-Ishtar's personality may well be rooted in historical events, it would have had profound theological significance for the ancients.[11] The contraries that led to disorder added a dimension that should not be quickly dismissed or denigrated. Inanna-Ishtar was far more than "truly all woman and of infinite variety."[12]

The texts reveal both the benign and the horrific sides of the goddess's personality. All too often, as others have noted, myths about her reveal her capriciousness.[13] Inanna-Ishtar frequently acts in ways that disrupt the social order. She can be wild and savage, excessive in her sexuality and love of war. Her sexual encounters mingle eroticism with violence.

In the *Gilgamesh Epic* she is depicted, on one hand, as a compassionate, maternal goddess, distraught at the destruction of mankind by flood: "Ishtar cries out like a woman in travail."[14] On the other hand, as in the scene where she proposes marriage to Gilgamesh, she is described as a lusty, aggressive goddess, vindictive and vengeful when rejected by the hero.[15] The composer of the so-called Standard Babylonian Version of the *Gilgamesh Epic* incorporated the originally separate flood story into his version, surely aware of the contradictory depictions of the goddess. They apparently presented no problem to him.

The goddess's hypersexuality is frequently noted in the texts, especially in the *Gilgamesh Epic*. But it comes as no surprise that a recently published myth emphasizes her sexual innocence: "I am one who knows not that which is womanly—copulating. I am one who knows not that which is womanly—kissing."[16]

Inanna-Ishtar is a liminal figure; she is androgynous, marginal, ambiguous. She is neither here nor there. She is betwixt and between. And as V. Turner observed, "ambiguous and indeterminate attributes are expressed by a rich variety of symbols."[17]

The powerful hymn of the *entu* priestess Enheduanna, daughter of Sargon, ruler of Akkad (2370–2316 B.C.E.), to Inanna highlights the anomalies of the goddess. She is the "lady (who) soothes the reins, the lady (who) gladdens the heart," but of her it is also said: "Like a dragon you have deposited venom on the land."[18] She is both a loving spouse to Dumuzi and a hostile wife.[19]

The most vivid expressions of the goddess's innate contradictions appear in the following passage:

> To run, to escape, to quiet and to pacify are yours, Inanna . . .
> To destroy, to build up, to tear up and to settle are yours,
>   Inanna . . .
> To turn a man into a woman and a woman into a man are
>   yours, Inanna . . .
> Business, great winning, financial loss, deficit are yours,
>   Inanna . . .
> Neglect, careful preparation, to raise the head and to
>   subdue are yours, Inanna . . .
> Slander, untruthful words, to speak inimical (words) (and)
>   to add hostile words are yours, Inanna . . .

To initiate a quarrel, to joke, to cause smiling, to be base and
to be important are yours, Inanna.[20]

Even more pointed are the following lines:

You have thrown into confusion those threads which have
been ordered . . .
You organize those threads which bring confusion . . .
Inanna, you have destroyed what should not have been
destroyed, you have made what should not have been
made.[21]

Inanna-Ishtar as the source of human conflict and destruction is
frequently underlined in prayers:

Star of the battle-cry, who can make brothers who have
lived together in harmony fight each other.[22]

When you put clean festive garments on them
You soil one,
and another you neglect even though his is clean(!) . . .
"You, Ishtar, thus always finish men off.[23]

Inanna-Ishtar is ambiguity incarnate. She is, to quote S. Stewart's
definition of ambiguous, "that which cannot be defined in terms of
any given category[: she] threatens the integrity of individual
categories being 'either this or that something else.' [She] belongs to
more than one domain at a time and will not fix [her] identity in
any one member of this set of domains. [She] is both this and that."[24]

Two myths seem to imply the great vulnerability of the goddess
to madness, the enormous potential of her raw power for incal-
culable destructiveness if uncurbed. Her wildness and unpredict-
ability, they suggest, are dangerous to both humans and gods. She
cannot in her marginality be a symbol of unchecked power. The
Sumerian myth several times repeats the refrain, "How you

(Inanna) torment heaven and earth."[25] It is the wily Sumerian trickster god Enki who comes to the aid of gods and men by fashioning the *gala*, the lamentation priest, providing him with prayers and laments as well as with musical instruments. With their aid, the *gala* soothes the fierce and angry goddess.

More curious is the Akkadian myth incorporated into a hymn in praise of Ishtar.[26] It relates the creation by Ea, the Akkadian counterpart of Enki, of the goddess's double, Ṣaltu, literally "Strife."[27] He creates her from the dirt of his fingernails, as he does the sexless creatures in the Sumerian version of the goddess's descent to the netherworld.[28] (That strife is personified may indicate the high value the Mesopotamians placed on it and the importance of the role attributed to it.) Ṣaltu is formed to do battle with the ferocious Ishtar and so to tame her. But this proves unnecessary. The sight of Ṣaltu, "a gross travesty of Ishtar herself," is sufficient to curb the goddess.[29] The hymn ends with Ea conciliating Ishtar by instituting an annual whirling dance in her honor, a dance associated with men.[30]

W. W. Hallo has noted, "Ishtar's preoccupation with the *me*s may almost be said to approach the character of an obsession in Sumerian literature. In 'Inanna and Enki' we have one version of the manner in which, with a good deal of deviousness, the goddess acquired the *me*s from Enki."[31] The *me*s are especially important in Enheduanna's hymn to the goddess.

The meaning of the term *me*, basic to civilization, has long been discussed and debated.[32] What is significant for us is the intimate relationship between the goddess and the *me*s, for both embody antitheses. Among other things, the *me*s include

> the art of lovemaking . . .
> the art of prostitution . . .
> the art of forthright speech . . .
> the art of slanderous speech . . .
> the art of treachery . . .
> the art of straightforwardness . . .
> the plundering of cities . . .

deceit . . .
the art of kindness . . .
fear . . .
consternation . . .
the kindling of strife . . .
counseling . . .
heart-soothing.[33]

Central then to the Mesopotamian perspective is the existence of antitheses and contradictions, the delicate balancing of order and disorder. The observation by F. Zeitlin on the personality of the Greek god Dionysus seems particularly appropriate to Inanna-Ishtar: in her own person she "attests to the *coincidentia oppositorum* that challenge the hierarchies and rules of the public masculine world, reintroducing into it confusions, conflicts, tensions, and ambiguities, insisting always on the more complex nature of life than masculine aspirations would allow."[34]

Central to the goddess as paradox is her well-attested psychological and more rarely evidenced physiological androgyny.[35] Inanna-Ishtar is both female and male. Over and over again the texts juxtapose the masculine and feminine traits and behavior of the goddess. She can be at one and the same time compassionate, supportive, and nurturing as well as assertive, aggressive, and strong-willed. In short, she breaks the boundaries between the sexes by embodying both femaleness and maleness.

The primary sources provide ample evidence of this reading, including the following brief examples:

Though I am a woman I am a noble young man.[36]

Her coming forth is that of a hero . . . lordship and kingship he placed in her hand.[37]

When I take my stand at the rear of battle, verily I am the woman who comes and draws near. When I sit in the ale-

Figure 4. Modern impression of a Neo-Assyrian seal (ca. 700 B.C.E.), showing the seal's owner worshipping before the armed warrior-goddess Ishtar. Courtesy of the Trustees of the British Museum, neg. no. 175906.

house, I am a woman (but) verily I am an exuberant man.

When I am present at a place of quarreling, verily I am a woman, a perfect pillar.

When I sit by the door of the tavern, verily I am a prostitute who knows *the penis*. The friend of a man, the girl-friend of a woman.[38]

Though Inanna-Ishtar is a wife and mother, neither is of great significance in her mythology.[39] She is not involved with the normal feminine pursuits of weaving and child care. The goddess's roles as prostitute and warrior place her outside of the female domestic domain and in the extradomestic world of the former and in the public arena of men who quest for power and fame.[40] Over and over again the texts stress her bloodthirstiness, her love of war and carnage:

> Battle is a feast for her.[41]
> She washes the tools in the blood of battle. She opens the "door of battle."[42]
> Inanna, you pile up heads like dust, you sow heads like seeds.[43]

Yet at the same time, the maternal, solicitous love of Inanna-Ishtar for Mesopotamian kings is noted again and again:

> She (Ishtar) held you in her kind arm (like a child).[44]
> In her loving bosom she embraced you and protected your whole figure.[45]

The significance of Ishtar-Inanna's androgyny is aptly described by B. Groneberg as a bipolarity that overturns the existing order and yet nevertheless incorporates an ordered whole.[46] Her androgyny also manifests itself ritually in the transvestism of her cultic personnel. The awesome power of the goddess shows itself in the shattering of the human boundary between the sexes: "She (Ishtar)[changes] the right side (male) into the left side (female), she [changes] the left side into the right side. She [turns] a man into a woman, she [turns] a woman into a man. She ador[ns] a man as a woman, she ador[ns] a woman as a man."[47] Mesopotamians believed that the transforming of men into women and women into men through the frightening power of the goddess was done "to teach the people religious fear."[48]

Inanna-Ishtar combines male aggressiveness with the force of a superabundance of female sexuality. She encompasses the two forms of potential disorder and violence—sex and war.[49]

The goddess also confounds the boundaries of status, of high and low. Her very special relationship with kings extends from early times down to Ashurbanipal, the last Assyrian king. Of notable prominence is her relationship with Sargon of Akkad, the Semitic ruler who "laid the basis for the new departure in Mesopotamian political organization and ushered in a complex of social, religious, and artistic innovation that deserve[s] to be regarded as a kind of cultural explosion."[50] The term "dynasty of Ishtar" is, as B. Foster describes it, "a tantalizing late sobriquet" for the Old Akkadian dynasty of Sargon and his successors. He makes the provocative comment that "the way of Ishtar points to something in the early Mesopotamian view of warfare . . . a paradox neatly drawn in an Old Babylonian Sargon epic where the undulating lines of battle are compared to two women in the act of giving birth, gushing blood in their climactic agony."[51] When Ishtar turns away from her dynasty, ruin and devastation inevitably follow.

At the same time that the goddess is associated with the most powerful in the land, with those who wield the greatest human power, she is also the patroness of prostitutes, those who belong to the fringes of society, to its marginal members (see chapter 7). In the *Gilgamesh Epic*, Ishtar assembles her devotees to mourn the killing of the Bull of Heaven by Gilgamesh and Enkidu: "(There-upon) Ishtar assembled courtesans, hierodules and prostitutes."[52] She is herself as the *harimtu*, the harlot of heaven, the role model for her votaries:

> O harlot, you set out for the alehouse
> O Inanna, you are bent on going into your (usual) window
> (namely to solicit) for a lover . . .
> You, my lady, dress like one of no repute in a single garment
> The beads (the sign) of a harlot you put around your neck[53]

Inanna-Ishtar thus breaks down the category of status, as noted quite explicitly in the following proverb: "At Ishtar's command the noble's wife gets a bad name."[54]

Inanna-Ishtar shatters the boundaries that differentiate the species: between divine and human, divine and animal, human and animal. But evidence for this is harder to come by than her confusion of the sexual categories. An episode in the *Gilgamesh Epic* is perhaps the most telling. When Inanna proposes marriage to Gilgamesh, he rejects her proposal in a long, devastatingly critical speech in which he enumerates her past sordid affairs, her previous lovers and their fates. The lovers—Dumuzi, a bird, a lion, a war-horse, a shepherd, and a gardener—all came to grief. The shepherd she turned into a wolf. In her choice of lovers Ishtar thus confused the boundaries between divine and human, divine and animal, and (in the transformation of a human into a wolf) human and animal: the divisions, then, between species.[55]

Lions especially are associated with Ishtar.[56] She is the only goddess to have the epithet of "lioness" (*labbatu*), and with her fierceness and raging power it is indeed a fitting epithet, even more befitting the maleness of the goddess.[57]

Relevant here is the new interpretation by Jacobsen of the well-known Burney Relief.[58] The winged goddess of the plaque, bearing bird's claws, being flanked by owls, and standing on two lions couchant, he believes, is Inanna as "Lady Owl," who, when named Kilili, "denotes the harlot who like the owl comes out at dusk." He suggests that the Burney Relief may have "served as a cult-relief at the house altar of an ancient bordello." If so (and Jacobsen makes a convincing case), then the depiction of the goddess breaks down the boundary between divine and animal.

There is the strong possibility that the cultic celebrations enacted in worship of the goddess shattered and confused the boundaries that separated the generations, for on these occasions adults played at children's games.[59] The festivals of the goddess were the time for disorder and antistructure, when reversals in categories of age, species, status, and sex all came into play.

Inanna-Ishtar's cultic celebrations and cultic personnel above all reflect her anomalousness and liminality. She was, one might say, externalized into unordered, carnivalesque celebration that demonstrates a reaching beyond the normal order of things and the breakdown of norms. The goddess's festivals were institutionalized license. They celebrated and tolerated disorder. They were occasions when social rules were in abeyance and deviance from norms was articulated. Through symbolic inversion they attacked the basic categorical differences between male and female, human and animal, young and old. Crucial in contributing to our understanding of the underlying elements of Ishtar's festivals is a very difficult text that was long thought to be a list of children's games. A. Kilmer has convincingly demonstrated through painstaking analysis that this text "is at home, so to speak, among the Inanna/Ishtar cultic texts."[60] That it was long thought to be a list of children's games is not surprising, for it does mention children's games: jump-rope, disappear, and hide-and-seek, to name a few. It is striking to find that the types of games mentioned here fit very well into the classification of games set up by R. Caillois: competition (races, combat), chance (dice), pretense (masks, costumes, theater), and vertigo (swings).[61]

Play (*mēlulu*) is an integral part of Inanna-Ishtar's personality.[62] She is "the player" (*mummiltu*) par excellence.[63] The semantic range of the Akkadian word for play includes dancing and acting and, not surprisingly when we think of the goddess, involves the arena of war, for her playground was the battleground:

> Goddess of fights, let the battle proceed like a play of puppets.
> Do not turn away in battle (literally, in the play of Ishtar).
> Ishtar, whose play is fighting.[64]

The interrelationship between play and ritual has been the subject of much interdisciplinary study since J. Huizinga's pioneering *Homo Ludens*.[65] "During carnivalesque occasions the indeterminacy of play serves as a mediating prelude to the transcendence of a social collective preparing it to be recast as a religious community."[66] As U. Eco observes, "Comedy and carnival are not instances of real transgressions; on the contrary they represent paramount examples of law reinforcement. They remind us of the existence of rule."[67] Play in Ishtar's festivals was related to the carnivalesque. It "embodied the essential carnival spirit, strongly characterized by the transgression of daily conventions and excesses of behavior."[68]

In what must have been boisterous, noisy entertainment, disorder was celebrated in honor of the goddess of disorder. In the "Games Text," reference is made to "improper speech":

obscenity, in other words. Mockery, abuse, and hostile words were very much part of the goddess's repertory. They form part of the *me*s with which the goddess was obsessed.[69] Pornographic language characterizes the so-called love lyrics that were recited in the cultic performances of her celebrations. These texts are described by their editor, W. G. Lambert: "Imagery of the boldest kind is commonplace, and the eroticism is the most explicit for Mesopotamia. . . . How should we take it? As factual record merely, as jest, as innuendo or as something else?"[70] Bawdy theater was very much a part of the celebration in which the goddess's personnel enacted (probably with appropriate costumes and masks) the roles of their goddess (paramour of the god Marduk in the "love lyrics") and other deities (e.g., Marduk and his spouse Ṣarpanitum). The "Games Text" also seems to be formulated as a dialogue. The "improper speech" of the text suggests that scatological jokes were part of the entertainment, the scatological that "is the explosive flaunting . . . of taboos" along with "a foisting off of the terror of breaking the taboos."[71] Ritual obscenity thus also attacked the conventional limits. Through farce and bawdy songs the goddess's celebrants would find temporary release from societal restrictions.

There are suggestions in the "Games Text" and tantalizing hints from cylinder seals that masked men (and possibly women) may have worn lion masks and special cloaks during the festivities honoring "the lioness." Thus once again Inanna's symbols would have shattered the boundaries between human and animal.[72]

Dancing too was part of the celebration for the goddess, who danced "the whirl like a man."[73] Dance suggests the power of movement as opposed to stasis and limitation.

Inanna-Ishtar's celebrations were then "creative negation" that reminded her devotees "of the need to reinvest the clean with the filthy, the rational with the animalistic, the ceremonial with the carnivalesque in order to maintain cultural vitality. And they confirm[ed] the endless potentiality of dirt and the pure possibility of liminality."[74]

The chief participants and actors in the goddess's cult are well known by name: *assinnu, ḫabbūbu, kurgarrû, kulu'u, pilpilu*. What is uncertain is how best to describe them.[75] There is even ambiguity about their sexuality—whether they were eunuchs, hermaphrodites, or simply transvestites. *The Assyrian Dictionary* describes the *assinnu* as seeming "to have functioned mainly in the cult of Ishtar, to have sung specific songs and dressed in distinctive garments. There is no specific evidence that [the *assinnu*] was a eunuch or a homosexual."[76] The *kurgarrû* (as well as *assinnu* and *kulu'u*) are described as "performing games, plays, dances and music as part of the ritual (of the great festivals). There is no evidence that they were eunuchs or homosexuals. However, in the *Descent of Ishtar* the reference to the *kurgarrû* as neither male nor female may indicate they were transvestites performing in female apparel. On the other hand, the mention of daggers seems to suggest that they were devotees of Ishtar's performing some sword dance."[77] Through their war dance, Groneberg observes, they reenact the attribute of Ishtar as warrior.[78] And self-mutilation may well have been part of their ritual:

> The male prostitutes comb their hair before her . . .
> They decorate the napes of their necks with colored bands . . .
> They gird themselves with the sword belt, the "arm of
>   battle" . . .
> Their right side they adorn with women's clothing . . .
> Their left side they cover with men's clothing . . .
> With jump ropes and colored cords they compete before
>   her . . .
> The young men, carrying hoops, sing to her . . .
> The ascending *kurgarra* priests grasped the sword . . .
> The one who covers the sword with blood, he sprinkles
>   blood . . .
> He pours out blood on the dais of the throne room.[79]

Their transvestism simulated the androgyny of Inanna-Ishtar. It was perhaps the inversion of the male/female binary opposition that thereby neutralized this opposition. By emulating their goddess who was both female and male, they shattered the boundary between the sexes. Thus at her festival time the full range of human emotions might be freely manifested without regard to the stereotypical notions of masculinity and femininity. The function of transvestism, as M. Eliade observed, was "a coming out of one's self, a transcending of one's own historically controlled situation . . . a paradoxical situation impossible to maintain in profane time, in an historical epoch, but which is important to reconstitute periodically in order to restore, if only for a brief moment, the initial completeness, the intact source of holiness and power."[80] The cultic personnel of the goddess in their costumes, words, and acts had but one goal: "To delight Ishtar's heart, give themselves up to (otherwise) for[bidden] actions."[81]

Inanna-Ishtar thus cuts across socioeconomic and gender distinctions: "Be it slave, unattached girl, 'Ishtar' preserves her. Women and men indeed revere her."[82]

Perhaps C. Geertz's words best explain her enormous and abiding popularity: "The strange opacity of certain empirical events, the dumb senselessness of intense or inexorable pain, and the enigmatic unaccountability of gross inequity all raise the uncomfortable suspicion that perhaps the world, and hence man's life in the worlds, has no genuine order at all—no empirical regularity, no form, no moral coherence. And the religious response is the same: the formulation, by means of symbols, or an image of such a genuine order which will account for and even celebrate the perceived ambiguities, puzzles and paradoxes in human experience."[83]

GLOSSARY

Adad-guppi
: The incredibly long lived mother of Nabonidus, last king of Babylonia.

Addu-duri
: Probably the mother of Zimri-Lim, king of Mari (ca. 1771–1761 B.C.E.).

Akkadian
: Designation of the closely related Semitic dialects, which are also called Assyrian and Babylonian.

Assyriology
: The academic discipline that deals with the history, language, and antiquities of ancient Mesopotamian civilization.

Cuneiform
: The wedge-shaped writing on clay of Mesopotamia. This writing system was also adopted by the Elamites and the Hittites.

Enheduanna
: The daughter of Sargon of Akkad, she was high priestess (*entu*) of the moon god of the city of Ur. She has been considered by many scholars as an author of temple hymns.

Enkidu
: The primitive, wild man of the *Gilgamesh Epic* who was domesticated by the prostitute Shamhat, then became Gilgamesh's friend and companion.

Enlil
: One of the most important gods in the Mesopotamian pantheon. Nippur is his major cult center.

Enuma Elish
: The so-called Babylonian story of creation, centering on the conflict between the older and younger gods, with ultimate victory by the young god Marduk. Most of the tablets date to the first millennium B.C.E.

Ereshkigal   "The Lady of the Great Land" (=netherworld). The myth of *Nergal and Ereshkigal* relates how Ereshkigal gave up being sole ruler of the netherworld when Nergal became her husband.

Gilgamesh   A ruler of the Sumerian city-state Uruk who lived ca. 2700 B.C.E. His fame lived on long after his death.

Gilgamesh Epic   Relates the adventures of the Sumerian king and hero Gilgamesh. His exploits were written down at first in Sumerian (ca. 2000 B.C.E.). Later, three different Akkadian versions were composed over a period of nearly a thousand years, each with somewhat different motifs.

Inanna   The Sumerian goddess of love and war who was lover and wife of Dumuzi. She was later identified with the Semitic goddess Ishtar.

Ishtar   The Semitic goddess of love and war who was lover and wife of Tammuz. Identified with the Sumerian goddess Inanna, she was the most important female deity of ancient Mesopotamia in all periods.

Maqlu   An incantation series for use by priests specializing in exorcism. Its conjurations are addressed to gods or to the means, especially fire, used to destroy figurines representing the enemies of sufferers.

Marduk   Patron god of Babylon from at least as early as the Ur III period. He is the young god who defeats Tiamat and her forces in *Enuma Elish*.

Mari   (=Tell Hariri) Thousands of cuneiform tablets excavated here roughly cover the period of the first half of the eighteenth century B.C.E. They are a rich source of information on the socioeconomic and religious life of the kingdom's rulers and their families.

Mesopotamia   The civilization that arose along and between the Tigris and Euphrates Rivers and endured for some three thousand years—from the fourth millennium B.C.E. until the beginning of the Common Era. It was made up of two basic components: the Sumerians and the Akkadians.

Nadītu   Girls who, during the Old Babylonian period, entered a cloister (*gagû*) on reaching the age of marriage. There they lived celibate lives dedicated to the god Shamash

	and his consort for their lifetime. Mostly women of means, many were involved in a variety of business activities.
Naqi'a-Zakutu	Favorite wife of Sennacherib, mother of Esarhaddon and grandmother of Ashurbanipal. She was instrumental in her son's and grandson's succeeding to the throne despite their having older siblings.
Nergal	Patron god of Cutha in central Babylonia. He and his spouse, Ereshkigal, were rulers of the netherworld. He was the source of plagues.
Sammuramat	Identified with the Semiramis of Greek literature, she was the wife of Shamshi-Adad V and mother of Adad-nirari III. She was outstanding as a matriarch and queen mother and probably served as regent for her son.
Sumerians	The inhabitants of southern Mesopotamia who spoke and wrote a language with no close resemblance to any known language. The earliest texts from Mesopotamia were written in Sumerian. In the course of time the Sumerians became integrated into the Semitic population, but their language continued as the language of the learned.
Sumerology	The academic discipline that deals with the history, language, and antiquities of ancient Sumer.
Šumma Ālu	A long and complex omen series consisting of at least 107 tablets, of which only one-fourth are preserved. It contains omens referring to cities, houses, behavior of insects, and large and small animals. Some also concern human relations, especially regarding sexual matters.
Tiamat	The primeval goddess, mother of the first generation of gods in *Enuma Elish*. She was the spouse and later the widow of Apsu, progenitor of the primeval gods.
Utnapishtim	The one man who, with his wife, was permitted to survive the great flood and was then granted immortality. His name means "He Found Life."

ABBREVIATIONS

AHw   W. von Soden. *Akkadisches Handwörterbuch* (Wiesbaden, 1959–1981).

ANET   J. B. Pritchard, ed. *Ancient Near Eastern Texts Relating to the Old Testament* (Princeton: Princeton University Press, 1950).

CAD   *The Assyrian Dictionary of the University of Chicago* (Chicago, 1956–).

CANE   J. M. Sasson, et al., eds. *Civilizations of the Ancient Near East*. 4 vols. (Charles Scribner's Sons: New York, 1995).

Dumu-e$_2$-dub-ba-a   H. Behrens, D. Loding, and M. T. Roth, eds. *Dumu-e$_2$-dub-ba-a: Studies in Honor of Åke W. Sjöberg* (Philadelphia: University Museum, 1989).

La Femme   J.-M. Durand, ed. *La femme dans le Proche-Orient antique*. Compte rendue de la 33e Rencontre Assyriologique Internationale (Paris: Éditions Recherche sur les Civilisations, 1987).

JANES   *Journal of the Ancient Near Eastern Society of Columbia University* (New York).

JAOS   *Journal of the American Oriental Society* (New Haven).

JCS   *Journal of Cuneiform Studies* (New Haven, Philadelphia).

JNES	*Journal of Near Eastern Studies* (Chicago).
RA	*Revue d'Assyriologie et d'archéologie orientale* (Paris).
RLA	*Reallexikon der Assyriologie* (Berlin, 1932–).
The Tablet and the Scroll	M. E. Cohen, D. Snell, and D. Weisberg, eds. *The Tablet and the Scroll: Near Eastern Studies in Honor of William W. Hallo* (Bethesda, Md.: CDL Press, 1993).
Women's Earliest Records	B. Lesko, ed. *Women's Earliest Records from Ancient Egypt and Western Asia.* Brown Judaic Studies 66 (Atlanta: Scholars Press, 1989).
ZA	*Zeitschrift für Assyriologie und Verwandte Gebiete* (Berlin).

NOTES

PREFACE

1. Clark, *Women in Late Antiquity*, 4.
2. Cooper, "The Fate of Mankind," 20.
3. Skinner, "Introduction," 3.
4. For an anthology of essays on the *Gilgamesh Epic* see Maier, *Gilgamesh: A Reader*.
5. Perera, "The Descent of Inanna," 148.
6. Oppenheim, *Ancient Mesopotamia*, 30

CHAPTER 1. THE LIFE COURSE

1. The following articles are relevant to the subject: Malamat, "Longevity"; van der Toorn, *From Her Cradle to Her Grave*; Wilcke, "Familiengrundüng im Alten Babylonien"; Glassner, "De Sumer à Babylone"; Kramer, "The Woman in Ancient Sumer"; Roth, "Age at Marriage"; Hoffner, "Hittite Terms for the Life Span"; Klein, "The 'Bane' of Humanity"; and Stol, "Private Life in Ancient Mesopotamia." The prestigious *Reallexikon der Assyriologie* has no entry for the topic.

2. See, for example, the cogent comments by Gaffney on "the vast indifference to time" during the Middle Ages in "The Ages of Man in Old French Verse, Epic and Romance," 570f.

3. Note the use of *alāku* "to go" in idioms such as *am īlūtu alāku* "to reach old age" (CAD A/2 62b) and *šībūtu alāku*, also meaning "to reach

old age" (CAD A/1 316b), as well as "they (the forefathers) must go 'the way of death' (*uruḫ mūt[u]*)" (Lambert, *Babylonian Wisdom Literature* 70:16).

4. See Simpson, ed., *Literature of Ancient Egypt*, 162:5.

5. Klein, "The 'Bane' of Humanity," 65 n. 18.

6. Alster, "The Paradigmatic Character of Mesopotamian Heroes," 58 n. 2.

7. Jacobsen, "Death in Mesopotamia (Abstract)," 21.

8. Ibid.

9. Lambert, "The Theology of Death," 57.

10. Jacobsen, *The Sumerian King List*.

11. Kovacs, *The Epic of Gilgamesh*, 17 II 93–94.

12. Foster, "Gilgamesh," 37.

13. For kissing each other see Kovacs, *The Epic of Gilgamesh*, 18 II 29; for holding hands see ibid., 19 II 164; 20 II 249; 25 III 19; 56 VI 168.

14. For the many references to *eṭlu* in the *Gilgamesh Epic* see CAD E 408b.

15. For a discussion of the many shades of meaning of *šīmtu* see Oppenheim, *Ancient Mesopotamia*, 202–204. For references to *šīmtu* see CAD S/3 17–18; for *lalîšu* see CAD L 50b–51a.

16. See Bayliss, "Cult of the Dead in Assyria and Babylonia."

17. For references to *mār māri* see CAD M/1 259–260; for *inbu* see CAD I/J 144–146, especially 146b; for *liblibbu* see CAD L 179–180; for *lillidu* see CAD L 183; for *zēru* see CAD Z 94–96; for *per'u* see AHw 856. See CAD Z 95 for references to such curses. For references to the idiom *kinūnšu belû* see CAD B 191b.

18. Oppenheim, *Ancient Mesopotamia*, 257f.

19. Kovacs, *The Epic of Gilgamesh*, 116.

20. Jacobsen, *The Harps*, 461:228–229.

21. Ibid., 138:176.

22. For references see, for example, Cooper, *The Curse of Agade*, 53 I 29–33: old women (*um.ma*), old men (*ab.ba*), young women (*ki.sikil*), young men (*guruš*), little ones (*di₄.di₄.lá*). See also Farber-Flügge, *Der Mythos "Inanna und Enki,"* 50:33–36; and Kramer, "BM 96927: A Prime Example of Ancient Scribal Redaction," 260 r. ii 106–110. In all these literary passages only the "little ones" are not gender-differentiated.

23. For the early period see Gelb, "The Ancient Mesopotamian Ration System," especially 238–241. For the later period see Brinkman, "Sex, Age, and Physical Condition" and idem, "Forced Laborers in the Middle Babylonian Period," especially 18.

24. Stol, "Private Life in Ancient Mesopotamia," 485.

25. Brinkman, "Sex, Age, and Physical Condition," 2. He also includes the feminine equivalent for each age category.

26. Burrow, *The Ages of Man*, 22.

27. Gelb, "The Ancient Mesopotamian Ration System," 239.

28. Gordon, *Sumerian Proverbs*, 126 1.160.

29. Golden, *Children and Childhood in Classical Athens*, 83. On longevity and infant mortality in ancient Rome see Wiedemann, *Adults and Children in the Roman Empire*, 11–17.

30. Foster, *Before the Muses*, vol. 1, 136. See also ibid., vol. 2, 890. For the best discussion to date, to my knowledge, on infants in Mesopotamia see Limet, "La condition de l'enfant en Mésopotamie." For another childbirth incantation, with more references, see G. Farber, "Another Old Babylonian Childbirth Incantation."

Following generally accepted Assyriological practice, parentheses enclose material added to the English translation while square brackets mark restoration of broken text in the original. Some exceptions do appear in this book where translators or editors deviated from this practice. Ellipses mark untranslatable passages as well as gaps in the quoted material. Some modifications of capitalization and punctuation have been made to enhance readability.

31. On Lamashtu and the *lilû* see W. Farber, "Lamaštu" and "*lilû, lilîtu, ardat lilî*," respectively. For a description of Lamashtu see also Black and Green, *Gods, Demons, and Symbols of Ancient Mesopotamia*, 115f.

32. For comments on the illnesses of infants and children, as well as for a bibliography, see Biggs, "Medizen A," 625. He observes that the treatment of babies' illnesses "seems to have belonged to the domain of magic." See also idem, "Medicine, Surgery, and Public Health in Ancient Mesopotamia," 1917. Limet (in "La condition de l'enfant en Mesopotamie," 14) notes that because there were no advances in either treatment or hygiene down the centuries, children's illnesses probably remained very much the same. For a survey of children's illnesses see also Labat, *Traité akkadien de diagnostic et prognostic médicaux*.

33. For this view see Kilmer, "The Mesopotamian Concept of Overpopulation."

34. Dalley, *Myths from Mesopotamia*, 35.

35. Porada, "An Emaciated Male Figure of Bronze in the Cincinnati Museum," especially 164–166. For an example of such a clay plaque see ibid., Fig. 9.

36. For references to *ša libbiša* see CAD L 175a–176a. For a discussion of the Sumerian terminology see Limet, "La condition de l'enfant en

Mésopotamie," 5. The Sumerian word for infancy is *u₄.tur.ra* "the days when one is small," equivalent to Akkadian *ūm ṣeḫēri*. See ibid., note 1. For references to *izbu* see CAD I/J 317f. For the edition and study of the birth omens see Leichty, *The Omen Series šumma izbu*. For references to *ina mêšu* see CAD M/2 154b; for *šilip rēmim*, which appears to be a scribal idiosyncrasy, see CAD Š/2 447–448. For a recent discussion, with bibliography, on the problems preventing full understanding of the idiom see Veenhof, "Two *šilip rēmim*, Adoptions from Sippar."

37. For references to *šerru* see CAD Š/2 317–320; for *ṣiḫru* see CAD S 179 and 182–183. For the incantations see Farber, *Schlaf, Kindchen, Schlaf!* 34.

38. For *daqqu* see CAD D 107; for *qudādu* see CAD Q 293b; for *dumugabû* see CAD D 107; for the Sumerian *tur.gaba* see Stol, "Private Life in Ancient Mesopotamia," 491; for *lakû* see CAD L 45–46; for *la'û* see CAD L 114; for *mār irti* and *mārat irti* see CAD I/J 186a; and for *ginû* see CAD G 83. Another designation for a nursing child is *(ša) šizbu*, which appears in late texts (CAD Š/3 151f), also used of suckling animals. The weaned child is *pirsu* "withdrawn (from the breast)" (AHw 867a s.v. *pirsu*). For an informative study of breast-feeding in ancient Mesopotamia see Gruber, "Breast-Feeding Practices in Biblical Israel and in Old Babylonian Mesopotamia."

39. For references to the ages of young children see CAD M/1 311 and 312a.

40. Finkelstein, "Documents from the Practice of Law," 547.

41. For *mār(at) šatti* see CAD Š/2 205.

42. See CAD M/1 303a. For comments on and references to the age and height of children see Roth, "Age at Marriage," 732 and 735. She notes that the Assyrian Domesday book follows descending age categories: the shorter, the younger, the smaller the ration. On rations issued for infants or nursing infants see Gelb, "The Ancient Mesopotamian Ration System," 240.

43. Finkelstein, *Late Old Babylonian Documents and Letters*, 14–16. See also the stimulating article by Zaccagnini, "Feet of Clay at Emar and Elsewhere," in which he uses the size of footprints of very young children impressed on lumps of clay, accompanying two Emar sale contracts in which children are sold, to recover their ages. One was a girl of about three months; a set of twin boys were about two years old.

44. Canby, "The Child in Hittite Iconography," 65.

45. For references to *kirimmu* see CAD K 406.

46. For this myth see Kramer and Maier, *Myths of Enki, the Crafty God,* 31–37. For Kilmer's interpretation see her "Speculations on Umul, the First Baby."

47. See the myth of *Erra and Ishum* in Foster, *Before the Muses,* vol. 2, 774:48 for "Why sitting at home like a helpless child."

48. There is, to my knowledge, no data on accidental deaths in Mesopotamia. Whether infants and young children would be left alone would of course be relevant to the issue of accidental death.

49. See W. Farber, *Schlaf Kindchen Schlaf!* and idem, "Magic at the Cradle."

50. Foster, *Before the Muses,* vol. 2, 896. See also ibid., 894 and vol. 1, 137.

51. Jacobsen, *The Harps,* 83:368–369.

52. For *rigmu,* used of both animals and babies (*šerru*), see AHw 982b.

53. See Kramer, "Ua-aua: A Sumerian Lullaby," 652. Lullabies appear to be particularly associated with wet nurses in Sumerian literature. For this see Michalowski, *The Lamentation over the Destruction of Sumer and Ur,* 72:16. W. Farber (in "Magic at the Cradle," 140 n. 3) questions Kramer's description of the text. He believes that "although ultimately serving a similar purpose, [it] clearly belongs to the realm of cult-related literature and shows no recognizable features of folk poetry." In my view there is much in this lullaby, especially in its ambiguities, that is very similar to lullabies cross-culturally.

54. See, for example, the discussions by Tucker, "Lullabies"; and K. Achte et al., "Themes of Death and Violence in Lullabies of Different Countries."

55. See Cooper, *The Curse of Agade,* 50:37; and Farber-Flügge, *Der Mythos "Inanna und Enki,"* 50:36 and ibid., 84 n. 14.

56. For kissing as a gesture of familial affection see Cooper, "Kuss," especially 376b and 377a.

57. Jacobsen, *The Harps,* 226:349.

58. Cited in the lexical section of CAD Š/1 483a. All of Inanna's listed powers involve the setting up of a household, which would also include having children.

59. Cited in CAD N/2 57b.

60. Livingstone, *Mystical and Mythological Explanatory Works of Assyrian and Babylonian Scholars,* 121 K 3476 (obverse):5. Here a state ritual is explained in terms of a mythological event.

61. See Albenda, "Woman, Child, and Family." See also Canby, "The Child in Hittite Iconography," especially 61, and 67 n. 17.

62. For references to *birku* see CAD B 256b. See also the comments by Canby in "The Child in Hittite Iconography," 59 and 68 n. 25.

63. Jacobsen, *The Harps*, 226:350.

64. Kramer, "The Death of Ur-Nammu and the Descent to the Netherworld," 119:151.

65. Jacobsen, *The Harps*, 461:229–230 and 476:26.

66. For references see CAD S 388b s.v. *sūnu*.

67. For references see CAD K 540–542 s.v. *kunnû*, as well as Sperling, "A *šu-il-lá* to Ishtar," 13. Ishtar is here described as "the darling of the goddesses (*kanūt ilāti*)."

68. See Kilmer, "Games and Toys in Ancient Mesopotamia." For rattles, see ibid., 362.

69. Malul, "Adoption of Foundlings in the Bible and Mesopotamian Documents," 104–118. For the sale of children see the comments of Limet, "La condition de l'enfant," 15–17; and Kienast, "Kinderkauf."

70. Golden, *Children and Childhood in Classical Athens*, 87. Nor was it uncommon in later times either.

71. Van de Mieroop, *Society and Enterprise in Old Babylonian Ur*, 37.

72. For a discussion of these burials see Ellis, *Foundation Deposits in Ancient Mesopotamia*, 35–39 and 41. At least one child was buried in a mausoleum at Ur. See Michalowski, "The Death of Šulgi," 233.

73. Jacobsen, *The Harps*, 475 n. 1.

74. Golden, *Children and Childhood in Classical Athens*, 82–93.

75. Ibid., 85. This is in sharp contrast to the view expressed by Black and Green (in *Gods, Demons, and Symbols of Ancient Mesopotamia*, 59f.) that children's burials is evidence that "they were regarded as subhuman."

76. For the profound sorrow expressed in the laments of Dumuzi's mother see Jacobsen, *The Harps*, 65–72.

77. Alster, "The Paradigmatic Character of Mesopotamian Heroes," 58.

78. Dalley, *Mari and Karana*, 98.

79. Ibid., 97.

80. CAD Ṣ 179 s.v. *ṣiḫru*. It has been suggested that in literary texts the Sumerian equivalent for *ṣiḫru*, *lú.tur*, refers to a newborn baby or small child and should be read *šerru* but in Middle Babylonian and Neo-Assyrian ration lists probably should be read *batultu*. See CAD Ṣ 185b. Brinkman (in "Sex, Age, and Physical Condition," 2) finds that a distinction is made in Middle Babylonian ration lists between *guruš.tur* and *sal.tur* "adolescent" and *guruš.tur.tur* and *sal.tur.tur* "child," or in other words between an older child and a younger child. Dandamaev (in *Slavery in Babylonia from Nabopolassar to Alexander the Great*, 98) suggests that in the very late period *ṣiḫru/ṣaḫru* describes slaves from the ages of one through

fifteen or sixteen! For *ṣuḫāru* see CAD Ṣ 231–232; the Sumerian equivalent is *tur.tur*. It can include the infant too, as some of the citations show. See also the derivatives *meṣḫerūtu* "childhood," *ṣuḫārtu, ṣuḫru* "(early) youth." The same wide range is also true of *ṣuḫartu* "young woman," "female child." For this see CAD Ṣ 229–231.

81. Golden, *Children and Childhood in Classical Athens,"* 12f.

82. For a discussion of this range of meanings of *ṣuḫāru* see Finet, "Le *ṣuḫārum* à Mari." For a parallel example in Greek see Golden, *"Pais,* 'Child' and 'Slave.'"

83. Evans, "Ancient Mesopotamian Assemblies," 8.

84. Marcus, "Juvenile Delinquency in the Bible and the Ancient Near East," 32. The term "minor" itself denotes inferiority.

85. Lambert, *Babylonian Wisdom Literature*, 233 IV 31f.

86. Cited in CAD Ṣ 183b. Both references are from Mari.

87. Gordon, *Sumerian Proverbs*, 58 1.37.

88. See the citation in CAD M/2 37b s.v. *meṣḫerūtu*.

89. See Jacobsen, *The Harps*, 322:3–4. For references to *arû A*, used of both children and boats, see CAD A/2 315a.

90. Kovacs, *The Epic of Gilgamesh*, 6 I 86–93.

91. Ibid., 16 n. 2, *awēliš īwi* "he became a human being."

92. Jacobsen, *The Treasures of Darkness*, 147.

93. Kovacs, *The Epic of Gilgamesh*, 85 n. 1. Little work has been done to date on kinship relations. The little that has been written focuses primarily on mother-children ties. See, for example, Frymer-Kensky, *In the Wake of the Goddesses*, 16–19. See also my comments in chapter 7.

94. Saporetti, *The Status of Women in the Middle Assyrian Period*, 12.

95. On the school and its curriculum see Kramer, *History Begins at Sumer*, 3–17; and Sjöberg, "The Old Babylonian Eduba." See most recently Vanstiphout, "Memory and Literacy in Ancient Western Asia," 2189f.; and Pearce, "The Scribes and Scholars of Ancient Mesopotamia," 2270–2272.

96. Pearce, ibid., 2276.

97. Ibid., 2277.

98. Kramer, *The Sumerians*, 240 and 249, respectively.

99. Oppenheim, *Letters from Mesopotamia*, 84f.

100. On apprenticeships see Petschow, "Lehrvertrag."

101. Golden, *Children and Childhood in Classical Athens*, 32f.

102. See Janssen and Janssen, *Growing Up in Ancient Egypt*, 49.

103. Jacobsen and Kramer, "The Myth of Inanna and Bilulu," 173:45.

104. Dalley, *Mari and Karana*, 99. Payment was therefore according to need and not just a standard wage. Earlier in the Ur III period, also, very

young children and babes-in-arms received food and wool allotments even though they did not work. See Waetzoldt, "Compensation of Craft Workers and Officials in the Ur III Period," 134.

105. For picking of clods see CAD K 402b. For children as "teaselers" see Brinkman, "Sex, Age, and Physical Condition," 4. For a reference to three girls (*sal.tur*) gathering something that is no longer preserved see CAD L 102a. For children fetching bitumen see Dalley, *Myths from Mesopotamia*, 30 ii.

106. Waetzoldt, "Compensation of Craft Workers and Officials in the Ur III Period," 132–135. But even when postpubescent boys were receiving adult rations, they were still referred to as boys (*dumu.nita*) in the subtotal.

107. Ibid., 140.

108. Brinkman, "Sex, Age, and Physical Condition," 5.

109. On sale of children see Limet, "La condition de l'enfant," 15–17; and Kienast, "Kinderkauf." Limet (ibid., 15f.) notes that more girls than boys are sold in texts published by Falkenstein, which suggests a preference for male children.

110. See Oppenheim, "'Siege Documents' from Nippur."

111. Lambert, *Babylonian Wisdom Literature*, 248 iii 7–10.

112. See Cohen, *Canonical Lamentations of Ancient Mesopotamia*, 336:f+239. See also CAD M/2 15b, lexical section: "Lord, do not step into the playground (*ašar mēlultu*), do not drive out the young ones (*ṣeḫrūtu*) from the playground."

113. Foster, *Before the Muses*, vol. 1, 425:18–20.

114. I owe this information to Robert D. Biggs, who generously gave me permission to quote from his forthcoming essay, "The Human Body and Sexuality in Mesopotamian Medical Texts."

115. Jacobsen *apud* Gordon, *Sumerian Proverbs*, 453.

116. For a photograph of this plaque see Glassner, "De Sumer à Babylone," 116.

117. For this statue see Frankfort, *Sculpture of the Third Millennium B.C. from Tell Asmar and Khafajah*, Plate 5 B and C. For his reconstruction of what the statue must have looked like see the frontispiece.

118. See Albenda, "Woman, Child, and Family," 19, on this depiction. Nudity is one aspect of generic young childhood in Egyptian art, where both boys and girls are shown nude; sometimes with finger to the mouth and boys with side-locks. See Janssen and Janssen, *Growing Up in Ancient Egypt*, 160.

119. For *batultu* and *batūlu* see CAD B 173 and 174, respectively. Leick, (in *Sex and Eroticism in Mesopotamian Literature*, 42) calls her chapter 4

"From Adolescence to Maturity." Here she characterizes the goddess Ninlil as acting "like any curious adolescent."

120. For *eṭlu* see CAD E 407–411a, especially 407.

121. For this translation see Sasson, "A King of Early Assyria," 799.

122. CAD E 397a s.v. *eṭēlu*.

123. For changes in beard styles see Collon, "Clothing and Grooming in Ancient Western Asia." For clothing see also Waetzoldt, "Kleidung A: Philologisch"; Strommenger, "Kleidung B: Archäologisch."

124. Cited in CAD M/2 88b s.v. *minîtu*. For *dûtu* see CAD D 202; for *banû* see CAD B 81; for *baštu* see CAD B 142–144. These are adjectives that describe Gilgamesh, the youth, before he has reached mature adulthood. See chapter 2 for these and other characteristics associated with the youth stage of life.

125. See Cooper, *The Curse of Agade*, 53:32. Here both young and older (but not old) male adults are included in the term *guruš*.

126. For citation see CAD I/J 197a. Jacobsen (in *The Harps*, 46 n. 21) suggests that the phrase "battle is the festival of young men" is "a stereotype for recording the death of a young soldier."

127. For *meṭlūtu* see CAD M/2 45; for *mūtu* see CAD M/2 3/4a, lexical section; for *mutūtu* see CAD M/2 319b.

128. Cited in CAD A/2 55a. Learning civility was part of the *eduba*'s curriculum. For this see Alster, *The Instruction of Suruppak*, 96: the teacher teaches "pleasant mouth and politeness." For additional comments on this concept see also van der Toorn, *Family Religion in Babylonia, Ugarit, and Israel*, 27. For *amīlu* see CAD A/2 54a–55. See also CAD A/2 62 for *amīlūtu* "behavior of a gentleman." The references are limited in time (Old Assyrian and Old Babylonian), but the concept may have had much wider currency than the remaining texts indicate. The ancient Egyptian didactic texts provide a far more detailed profile of the "gentleman," equating etiquette with morality.

129. Jacobsen, "Note on the Word *lú*."

130. With the exception of princesses destined to become *entu*-priest-esses or girls of mostly elite strata who in the Old Babylonian period entered the cloister (*gagû*) as *nadītu* at the age they would otherwise marry. On such institutions see Renger, "Untersuchungen zum Priestertum in der altbabylonischen Zeit"; on the *nadītu* see R. Harris, "Independent Women in Ancient Mesopotamia?"

131. For a survey on Mesopotamian women see Stol, "Women in Mesopotamia."

132. Roth, "Age at Marriage," 737.

133. I quote from his forthcoming essay "The Human Body and Sexuality in Mesopotamian Medical Texts."

134. Baba is a pet name for Inanna.

135. Jacobsen, *The Harps*, 18.

136. Leick's *Sex and Eroticism in Mesopotamian Literature* is to date the most informative general study on sexuality in ancient Mesopotamia.

137. Roth, "Age at Marriage," 742–746. What is crucial, as Roth notes, is that neither *batultu* nor **nu'artu* is used to characterize women who act independently and hence neither term refers to more mature women (I would add, probably widowed) or women with children (ibid., 745).

138. Garland, *The Greek Way of Life*, 190.

139. See Jacobsen *apud* Gordon, *Sumerian Proverbs*, 453. The Sumerian term for boy is *guruš.tur* (Akkadian *batūlu*), and *guruš* is the Sumerian for *eṭlu*.

140. For *ardatu* see CAD A/2 242–243. This usage parallels "a young man who has not (yet) changed (to adulthood)." See CAD M/2 288b s.v. *muštēnû*.

141. Jacobsen, *The Harps*, 3–23. See the important study on marriage by Greengus, "Old Babylonian Marriage Ceremonies and Rites." See also idem, "Bridewealth in Sumerian Sources." For comments on marriage practices see also Westbrook, *Old Babylonian Marriage Law*; and Stol, "Private Life in Ancient Mesopotamia," 488–490.

142. For references to *mašraḫū* see CAD M/1 385a; for *kuzbu* see CAD K 614–615a; for *duššupu* see CAD D 200. Girls were given pleasing names such as Kuzubatum and Duššuptum at birth. On *ḫi.li* see Leick, *Sex and Eroticism in Mesopotamian Literature*, especially 74f. and 195. Her chapter "Bridal Songs" (ibid., 64–79) is informative on the characteristics of about-to-be married girls as represented by the goddess Inanna.

143. Civil, "Enlil and Ninlil—The Marriage of Sud."

144. See Cooper, *The Curse of Agade*, 53:31.

145. Jacobsen, *The Harps*, 10.

146. Kilmer, "Music and Dance in Ancient Western Asia," 2610f.

147. For references to *sinništu* see CAD S 286–292; for *amīltu* "free woman" see CAD A/2; for *aššatu* see CAD A/2 462–465.

148. M. I. Marcus, "Dressed to Kill: Women and Pins in Early Iran," 7 and 8, respectively.

149. Jacobsen, *The Harps*, 95.

150. Gurney and Hulin, *The Sultantepe Tablets*, 400 r. 45–47. The text is usually referred to as STT 400 and will be here too. It has been discussed, mostly in passing, down the years: see Nougayrol, "Notes brèves";

Sjöberg, "Der Examenstat A," 164; Malamat, "Longevity," 215; Wilcke, "Familiengründung im Alten Babylonien," 217f.; Roth, "Age at Marriage," 717; and Weinfeld, "The Phases of Human Life in Mesopotamia and Jewish Sources."

151. Roth, "Age at Marriage," 717 and 717 n. 3, respectively.

152. Shakespeare, *As You Like It*, 38–39.

153. For an in-depth discussion of this text see Falkner, "The Politics and the Poetics of Time in Solon's 'Ten Ages.'"

154. See Herlihy, "Growing Old in the Quattrocento," 104; and Gilbert, "When Did Renaissance Man Grow Old?" For a general survey see Covey, "The Definitions of the Beginning of Old Age in History."

155. For the Ptolemaic Papyrus Insinger scheme see the sixteenth instruction in Lichtheim, *Ancient Egyptian Literature*, vol. 3, 198f.

156. Perhaps the pervasive elasticity of Akkadian age terminology is an aspect of the fairly undifferentiated stretch of time applied to the years before mature adulthood.

157. For the widespread view of young–old age and old–old age see Covey, "The Definitions of the Beginning of Old Age in History."

158. Dandamaev, "About Life Expectancy in Babylonia," 185.

159. Roth, "Age at Marriage," 719 n. 9.

160. R. Harris, *Ancient Sippar*, 289 (for scribes). See also ibid., (p. 155) for the *sanga* priest Annum-pi-Aja, who held office for some fifty-nine years. There are many more examples of long-lived administrators of other institutions.

161. Falkner and de Luce (in "A View from Antiquity," 11) discuss the "graying of Greece" among intellectuals and creative artists.

162. For *lalûtum* see CAD L 526. For *lalû*, as a synonym for *nîš libbi* (*šà.zi.ga*) "desirability, (sexual) potency" see ibid., 49, lexical section and Biggs, *šà.zi.ga: Ancient Mesopotamian Potency Incantations*, 2.

163. In Lattimore, *Greek Lyrics*, 23.

164. For these various shades of meaning for *meṭlūtu* see CAD M/2 45.

165. For references see CAD Š/2 201a s.v. *šattu*.

166. For this reference see CAD Z 126a s.v. *ziqnu*.

167. Bottéro, *Mesopotamia: Writing, Reasoning, and the Gods*, 250.

168. Kovacs, *The Epic of Gilgamesh*, 106.

169. Klein, "The 'Bane' of Humanity," 62.

170. Medina, *The Clock of Ages*, 313. That life was by nature limited to 120 years was a widespread view among the Romans. See Eyben, "Roman Notes on the Course of Life," 230.

171. Klein, "The 'Bane' of Humanity," 64 n. 15.

172. Kirk, "Old Age and Maturity in Ancient Greece," 156.
173. For *littūtu* see CAD L 220–221.

CHAPTER 2. GILGAMESH'S COMING OF AGE

1. Jacobsen, *The Treasures of Darkness*, 219. Vanstiphout (in "The Craftsmanship of Sin-leqi-unnini," 65f.) agrees with Jacobsen that the *Gilgamesh Epic* is "about growing up."

2. For a discussion of the additions see the seminal study by Tigay, *The Evolution of the Gilgamesh Epic*. On the different versions see ibid., 10–13. Abusch notes that Siduri, for example, loses her earlier function and becomes in the Standard Babylonian Version just another person whom Gilgamesh meets along the way and who listens to his story, "bears witness to his state," and directs "him toward Utnapishtim." Abusch, "Gilgamesh's Request and Siduri's Denial," 12.

3. Bing, "On the Sumerian Epic of Gilgamesh," 4.

4. For the ancient identification of Sin-leqi-unnini as the author of the *Gilgamesh Epic* see Lambert, "A Catalogue of Texts and Authors," 66 K9717:10. Vanstiphout (in "The Craftsmanship of Sin-leqi-unnini," 46) believes "in one individual composer for this version." However, W. Farber (in "Forerunners and 'Standard Versions,'" 97) refers to Sin-leqi-unnini as the "alleged" author, noting there is no proof that he "actually owned and made use of a set of older tablets with earlier versions of the story." If my contention is valid, one must assume that Sin-leqi-unnini had access to these and deliberately transformed the older versions. Foster (in "On Authorship in Akkadian Literature") does not include him as author of a major Akkadian literary work. However, von Soden (in *The Ancient Orient*, 214 n. 18) suggests that not only was he the author of the Standard Babylonian Version of the *Gilgamesh Epic* but that he probably composed the Akkadian version of the myth "Inanna's Descent into the Netherworld." Interestingly, "a late roster of scholars, copied in the second century, lists Sin-leqi-unnini as a contemporary of Gilgamesh," so associated had he become with the Sumerian hero down the generations. Tigay, *The Evolution of the Gilgamesh Epic*, 12.

5. Kovacs, *The Epic of Gilgamesh*, 3. I use her translation throughout this chapter unless otherwise noted.

6. Tigay, *The Evolution of the Gilgamesh Epic*, 143.

7. Foster, "Gilgamesh," 21f. Foster here presents an insightful analysis of what he considers to be the themes of the Nineveh version, the later

copy of the Standard Babylonian Version. The richness and multivalence of the *Gilgamesh Epic* calls forth many different perspectives on the ancient classic. I am not arguing against other interpretations of the Standard Babylonian Version but instead call attention to a dimension that has hitherto not been appreciated.

8. See most recently Denning-Bolle, *Wisdom in Akkadian Literature*, 3, 13, 20, 88–105, and passim.

9. See Foster's excellent "Review of *Das Gilgamesch-Epos*," 187.

10. Idem, "Gilgamesh," 22.

11. Buccellati, "Wisdom and Not," 38.

12. Oppenheim, "Mesopotamian Mythology II," 18.

13. See CAD N/2 276f for the use of *niṣirtu* to mean "the body of exclusive or special knowledge" of ritual experts, scholars, and sages. See most recently Limet, "Le secret et les écrits." For references to the use of *idû* and *amāru* in the context of initiation see CAD I/J 56a. The noun *mudû* is used for the "initiate"; the uninitiated is *la mudû*. The term *katimtu* of line 5 is also part of esoteric terminology; see especially CAD K 307 s.v. *katmu*. The term *petû* "to reveal" the secrets of gods appears in Tablet XI 9, 193. Perhaps the *nagbu* "everything" of the very first line of Tablet I can be linked to the *nagbu* associated with "the totality" of esoteric knowledge; see CAD N/1 111b. On wisdom terminology applied to cult officials, diviners, exorcists, etc., see Sweet, "The Sage in Akkadian Literature," 59–61. Lambert noted long ago (in *Babylonian Wisdom Literature*, 1) that "generally, 'wisdom' refers to skill in cult and magic lore, and the wise man is the initiate."

14. Ritter, "Magical Expert (= *Ašipu*) and Physician (= *Asû*)," 301 and 321, respectively.

15. Sweet, "The Sage in Akkadian Literature," 61.

16. See the important article by Parpola, "The Assyrian Tree of Life," especially 169 (and footnote 39 for bibliography). Parpola views the *Gilgamesh Epic* as presenting "a mystical path of spiritual growth culminating in the acquisition of superior esoteric knowledge" (ibid., 192). He discusses the epic on pages 192–195. I am not convinced that "mystical" and "spiritual" are terms applicable to Mesopotamian thought.

17. For translation of and comments on Utnapishtim's speech on death, which is found only in the late version, see Lambert, "The Theology of Death," 54–57.

18. On this view of Tablet XII see Kovacs, *The Epic of Gilgamesh*, 116f. Jacobsen (in *The Treasures of Darkness*, 229) finds its addition "mechanical," having no connection with the story.

19. Oppenheim, "Mesopotamian Mythology II," 18. Relevant here is a passage quoted by Lambert (in *Babylonian Wisdom Literature*, 70:16): "(They) go the way of death (*urḫu mūt[u]*)."

20. Kirk, *Myth*, 149, 151.

21. There continues to be great interest by nonspecialists in the *Gilgamesh Epic*, especially by classicists. For a bibliography see the notes to chapter 4, "Heroes and Pals," in Halperin, *One Hundred Years of Homosexuality and Other Essays on Greek Love*.

22. Abusch, "Gilgamesh's Request and Siduri's Denial," 7 n. 30.

23. Van Nortwick, *Somewhere I Have Never Travelled*, 27. He also views the heroic journey as "a metaphor for the process of growing up."

24. Ibid., 23. For a recent Jungian interpretation of the *Gilgamesh Epic* see Kluger, *The Archetypal Significance of Gilgamesh*.

25. Eliade (in *Rites and Symbols of Initiation*, 64) speaks of "the goal of heroic initiations from the time of Gilgamesh." See Prévot, "L'épopée de Gilgamesh."

26. Wolfe, *The Narrative Structure of Three Epic Poems*, 56.

27. Jacobson, *The Treasures of Darkness*, 218f. and asterisked note. Jacobsen's quotation from Sullivan dates from before the appearance of a plethora of writings focusing on child development. Sullivan discusses the period between preadolescence and adolescence, where Jacobsen would locate the young Gilgamesh. In my view Gilgamesh is an "adolescent," that is, in the stage between childhood and adulthood.

28. See Roth, "Age at Marriage," 718 n. 8 and 718f. n. 9. For a survey of Roman sources that shows that age-awareness among the Romans was "seriously defective" see Duncan-Jones, *Structure and Scale in the Roman Economy*, 79–92.

29. See, for example, CAD E 407b, where *eṭlu* is defined as "an age group between the full-grown man and the *baṭūlu* . . . 'adolescent' male." Davis (in *Society and Culture in Early Modern France*, 108) suggests that the term "adolescence" be applied to young people in all societies from the onset of puberty to their becoming adults.

30. For such a rite of passage see Eyben, *Restless Youth in Ancient Rome*, 6f. For more on the ceremony that marked the transition in status from child to adult see also Wiedemann, *Adults and Children in the Roman Empire*, 114–117. On Greek initiatory rites see Vidal-Naquet, "The Black Hunter and the Origin of the Athenian Ephebia" and idem, "Recipes for Greek Adolescence." Turner (in *The Forest of Symbols*, 93) asserts that "*rites de passage* are found in all societies but tend to reach their maximal expression in small-scale, relatively stable and cyclical societies, where change is

bound up with biological and meteorological rhythms and recurrences rather than with technological innovation." The latter describes Mesopotamia except for the adjective "small-scale." The lack of information on Mesopotamian rites of passage may be simply due to the fragmentary nature of the extant sources.

31. See, for example, Vanstiphout (in "The Craftsmanship of Sin-leqi-unnini," 49), who mentions in passing Gilgamesh's "youthful exuberance" and "adolescent spleen." Jacobsen's contribution has already been noted. See chapter 4 for my assessment of the effects of some age-specific behavioral traits. As in ancient Rome, I think that the young "were not seen as real adults, that physiological maturity did not coincide with psychological or social maturity." Eyben, *Restless Youth in Ancient Rome*, 42.

32. Oppenheim, "Mesopotamian Mythology II," 27 n. 2, and 42.

33. Very helpful have been Schlegel and Barry, "Adolescent Initiation Ceremonies," 277–288, and idem, *Adolescence*, especially 173–175. The authors note (p. 3) that researchers have been far more concerned in recent years with problems of stage transition than with the stages themselves. This in my view was also the interest of the ancient author.

34. See Schlegel and Barry, *Adolescence*, 134f.

35. In Oppenheim's opinion (in "Mesopotamian Mythology II," 23), "the old saga motif of royal building craze [was introduced] in order to avoid a motivation which would have fallen short of the moral and ideological standards of the public." Foster (in "Gilgamesh," 24) suggests that the exact nature of Gilgamesh's wrongdoing is deliberately made vague.

36. Schlegel and Barry, *Adolescence*, 74–75, and idem, "Adolescent Initiation Ceremonies," 283.

37. The issue of whether the relationship between the two is a homosexual one or not is of no special relevance here. See chapter 7; see also Foster, "Gilgamesh," 22; and Halperin, *One Hundred Years of Homosexuality and Other Essays on Greek Love*, 25. Halperin's stimulating work on their friendship, studied in the context of the friendships of Achilles and Patroclus and of David and Jonathan, finds a "common set of structures which serve to organize the basic elements that constitute each friendship" (ibid., 77). Jacobsen (in *Treasures of Darkness*) seems to skirt the issue. See also von Weiher, "Gilgames und Enkidu"; and Van Nortwick, *Somewhere I Have Never Travelled*.

38. Foster, "Gilgamesh," 24.

39. Garber, *Coming of Age in Shakespeare*, 31.

40. Foster's translation makes this identification more strikingly: "Let the two be doubles to each other (*ištannanuma*)."

41. Lambert, "Gilgamesh in Literature and Art," 47.

42. Dalley, "The Gilgamesh Epic and Manichaean Themes," 26.

43. Might this suggest that a tradition of insulting may have defined Mesopotamian youthful masculinity, at least of the elite? For age-specific characteristics of the adolescent see Schlegel and Barry, *Adolescence*, 157–165.

44. Foster, "Gilgamesh," 23.

45. Kovacs, *The Epic of Gilgamesh*, 9.

46. Ibid., 10 n. 13. The Akkadian is *ḫadī-ū'a amēlu*.

47. See Schlegel and Barry, *Adolescence*, 173–176. Oppenheim (in "Mesopotamian Mythology II," 27) remarks that "the epic always stressed the beauty of its heroes, not their wisdom." "Outstanding prowess and beauty" were also desirable attributes for the youth of medieval times, training for the knighthood. See Shahar, *Childhood in the Middle Ages*, 27.

48. See Eyben, *Restless Youth in Ancient Rome*, 98f., 101–102. Do we have here perhaps the earliest example of the eroticized young man who will appear prominently much later in late medieval and early modern European art and literature?

49. The relationship between mother and son is especially close. No conflict between the two is at all hinted at.

50. There may be other features that suggest Gilgamesh's youthfulness, particularly the frequent mention of Gilgamesh and Enkidu holding hands (II 164f., 249; III 19; VI 168). Tigay (in *The Evolution of the Gilgamesh Epic*, 184 n. 22) sees this as an expression of friendship. Is the omission of any mention of Gilgamesh's beard perhaps significant? In Mesopotamia, growing up, being an *eṭlu*, is associated with the beginning of beard growth: see the lexical section in CAD E 397a s.v. *eṭēlu*. See also the poorly preserved passage in Tablet V 90–98 in which Gilgamesh, despite his bravado, is so frightened by Humbaba's face after the monster's capture that he has to be encouraged by Enkidu. Note should be made of one ambiguous passage that seems to contradict my contention that Gilgamesh is young. In Tablet XI 285–291 Gilgamesh speaks to Urshanabi about bringing home the magical plant whose name is "The-Old-Man-Becomes-Young" (incidentally, the apparent meaning of the hero's name). He says, "I will bring it to Uruk-Haven and have an old man test it. . . . Then I will eat it and return to the condition of my youth." One can perhaps assume that Gilgamesh is speaking of his rejuvenation at some future time when he is older. Vanstiphout (in "The Craftsmanship of Sin-leqi-unnini," 58 n. 61) comments cogently on this passage.

51. Stevenson, "The Fear of Death in Childhood," 126.

52. McNeil et al., "Helping Adolescents Cope with the Death of a Peer," 133.

53. See Oppenheim, *The Interpretation of Dreams*, 187, 204, 208, and passim. For a discussion of the differences between the dreams in the Standard Babylonian Version and in the Old Babylonian Version see Cooper, "Gilgamesh Dreams of Enkidu," 39–40.

54. Cooper, "Gilgamesh Dreams of Enkidu," 40.

55. Bulkley, "The Evil Dreams of Gilgamesh," 168f.

56. There is no evidence (as stated earlier) that there existed in Mesopotamia a ritual ceremony that marked the transition from childhood to adulthood. Circumcision may have served as such in ancient Egypt. See Janssen and Janssen, *Growing Up in Ancient Egypt*, 90–98. Prévot (in "L'épopée de Gilgamesh," 225–241) suggests that there is an initiation paradigm in the *Gilgamesh Epic*, focusing on shamanistic features, which she links to sacred kingship. She finds these elements particularly in the Humbaba episode and quite rightly delineates initiatory themes there. However, I question her interpretation of these as a shamanistic experience. As Oppenheim stressed (in *Ancient Mesopotamia*, 221), ecstasis was of little importance in Mesopotamia proper as a means of communication between gods and men. One might say that the initiatory motifs of the Humbaba episode are proleptic to the major initiatory theme of the Standard Babylonian Version: the transition of the hero from youth to mature adult.

57. Turner, *Dramas, Fields, and Metaphors*, 253.

58. E. J. Leed, *The Mind of the Traveler*, 3.

59. Ibid., 7.

60. La Fontaine, *Initiation*. This includes a critical survey of earlier theories.

61. van Gennep, *The Rites of Passage*, 11. What B. Lincoln says (in *Emerging from the Chrysalis*, 97) about female initiates is applicable to Gilgamesh: "The goal of the cosmic journey is to transform her completely from what she had been and radically separate her from childhood existence."

62. van Gennep, *The Rites of Passage*, 24.

63. Turner, "Three Symbols of Passage in Ndembu Circumcision Ritual," 173.

64. La Fontaine, *Initiation*, 116.

65. Leach (in "Magical Hair," 103) notes that hair is a prominent feature of rites that mark the progressions of the individual through different stages of maturity.

66. Ibid., 98f.

67. Kovacs, *The Epic of Gilgamesh*, 85 n. 1.

68. On the appearance of these creatures see Black and Green, *Gods, Demons, and Symbols of Ancient Mesopotamia*, 131.

69. Gilgamesh's journey is truly a "territorial passage," to use van Gennep's term (in *The Rites of Passage*, 15).

70. Kovacs, *The Epic of Gilgamesh*, 74.

71. Ibid.

72. La Fontaine, *Initiation*, 100.

73. Oppenheim, "Mesopotamian Mythology II," 55f., and idem, *Ancient Mesopotamia*, 262 and 380 n. 42.

74. Tigay (in *The Evolution of the Gilgamesh Epic*, 238f.) thinks this was an addition by the author of the Standard Babylonian Version and not part of the Old Babylonian Version.

75. Kovacs, *The Epic of Gilgamesh*, xxvi.

76. Turner, *Dramas, Fields, and Metaphors*, 258.

77. van Gennep (in *The Rites of Passage*, 20) notes that washing and cleansing are elements in the stage of incorporation. Eating and dressing in new clothes are common integrative acts (La Fontaine, *Initiation*, 25).

78. Circumambulation is frequently associated with rites of passage. See Eck, "Circumambulation."

79. Kovacs, *The Epic of Gilgamesh*, 116f. See most recently Vulpe, "Irony and the Unity of the *Gilgamesh Epic*." Vulpe also views Tablet XII as an integral part of the *Gilgamesh Epic* but for very different reasons.

80. For Gilgamesh as judge of the netherworld see Falkenstein, "Gilgameš," 360a.

81. This is also the case for women.

82. Gardner and Maier, *Gilgamesh*, 16.

83. Jacobsen, *The Treasures of Darkness*, 230–239. See also the observation by Foster (in "Review of Das Gilgamesch-Epos," 187) "that Mesopotamian belles-lettres as a rule, while admiring physical strength, looked with disgust on violence, particularly fighting."

CHAPTER 3. ON AGING AND THE ELDERLY

1. Falkner and de Luce, "A View from Antiquity," 4.

2. For relevant passages from Aristotle's *Rhetoric* see Burrow, *The Ages of Man*, 191–202. For a translation of Cicero's work see his *On Old Age*.

3. Some of these issues are discussed in chapters 4 and 5. The letters from Mesopotamia, a rich source of information, have barely been utilized in the present study. They remain to be examined at a later date.

4. But see Curchin, "Old Age in Sumer"; and Arnett, "Only the Bad Died Young in the Ancient Middle East" and idem, "Growing Old in the Cradle."

5. The focus here is on the Semitic Akkadian texts with very little attention paid to the Sumerian material. But there may not have been any major differences between Sumerian and Akkadian views, as Cooper has noted (in "The Fate of Mankind," 20). The question of when old age was thought to begin is considered in chapter 1. Old(er) women are treated separately below in chapters 5 and 6.

6. For references to *šību* and *šībtu* see CAD Š/2 390–392. In the Hebrew Bible, too, gray/white hair is "the primary trait of old age." See the succinct discussion of biblical old age in J. G. Harris, "Old Age."

7. See the lexical section for *šību* in CAD Š/2 390. So too in English "father" and "mother" can each be used to designate an old person. See *Webster's Third International Dictionary*.

8. For *šâbu* see CAD Š/1 19.

9. For *ṣalmāt qaqqadi* see CAD Ṣ 75b–76. Thrasher and Lamberg (in "Hair," 301) note that "by age 50, approximately half of the Caucasian population has at least 50% gray hair." Generally the two most obvious features associated with aging are balding and graying (ibid., 300).

10. See CAD Š/2 126b s.v. *šartu*. I am grateful to Robert Biggs for this reference. For evidence that the ancient Egyptians colored their hair to cover up gray hair see Manniche, *An Ancient Egyptian Herbal*, 46 (with juniper) and 114 (with henna). There are few examples of gray-haired people in Egyptian art. The ideal was youthfulness with full heads of black hair. For these observations see L. Green, "More Than a Fashion Statement," 35 and 38 n. 30.

11. For these phenomena see A. Foner, *Aging and Old Age*, 23.

12. See CAD L 13–16 s.v. *labāru*; CAD L 26 s.v. *labīru*; CAD L 33 s.v. *labīrūtu alāku*.

13. See S. R. Smith, "Growing Old in Early Stuart England," 131.

14. For references to *amēlūtū alāku* see CAD A/1 315. In the Old Assyrian period the same idiom means "to act as a free man."

15. For *puršumû* see AHw 881. In Sumerian it is used only of women with the meaning of "old." See chapter 6.

16. See CAD Š/3 202a for references to *šugû* in lexical texts.

17. For *šību* see CAD Š/2 390a lexical section; for *pisnuqu* see AHw 867b. See also CAD L 161, lexical section for *pisnuqu* equated with *la lē'u* "powerless, unprotected."

18. Lambert, *Babylonian Wisdom Literature*, 87:272.

19. CAD K 336 s.v. *kibrû*. It is somewhat similar to an old woman being perjoratively described as an "old bag." For "bag" as "a disparaging term for a woman, esp. one who is unattractive or elderly" see *The Oxford English Dictionary*, vol. 1, 880:17.

20. CAD L 220 s.v. *littu* D.

21. CAD Š/2 399–400 s.v. *šibūtu*.

22. STT 400 r. 45–47 published in Gurney and Hulin, *The Sultantepe Tablets*, 20.

23. For a discussion and bibliography on life expectancy in ancient Mesopotamia see Roth, "Age at Marriage," 718 n. 8 and 718f. n. 9. Saller and Shaw (in "Tombstones and Roman Family Relations in the Principate," 136) have detected a pattern that would be applicable to Mesopotamia: "Short life expectancy and late age of marriage for men meant that only a small minority of children would have had a paternal grandfather alive." So too are Saller's comments on the life expectancy of Roman babies (in *"Patria Potestas,"* 12) applicable to Mesopotamian babies: "Approximately one-third of babies did not survive the first year and half did not live to age 10. Of those who did reach 10, about one in three then lived to 60, and only one in seven to age 70." Very much the same figures are cited for eighteenth-century France. See McManners, *Death and the Enlightenment*, 10.

24. Snell, "Plagues and Peoples in Mesopotamia."

25. Curchin, "Old Age in Sumer," 61f. For an extensive and careful study of the skeletal remains of 584 people of various ages found in different areas in Anatolia see Angel and Bisel, "Health and Stress in Early Bronze Age Population." Adult longevity for females was just under thirty; for males, thirty-four.

26. See R. Harris, "The *nadītu* Woman," 122.

27. Roth, "Age at Marriage," 719 n. 9.

28. Humphreys, *The Family, Women, and Death*, 145. On old age in Greece as a loathsome reality see also Falkner and de Luce, "A View from Antiquity," 7–9.

29. Jacobsen, *The Harps*, 186:22–23.

30. See Arnett, "Only the Bad Died Young."

31. Arnett, ibid., and "Growing Old in the Cradle." For other references see CAD B 48.

32. Pearce, "Statements of Purpose," 189–190. For other references to votive offerings presented to obtain long life see CAD B 48b–49a.

33. Longman, *Fictional Akkadian Autobiography*, 97–103. Beaulieu (in *The Reign of Nabonidus*, 68–76) finds no evidence that Adad-guppi was a high

priestess of the god Sin at Harran, as is usually assumed. Her piety, he says, was characteristic of members not of the clergy but of the royal family.

34. For this reference see CAD M/2 37a s.v. *mesherūtu*.

35. Foster, *Before the Muses*, vol. 2, 611:14–15. This passage occurs in a late prayer to the god Nabu. Foster calls it "An Old Man's Prayer," suggesting that old age is here perhaps "a metaphor for being bowed down by suffering."

36. Ibid., 613:13–14; 615:42–43. Noteworthy too is a long letter from Rib-Addi, prince of Byblus, to Akhenaton, king of Egypt, complaining about his plight as an old man in exile. Rib-Addi is plagued by illness, "and the pains are severe, for I com<mit>ted sins against the gods." For this letter see Moran, *The Amarna Letters*, 218–220.

37. Pritchard, ed., *Ancient Near Eastern Texts Relating to the Old Testament*, 312.

38. Beaulieu (in *The Reign of Nabonidus*, 70) thinks she may have been 101 or 102 when she died rather than 104.

39. Klein, "The 'Bane' of Humanity," 59.

40. Alster, *Studies in Sumerian Proverbs*, 90–99.

41. Ibid., 93:27–38.

42. For the ass as an example of high sexual potency see Biggs, *šà.zi.ga: Ancient Mesopotamian Potency Incantations*, 33:3: "Let the ass swell up! Let him mount the jenny." So too in the *Descent of Ishtar* (in Dalley, *Myths from Mesopotamia*, 158), among the signs of infertility is the fact that no ass impregnated a jenny.

43. Crenshaw, "Youth and Old Age in Qoheleth," 3. His interpretation of the mongoose image as a loss of appetite is more convincing than Alster's comment (in *Studies in Sumerian Proverbs*, 95) that the old man is unable to smell.

44. Kilmer, "An Oration on Babylon."

45. Greengus, *Old Babylonian Tablets from Ishchali and Vicinity*, 64:31f.

46. For references see CAD M/2 214 s.v. *muqqu*.

47. Ibid., 214a.

48. Gelb, "The Ancient Mesopotamian Ration System," 233.

49. Foster, *Before the Muses*, vol. 2, 774:47–51. Ancient Egyptians, despite the high regard for the elderly found in the proverbial literature, also expressed ageism at times. See, for example, the Old Kingdom Cannibal Hymn (in Lichtheim, *Ancient Egyptian Literature*, vol. 1, 37) in which the deceased king "consumes" big, middle-sized, and little deities to acquire their power but "the oldest males and females for his fuel." The aged are uneatable, probably because they are powerless.

50. I here follow the translation of Beaulieu of *dakkannu* as "bedroom" in IV 110–111 of the myth. See Beaulieu, "New Light on Secret Knowledge in Late Babylonian Culture," 102f. For the old as bedridden see also Livingstone, *Court Poetry and Literary Miscellanea*, 30:11–12: "I have received wealth, precociously I achieved my goal; (but) old age has confined me to my bed before my time."

51. Cited in CAD Q 45b.

52. See CAD Š/2 398b:5.

53. *Encyclopedia Americana* s.v. "Perseus."

54. L. Green, "More Than a Fashion Statement," 37 Fig. 7.

55. Hallo, "Individual Prayer in Sumerian," 85:23.

56. Starr (in "Sexuality," 607) notes that "after age 40 most men will experience an occasional erection problem." It is a common problem among elderly men.

57. Biggs, *ša.zi.ga: Ancient Mesopotamian Potency Incantations*, 3f.

58. For references to *muṭṭu* see CAD M/1 434 s.v. *maṭû*.

59. Falkner and de Luce, "A View from Antiquity," 7. On the "sloughing off of old age" in ancient Greece see Garland, *The Greek Way of Life*, 267.

60. Kovacs, *The Epic of Gilgamesh*, 109. Kovacs (in ibid., 109 n. 7) describes the scene as "an etiological story of how the snake came to shed its old skin after eating a 'plant of rejuvenation.'"

61. Foster, "Letters and Literature," 98f. See also ibid., 99 n. 7.

62. See the example of the sun god Re, who has become old and vulnerable (in Wilson, "The God and His Unknown Name of Power"). For more on Re as a "tired old man" see also Hornung, *Conceptions of God in Ancient Egypt*, 153–155. I can think of only one possible physical description of a Mesopotamian god as old. Nergal is disguised by Ea in the myth of *Nergal and Ereshkigal* to escape detection by Namtar. He is described as "[b]ald, with a tic, lame." See Foster, *Before the Muses*, vol. 1, 426:37. Leick (in *Sex and Eroticism in Mesopotamian Literature*, 251) also considers Nergal to be disguised as an old man. Of interest is the chapter "The God Description Texts: A Mystical Representation of a Deity" in Livingstone, *Mystical and Mythological Explanatory Works of Assyrian and Babylonian Scholars*, 92–112.

63. See, for example, Breslau and Hauge, eds., *Depression and Aging*. Blazer (in "Depression," 169) notes that "Depressive disorders are among the complaints of older adults and the leading cause of suicide in later life." For the Ammisaduga letter see Frankena, *Briefe aus dem Berliner Museum*, 190.

64. See the discussion on alcoholism by Wood (in "Alcoholism," 25–27), who notes: "Researchers have found that the effects of alcohol are

different on aged organisms compared to younger organisms." But "evidence that alcoholism and alcohol abuse are serious problems for a number of elderly has not been forthcoming."

65. Pangle, ed., *The Laws of Plato*, 47 Book II 666a–666c. From this passage it would appear that the onset of old age is at age forty.

66. See Bryce, *Historical and Social Documents of the Hittite World*, 23:19, 26–32. I am grateful to Harry Hoffner for sending me a copy of the relevant passage. See also *Proverbs* 31:6: "Give strong drink unto him that is ready to perish and wine unto those that be heavy of heart."

67. Jacobsen, "Primitive Democracy in Ancient Mesopotamia," 167.

68. Idem, *The Treasures of Darkness*, 227.

69. Black and Green, *Gods, Demons, and Symbols of Ancient Mesopotamia*, 129.

70. Foster, *Before the Muses*, vol. 2, 771.

71. For Marduk's speech see ibid., 778:130–160. See also 778 n. 6.

72. Idem, *Before the Muses*, vol. 1, 16.

73. Moran, "Atrahasis: The Babylonian Story of the Flood," 60.

74. The eminent gerontologist R. N. Butler (in "Life Review: Reminiscence," 398f.) suggests that as adults age they "engage increasingly in a process of reviewing and reinterpreting their past." Life review can also be considered an element in Adad-guppi's "autobiography."

75. Kovacs, *The Epic of Gilgamesh*, 97–103, Tablet XI. Its obtuseness is perhaps to be linked to its being esoteric knowledge. On this aspect of the *Gilgamesh Epic* see chapter 2.

76. I have discussed my view that the elderly are rarely depicted in art with several art historians in ancient Near Eastern art, and they have agreed. However, it is difficult to estimate the chronological age range for the extant sculptures. At a guess I would say anywhere from twenty-five to forty. See, for example, Schlossman's suggestion (in "Portraiture in Mesopotamia," 170) that "it is possible that youth and age are depicted in the beardless foundation figurines of Ur-Nammu . . . and in his bearded countenance on his famous stele now in Philadelphia." See also the note by Hansen and Dales (in "The Temple of Inanna, Queen of Heaven," 170), about "a statue of an old woman with long hair; such characterizations are rare in Early Dynastic sculpture." In Egyptian art, however, there are representations of elderly people. Spanel (in *Through Ancient Eyes*, 25) speaks of "generic elderly persons" in Egyptian art. Note also the comments by Aldred in "Some Royal Portraits of the Middle Kingdom," 19, 23. See Fischer's comments (in "Some Early Monuments," 166f.) about the representations on the false door of a tomb of its owner as a girl and

as an old woman. Most informative on the depiction of old age in Egyptian art is Riefstahl, "An Egyptian Portrait of an Old Man."

77. Curchin, "Old Age in Sumer," 62.

78. Frankfort, *The Art and Architecture of the Ancient Orient*, 56.

79. Spanel (in *Through Ancient Eyes*, 33f.) relates corpulence to prosperity. See also Smith, *The Art and Architecture of Ancient Egypt*, 111.

80. Barnett, *Sculptures from the North Palace of Ashurbanipal at Nineveh 668–627 B.C.*, 59–60, plate 68.

81. Reade, *Assyrian Sculpture*, 41 and Figure 59.

82. For references to *šībūtu* see CAD Š/2 392–394.

83. Reviv, *The Elders in Ancient Israel*, especially 163f.

84. Harris, *Ancient Sippar*, 59.

85. Alster, *Studies in Sumerian Proverbs*, 67. See more recently Alster's comments on fathers' instructions to sons (with bibliography) in "Interaction of Oral and Written Poetry in Early Mesopotamian Literature."

86. Denning-Bolle, *Wisdom in Akkadian Literature*, 2 n. 6, and 42f.

87. Ibid., 63.

88. R. Harris, *Ancient Sippar*, 81, 105, 155, and passim. For the lifelong and heredity aspects of temple offices see also Renger, "Untersuchungen zum Priestertum in der altbabylonischen Zeit."

89. Zettler, "The Genealogy of Ur-Meme."

90. For references to the elderly in work lists see CAD Š/2 391.

91. Steinkeller, *Labor in the Ancient Near East*, 78f. The question of the elderly in the labor force has not been treated at length. I present here a few comments on a difficult and elusive subject.

92. Ibid., 80f. P. Steinkeller in a personal communication interprets *šu.gi₄* as "old/retired worker." He thinks this type of worker was "either on pension or continued to work, though probably at a lower output. The sense of 'retired' was suggested by the context."

93. Brinkman, "Sex, Age, and Physical Condition" and idem, "Forced Laborers in the Middle Babylonian Period."

94. Idem, "Forced Laborers in the Middle Babylonian Period," 18.

95. Idem, "Sex, Age, and Physical Condition," 3 n. 8.

96. Gelb, "The Arua Institution," 9.

97. On the social responsibilities assumed by the temple see Oppenheim, *Ancient Mesopotamia*, 107.

98. Diakonoff, "Slaves, Helots, and Serfs in Early Antiquity," 71.

99. On the obligations of the living toward the dead see Bayliss, "Cult of Dead in Assyria and Babylonia"; Alster, "The Mythology of Mourning"; and Bottéro, *Mesopotamia: Writing, Reasoning, and the Gods*, 279–282.

100. Skaist, "The Ancestor Cult and Succession in Mesopotamia." For references to *kispu* see CAD K 425–427.

101. For this and other information on death and the dead see Scurlock, "Death and the Afterlife in Ancient Mesopotamia."

102. Foster, *Before the Muses*, vol. 2, 799 iv 94–98.

103. Translated by Oppenheim in *Letters from Mesopotamia*, 92.

104. For instances where family members other than children were derelict in caring for elderly relatives see Greenfield, "Adi Balṭu—Care for the Elderly and Its Rewards." On adoption generally see David, *Die Adoption im altbabylonischen Recht* and idem, "Adoption."

105. Stone and Owens, *Adoption in Old Babylonian Nippur*, 33. See also ibid., 9 and 10 (see footnote 22 for references to similar arrangements from other places and periods).

106. See D. Marcus, "Juvenile Delinquency in the Bible and the Ancient Near East," especially 36–44. On the proper attitudes toward parents see the next chapter.

107. See CAD L 220f s.v. *littūtu*.

CHAPTER 4. THE CONFLICT OF GENERATIONS IN ANCIENT MESOPOTAMIAN MYTHS

1. See RLA under such topics as "Erbe," "Gesetze," "Familie" for more information.

2. But see Kramer, "Modern Social Problems in Ancient Sumer," especially 118–120. See also Kramer's chapter "Father and Son" (in *History Begins at Sumer*, 14–17), where he discusses an angry diatribe between a scribe and his rebellious son who refuses to follow his father's profession, a case then of generational conflict. For a critical edition of this text see Sjöberg, "Der Vater und sein Missratener Sohn." More work has been done on generational tensions in other ancient Near Eastern societies. For ancient Israel see, for example, Wolff, "Problems between the Generations"; D. Marcus, "Juvenile Delinquency in the Bible and the Ancient Near East"; and Steinmetz, *From Father to Son*, especially her first chapter. In Egypt and Ugarit, mythological materials exist that are relevant to the topic. For the former see Hornung, *Conceptions of God in Ancient Egypt*, 153–155. For the latter see Caquot and Sznycer, *Ugaritic Religion*, 121. Especially important from Egypt are the instructional texts that teach the proper relations between young and old, children and parents.

3. For a sampling of Mesopotamian letters see Oppenheim, *Letters from Mesopotamia*.

4. Ibid., 64.

5. N. Foner, *Ages in Conflict*, ix. See also her extensive bibliography.

6. Note the comments by N. Foner (in ibid., 250–256) on "the question of the relative importance of age hierarchy" in comparison with gender inequalities. She believes that "inequality between young and old may turn out to be more significant than sex inequality in numerous societies."

7. Ancient Greek sources, for example, strongly suggest that fifth-century Athens was a time and place of enormous generational conflict. Gardner (in "Aristophanes and Male Anxiety," 59–61) finds its culmination in the last quarter of the fifth century B.C.E.

8. Mention should be made of the qualities admired and revealed in the so-called Sumerian schoolboy texts: ambition, competition, and aggressiveness. Therefore, the school system for Sumer's elite children upheld and furthered traits very much at variance with respectful restraint and obedience vis-à-vis one's elders. There is no reason to think that these desiderata changed with the political hegemony of the Semites. For this "will to superiority," as Kramer calls it, see his *Sumerians*, 264–270.

9. The extant inheritance documents, adoption texts, and lawsuits are a rich source, available from the third to the first millennium B.C.E.

10. For examples of a son receiving his inheritance during his father's lifetime see Klima, *Untersuchungen zum altbabylonischen Erbrecht* (74ff.). For the possibility that older sons might have taken "their patrimony early in the form of moveable wealth rather than wait until their father died" see Stone, *Nippur Neighborhoods*, 23f. In short, there may have been far more flexibility in inheritance division than the extant evidence reveals.

11. Powell, "Economy of the Extended Family," 10. On the problems of establishing the types of household patterns see Diakonoff, "Extended Families in Old Babylonian Ur." For recent surveys on the family in Mesopotamia see the excellent study by Glassner, "De Sumer à Babylone"; and the important contribution by Wilcke, "Familiengrundüng im Alten Babylonien." Of great ramification for our topic is the breakdown of kinship organization, which is replaced by occupational ties in Old Babylonian Nippur (Stone, *Nippur Neighborhoods*, 13–28).

12. CAD M/1 314f s.v. *māru*; CAD A/1 71 s.v. *abu*.

13. Alster, *The Instructions of Suruppak*, 45:177. The equation of eldest children with parents contains the seed for sibling rivalry. The Mesopotamian school, the *eduba*, with its identification of the teacher with father

and of the monitor with elder brother, may well have been a way of reinforcing paternal and fraternal dominance and authority.

14. *Gilgamesh,* III v. 10. For this translation see CAD S 184. Relevant too is the conflict in the Sumerian epic *Gilgamesh and Akka* between the elders and the *guruš* (the young citizens). The latter want to fight against the city of Kish; the former do not. The young Gilgamesh rejects the advice of the elders. He is backed by the *guruš* assembly, which confers kingship on him. Katz (in "Gilgamesh and Akka," 107) suggests that the "epic's representation of the elders versus *guruš* . . . should be regarded as a literary pattern, and not as evidence of a bicameral institution as scholars have assumed."

15. Roth, "Age at Marriage," 737. Late marriage for sons was perhaps a strategy for minimizing father-son conflict.

16. The mother as mediator is a common literary motif in Mesopotamian literature (see chapter 6). For examples of the ambivalence in mother-son relations see Kramer, "The Woman in Ancient Sumer," 112.

17. Zettler, "The Genealogy of Ur-Meme." In an appendix (ibid., 9–14), Roth presents a reassessment of the crucial text, which had been interpreted differently several years before. She clarifies the second lawsuit, which leads to the death of the accuser.

18. Parpola, "The Murderer of Sennacherib." On the rarity of royal parricide see Wiseman, "Murder in Mesopotamia." I owe this reference to one of the anonymous readers for *Comparative Studies in Society and History.*

19. For discussion of this terminology see Veenhof, "A Deed of Manumission and Adoption," 376–379. For the proper behavior of children toward parents in Mesopotamia and elsewhere in the ancient Near East see Greenfield, "Adi Balṭu—Care for the Elderly and Its Rewards."

20. von Soden, "Der grosse Hymnus an Nabu," 58:185f.

21. Alster, *Studies in Sumerian Proverbs,* 67.

22. Idem, *The Instructions of Suruppak,* 35:18.

23. Gordon, *Sumerian Proverbs,* 124.

24. Frankena, *Briefe aus dem Berliner Museum,* 17–19.

25. Gordon, *Sumerian Proverbs,* 139.

26. Ibid., 123.

27. Lambert, *Babylonian Wisdom Literature,* 85:245f. There are interesting and contradictory comments in the so-called *Babylonian Theodicy* on the differing temperaments of children, depending on their birth order. See ibid., 87:262f.

28. But see the critical article by Saller, *"Patria Potestas,"* which questions the stereotypical image of the Roman patriarch with almost absolute power over his extended family.

29. D. Marcus, "Juvenile Delinquency in the Bible," 33f. The law here is very severe: "If a son (intentionally) strikes his father, his hand will be cut off" (Section 195, the Code of Hammurapi). No age is here indicated. Assault against another person would subject the son to a lesser penalty. A person assaulting an unrelated individual would be fined or flogged, depending on the status of the attacker and the victim (Sections 202–208, the Code of Hammurapi). The Code thus served both to support and to check paternal authority.

30. The situation of the elderly *nadītu* women of Sippar, a unique institution of celibate women dedicated for life to the sun god Shamash, the chief deity of Sippar, is interesting. They usually adopted younger *nadītu*s, frequently a relative, or a slave to take care of them in their old age. See my recent discussion of this institution in R. Harris, "Independent Women in Ancient Mesopotamia?"

31. Both the very old and the very young may have performed the same kinds of tasks in the labor force and hence received equivalent rations. See below for more on the equation of the old with the very young.

32. Cited in CAD S 183. For the relegation of children, old men, women, and slaves to the margins of Roman society see Wiedemann, *Adults and Children in the Roman Empire*. He argues that their bond is their common physical weakness.

33. Cagni, *The Poem of Erra*, 28:47f.

34. Greengus, *Old Babylonian Tablets from Ishchali and Vicinity*. I am grateful to Samuel Greengus for this reference.

35. In the Ischali treaty, the death of a male slave is compensated with fifteen shekels of silver, a female slave with ten shekels (ibid.).

36. Greenfield, "Some Neo-Babylonian Women," 76.

37. For doubts about the usefulness of psychoanalytical perspectives in classical studies see Lloyd-Jones, "Psychoanalysis and the Study of the Ancient World."

38. N. Foner, *Ages in Conflict*, 147.

39. Wagner, *Lethal Speech*, 251.

40. M. W. Green, *Eridu in Sumerian Literature*, 126–128.

41. Like the ancient Greeks, the Mesopotamians may have, as Garland (in *The Greek Way of Life*, 149) observes, "fully appreciated the extent to which a propensity toward violence is engendered in the home and has its roots in one's relationship with one's parents."

42. Jacobsen, *The Treasures of Darkness*, 186–190.

43. See Dalley, *Myths from Mesopotamia*, 233–234.

44. For Plato, "generational struggle constituted virtually the basic mechanism in political change, the always disequilibrating factor in systems of government, the prime agent in the alternation of political forms." See Feuer, "Generational Struggle in Plato and Aristotle," 123.

45. For references to Marduk as "the avenger (*mutir gimilli*)" of his fathers see CAD M/2 229.

46. For references to Marduk as "the provider (*zaninu*)" of the gods see CAD Z 45.

47. Dalley (in *Myths from Mesopotamia*, 223) notes, "Anshar [and] Kishar were born, surpassing them. . . . Anu their first born son rivalled his forefathers. . . . He, Nudimmud, was superior to his forefathers."

48. Oppenheim (in "Mesopotamian Mythology I," 230 n. 1) suggests a "hidden rivalry" even between young Marduk and his father, Ea. In the case of Tiamat, the younger gods are dismayed when Tiamat turns against them: "Tiamat who bore us is rejecting us." See Dalley, *Myths from Mesopotamia*, 239. The depiction of the old Tiamat as aggressive and powerful reflects Mesopotamian views about gender differences in the personality of the elderly. In contrast to her, the old male gods appear as passive and timid. For more on this see the next chapter.

49. Ibid., 236. On relationships between grandparents and grandchildren, see N. Foner, *Ages in Conflict*, 55f.

50. Jacobsen, *The Treasures of Darkness*, 190.

51. See A. Sachs, "Temple Program for the New Year's Festivals at Babylon," 332.

52. Jacobsen, *The Harab Myth*, 26.

53. As discussed by Bamberger in "The Myth of Matriarchy."

54. The *Harab* myth could only have ended, as Jacobsen suggests, with the emergence of civilization. That this is characteristically the theme in those myths involving incest and violence, see Traube, "Incest and Mythology."

55. Jacobsen, *The Harab Myth*, 7:1–12.

56. Ibid., 9:39–42.

57. Dalley, *Myths from Mesopotamia*, 11.

58. Ibid., 13.

59. Ibid., 14f.

60. N. Foner, *Ages in Conflict*, 147. Moran (in "Atrahasis: The Babylonian Story of the Flood," 60) describes the unfavorable depiction of the senior god Enlil: "Throughout the epic Enlil cuts a sorry figure. He is not

only 'the counsellor of the gods' but *qurādu* Enlil, "the warrior Enlil," an epithet he often enjoys; and yet when his house is besieged by the rebel gods, the only occasion he has to display his valor, he pleads with his attendant Nusku for protection and cowers behind him in fear. Confronted with the stubbornness of the rebels, he breaks into tears. . . . Throughout the crisis he is singularly inept."

61. For references to the assembly of elders (*sŕbūtu*) see AHw 13, 1228f. This assembly acting as a judicial body was made up of the citizens of the city. The extent to which age was a criterion for membership is difficult to ascertain. See Evans, "Ancient Mesopotamian Assemblies," 114f.

62. There is the possibility that *Atrahasis* was recited to facilitate childbirth magically. See Speiser, *"Atrahasis,"* 104a.

63. Dalley, *Myths from Mesopotamia*, 203–207. For discussion of these myths see Jacobsen, *The Treasures of Darkness*, 129–134.

64. For the critical edition with commentary and bibliography see Cooper, *The Return of Ninurta to Nippur*. I am grateful to Jerrold Cooper for calling my attention to this myth. For the various interpretations of the myth see ibid., 5–8.

65. Ibid., 71:87f

66. Ibid., 75:106, 121f.

67. A special mother-son relationship between the two is tinged with subtle nuances. See ibid., 7 n. 7.

68. Ibid., 115.

69. For a translation of the myth, see Jacobsen, *The Harps*, 236–272.

70. Ibid., 245–246:183–191.

71. Ibid.

CHAPTER 5. GENDERED OLD AGE
IN *ENUMA ELISH*

1. Jacobsen, *The Treasures of Darkness*, 167. For a sensitive analysis of *Enuma Elish* see ibid., 167–191. For an analysis of the myth's play on words and intertextuality see the stimulating article by Michalowski, "Presence at the Creation."

2. Alter (in "Literary Refractions of the Jewish Family," 226) makes this comment regarding "mimetic fiction." I think it is also applicable to myths.

3. This view of myth is of course one of many, "for no one method [is] applicable to all myths. Each method offers insights into human ways

of life and thought, and no single method of analysis can possibly exhaust all the meanings inherent in any myth," as noted by Vecsey (in *Imagine Ourselves Richly*, 33). There is merit in Oppenheim's view (in *Ancient Mesopotamia*, 177) that "all these works which we are wont to call mythological should be studied by the literary critic rather than by the historian of religion." His comment on page 194 is noteworthy: "Seen typographically, [the gods] can be classified easily, though superficially, as old and young gods." Just what the relationship is between the "real" world and the "mythological" world can more precisely be delineated only by further study of other types of data such as letters and legal texts.

4. I am indebted to Van Nortwick's "'Do Not Go Gently . . . ,'" especially 133. His and the other contributions in *Old Age in Greek and Roman Literature*, ed. Falkner and de Luce, I found to be highly stimulating and instructive.

5. I will limit my quotations from Gutmann's book. They could easily be multiplied many times over.

6. Gutmann, *Reclaimed Powers*, 21, 49, 59, 102f., respectively.

7. See Speiser, "The Creation Epic," 61 I 38, 40, 50, and 62 I 116. I use Speiser's translation throughout this essay unless otherwise noted. This was the best English-language translation available at the time of its writing.

8. For the alterations in patterns of sleep and the reduction in a sense of well-being that accompanies them see, for example, Woodruff, "Arousal, Sleep, and Aging." Bertelson (in "Insomnia") discusses various studies that indicate that the elderly, compared with other adults, experience an increase in sleep disturbance. I am suggesting, therefore, that the complaints of the old gods are rooted in the realities of the aging process.

9. Michalowski, "Presence at the Creation," 384.

10. See Simmons, *The Role of the Aged in Primitive Society*, 131–140.

11. al-Rawi and George, "Tablets from the Sippar Library," 153:90, 114. I am grateful to Robert Biggs for calling my attention to this article.

12. See Foster, *Before the Muses*, vol. 1, 364:82, 106.

13. Ibid., 366:138–139; 363:57–71.

14. Perhaps a physical description is mentioned in I 121: *hummura īnātuni*, which Oppenheim (in "Mesopotamian Mythology I," 217:120) translated "[look how] our eyes are reddened(?) (by insomnia)." Interestingly, Davies (in "Youth and Old Age in the Thera Frescoes," 405) notes "the convention of lining the white of the eyes with red strokes to indicate old age." She thinks the red suggests "the bloodshot eyes of the

aged" (p. 404). For a vivid description of the decrepitudes of aging, see the Sumerian folktale "The Old Man and the Young Girl" in chapter 3.

15. Gutmann, *Reclaimed Powers*, 98–132, especially 103, 109, 110.

16. Silence too seems to be a characteristic of the gods' depression, an aspect of inactivity, just as noise (*rigmu, huburu*) is a metaphor for activity. On the latter see Michalowski's "Presence at the Creation." On the striking of the thigh as a form of agitation associated with depression see Gruber, *Aspects of Nonverbal Communication*, vol. 1, 350. The lips (*šaptu*) are mentioned three times in II 105–108. Twice, reference is made to Marduk asking his great-grandfather to open his lips (*piti šaptuk*). Closed lips also in II 88–89 suggest the withdrawal of the old god. For the association of closed lips with sadness see Gruber, ibid., vol. 2, 410–411.

17. Jacobsen, "Primitive Democracy in Ancient Mesopotamia," 167.

18. Cagni, *The Poem of Erra*, I:49f. (*alāk ṣēri ša eṭlūti kî ša isinnumma*).

19. Jacobsen, *The Treasures of Darkness*, 187. He explains the ambiguity by saying that "the author is here in the grip of conflicting emotions: love, fear, and a sense of guilt that requires palliation."

20. See the comments by Falkner, "The Wrath of Alcemene," especially 125. Cross-culturally there appears to be more frequently a greater repugnance toward old women than toward old men: so too in Mesopotamia.

21. Gutmann, *Reclaimed Powers*, 133, 152f., 173, respectively. Note that in the *Harab* myth too it is the mother who first takes the initiative to commit incest and encourages parricide. Gutmann's theory of the gender differences in aging is borne out in many other studies of aging in nonindustrial societies. See, for example, Cool and McCabe, "The 'Scheming Hag' and the 'Dear Old Thing.'" Faragher (in "Old Women and Old Men in Seventeenth Century Wetherford, Connecticut," 28) observes that widowhood gave older women "a significant island of opportunity . . . to move beyond the gender roles of the Puritan family." Simic and Myerhoff (in their conclusion to *Life's Career-Aging*, 236) state: "The fact is inescapable that male and female life trajectories differ markedly."

22. For an insightful discussion of *hubur* see Michalowski, "Presence at the Creation," 385–389.

23. I 136; II 22; III 26, 84 (*imtu kīma damī zumuršunu ušmalla*).

24. See Hallisey, *Venomous Woman*, xi. Her chapter "Mother Eve and Other Death Dealers" (pp. 15–56) deals with the connection between women and poison in ancient texts.

25. See V 51, where Marduk deposits her venom (*kamār imtiša*) in his creation of the universe.

26. The use of the masculine suffixes here and in II 2 (*pitikšu*) is perhaps deliberate.

27. One is reminded here of that paradoxical goddess Inanna/Ishtar. See chapter 10.

28. This is a difficult passage. Borger (in *"Lullû* in *Enuma eliš,"* 95f.) tentatively translates it as "She has lies upon her lips." Cassin (in "Mesopotamian Cosmogony," 159) translates this passage as "Like a primitive being, upon her lips she spoke falsehoods to him." CAD L 242 finds the passage obscure. Whatever the meaning, the passage is clearly critical of Tiamat.

29. al-Rawi and George, "Tablets from the Sippar Library," 153:87f., 111f. For Tiamat's powerful magic see also II 31; III 35, 93: "Her (magic) decrees are weighty, they are irresistable" (CAD G 43b).

30. Ibid., 153:92, 154:116.

31. Cassin, "The Death of the Gods," 319.

32. Cassin (in "Mesopotamian Cosmogony," 160), has an interesting interpretation of the use of *kūbu* and *lullû* as applied to Tiamat. The two terms "mutually valorize one another." "The living Tiamat is 'like a *lullû*,' i.e., like a human being that has not yet been enculturated; dead, she is nothing more than an embryonic being who dies before taking form." In my translation of *kūbu* I follow CAD K 487. For invectives against old women in Latin literature see Richlin, *The Garden of Priapus*, 109–116. Poking fun at old women is widespread in world literature.

33. CAD N/2 339b. See V 59 for Marduk twisting Tiamat's tail (*ēgir zibbatsa*), suggesting her form as a fish.

34. The alliance of Tiamat and her son Kingu fails, whereas the alliance of father and son, of Ea and Marduk, is successful. The warm relationship between grandfather and grandson is noted (I 101–106), as is that between father and son (I 90); whereas the hatred of Tiamat toward her offspring is repeated frequently (II 11; III 15, 73; IV 80).

CHAPTER 6. OLD(ER) WOMEN

1. See, for example, Stearns, "Old Women," 44. Banner (in *In Full Flower*, 6) remarks that "there is a history for aging women to discover and reclaim."

2. See Falkner, "The Wrath of Alcemene," especially 123–126; Esler, "Horace's Old Girls"; Henderson, "Older Women in Attic Old Comedy"; and Bremmer, "The Old Women of Ancient Greece."

3. See my comments in chapter 5. See also van der Toorn, *From Her Cradle to Her Grave*, 37–43, 116–128. Note that in Bottéro's excellent discussion, "La femme dans la Mésopotamie ancienne," no mention is made of older women. Little too is said about them in books devoted to studies of ancient Near Eastern women: *La femme dans le Proche-Orient antique*, ed. J.-M. Durand; or *Women's Earliest Records from Ancient Egypt and Western Asia*, ed. B. S. Lesko.

4. See Roth, "Age at Marriage," 716–722 and my comments in chapter 3. The focus here for the most part will be on women with grown children who may or may not be married.

5. Henderson, "Older Women in Attic Old Comedy," 108.

6. For *paristu* see AHw 835a s.v. *parsu(m)*.

7. Amundsen and Diers, "The Age of Menopause in Classical Greece and Rome." Henderson (in "Older Women in Attic Old Comedy," 108) notes that age forty was "the canonical end of youth" for ancient Greek women, and I suspect it may have been so for Mesopotamian women too.

8. For the translation of the letter with comments on the marital difficulties of Matanazi see Roth, "Age at Marriage," 717–718 and 718 n. 5.

9. See Buckley and Gottlieb, "A Critical Appraisal of Theories of Menstrual Symbolism," 44f.

10. For a brief discussion of differing views about age at the onset of menopause see Banner, *In Full Flower*, 183. For a bibliography on this question see ibid., 381 n. 50. Banner (in ibid., 381 n. 51) cites a paper on the fertility of Renaissance Florentine women, in which C. Kaplisch-Zuber found "that women ended giving birth at about thirty-five. She speculates either that they experienced an early menopause or that this was the point at which they were seen as entering old age and thus were required to end their procreative experience."

11. Jalland and Hooper, *Women from Birth to Death*, 284.

12. See Covey, "The Definitions of the Beginning of Old Age in History," 325–327, and especially 329.

13. Roth, "Age at Marriage," 718.

14. For the observation that the texts never note the ages at which even kings die see Michalowski, "The Death of Šulgi." Even the fact that a king has died is rarely mentioned.

15. See Asher-Greve, *Frauen in altsumerischer Zeit*, 145. See ibid., for references to these pathological studies.

16. For information on the *nadītu* women see Jeyes, "The *Nadītu* Women of Sippar." See ibid., for bibliography, to which now add R. Harris, "Independent Women in Ancient Mesopotamia?"

17. On their life expectancy see Renger, "Untersuchungen zum Priestertum in der altbabylonischen Zeit," 166–168; see also R. Harris, "The *nadītu* Woman," 122f.

18. Hallo, "Women of Sumer," 29–30. See also the example of Enanedu, the last known *entu* priestess, daughter of Kudur-Mabuk and sister of Rim-Sin, "who must have been at least sixty-nine years old to have survived her brother." Cited by van de Mieroop, *Society and Enterprise in Old Babylonian Ur*, 117 n. 62.

19. For references to sons usually living with their widowed mothers and providing them with allotments of grain, oil, and wool (clothing) for life see Gelb, "Household and Family in Early Mesopotamia," 76–77. See also the remark by Brinkman (in "Sex, Age, and Physical Condition," 4) that "elderly females seem to outnumber elderly males in these lists by a substantial margin." The fact that women may have been considerably younger than men at marriage may in part account for more mothers than fathers living with children. But all statements must be qualified because the data are not plentiful. Foster (in "Women in Sargonic Texts," 55) found that labor force texts from Susa mention "numerous old men but only a few old women." But this may be due to older women living with children and assisting with child care and household chores.

20. See Gelb, "The Ancient Mesopotamian Ration System," 233, 238f.

21. Maekawa, "Female Weavers and Their Children in Lagash," 109.

22. Waetzoldt, "Compensation of Craft Workers," 137 nn. 141 and 142.

23. Gelb, "The Ancient Mesopotamian Ration System."

24. See Kuhrt, "Non-Royal Women in the Late Babylonian Period," 231.

25. See Gelb, "Prisoners of War in Early Mesopotamia," 74.

26. Greengus, *Old Babylonian Tablets from Ishchali and Vicinity*, 75:7–8.

27. *The Sumerian Dictionary of the University Museum of the University of Pennsylvania*, 2:189.

28. See Partridge, *Origins*, 290 s.v. "hoary."

29. See the example of the Egyptian goddess Isis, who in the myth *Horus and Seth* (Lichtheim, *Ancient Egyptian Literature*, vol. 2, 217) transforms herself from a beautiful young woman into an old woman with a stoop. She thereby achieves mobility of movement, enabling her to cross to the Island-in-the-midst after bribing the ferryman.

30. The contributions to Lesko, ed., *Women's Earliest Records* amply illustrate the various arenas in which women, especially royal and elite women, participated in such activities. For a recent overall survey on women see Stol, "Women in Mesopotamia."

31. See CAD M/I 74b. Interestingly, the same metaphor is used by the nineteenth-century French historian Michelet in lamenting the pain and weakness endured by menstruating women: "[This] cicatrization of an interior wound [resulted in the fact that a] . . . woman is not only an invalid, but a wounded one." Cited by Murstein in "Love, Sex, and Marriage through the Ages," 22. See also the reference to Aristotle's *Historia Animalium* cited by R. Osborne (in "Women and Sacrifice in Classical Greece," 396), in which the menstrual blood of an adolescent girl is compared to "that of an animal that has just been stabbed."

32. See Labat, *Traité akkadien de diagnostic et prognostic médicaux*, vol. 1, 210–212. See also idem, "Geburt," 178f. The *qadištu* woman, who appears to play some role in childbirth, may have used purifying waters on women just after they have given birth to remove the impurity associated with parturition. On the *qadištu* see CAD Q 48–50.

33. See CAD E 104b. On issues of sexual impurity see van der Toorn, *Sin and Sanction in Israel and Mesopotamia*, especially 29–33. See also idem, *From Her Cradle to Her Grave*, especially 51–52. For textual references see CAD M/2 s.v. *musukku*.

34. Biggs, "The Human Body and Sexuality in Mesopotamian Medical Texts."

35. Livingstone, *Court Poetry and Literary Miscellanea*, 94:18.

36. See, for example, Oleander, "Aspects of Baubo," 100–104. See also Esler, "Horace's Old Girls."

37. For these demons see Scurlock, "Baby-Snatching Demons, Restless Souls, and the Dangers of Childbirth."

38. See chapter 4. Schlossman and York in "Women in Ancient Art" make no mention of women's life stages.

39. See Robins, *Egyptian Painting and Relief*, 27, and idem, "Some Images of Women in New Kingdom Art and Literature," 109.

40. For this statue see Hansen and Dales, "The Temple of Inanna, Queen of Heaven at Nippur," 81, Fig. 10.

41. I am grateful to Donald Hansen for his written and oral communications regarding this rare piece. Given the elaborateness of Mesopotamian women's hairstyles generally, this Early Dynastic sculpture is perhaps "making a statement" about women's aging. For sunken cheeks as an aspect of aging in ancient Egypt see the "realistic" head of Sesostris III in Aldred, *Egyptian Art in the Days of the Pharaohs 3100–320 BC*, 125, Illus. 83 and 84.

42. But L. Green (in "More Than a Fashion Statement") comments on elderly courtiers wearing long hair/wigs (p. 36) and kilts (p. 33).

43. See Barnett, *The Sculpture of Aššur-naṣir-apli II 883–859 B.C.* 51 pl. IV.

44. Starr, "Sexuality and Aging," 97. For a survey of medieval attitudes toward the sexuality of the elderly as well as a bibliography on the topic see Covey, "Perceptions and Attitudes toward Sexuality of the Elderly during the Middle Ages." See also idem, *Images of Older People in Western Art and Society*, 110–139. Finley (in "The Elderly in Classical Antiquity," 11) notes that "the jokes [about the aged] become especially brutal when they touch on the sexual desires of older women." Bertman (in "The Ashes and the Flames," 161f.) observes that Martial and Horace thought "that past a certain age making love (at least for a woman) can be obscene." He gives examples of ancient women who "felt that past a certain age it was time to retire from love."

45. See chapter 8 for attitudes toward male and female sexuality in general.

46. See R. Harris, "Representations of the Elderly in Ancient Mesopotamian Literature."

47. Cited by Pomeroy, *Goddesses, Whores, Wives, and Slaves*, 8. (But there was vast difference in prices fetched by a young slave-girl and an old one, as mentioned earlier.) This of course does not mean that prostitution was uncommon in Mesopotamia. But prostitutes were often foreigners or prisoners of war. Consorting with a prostitute was frowned upon. On prostitution see Lambert, "Prostitution"; and more recently, Leick, *Sex and Eroticism in Mesopotamian Literature*, 151–153, 160–169.

48. Lambert, *Babylonian Wisdom Literature*, 248. Jacobsen suggests (in *The Harps*, 112) that the maidens and crones described in a hymn to the goddess Inanna as curling their hair and parading before her may have been camp followers or women whose providers had fallen in battle and who became harlots in order to survive. The goddess was the patroness of prostitutes.

49. This may well underlie the repugnance toward marriage or a sexual relationship between an older woman and a younger man.

50. I borrow this information from Biggs's forthcoming article, "The Human Body and Sexuality in Mesopotamian Medical Texts."

51. Civil, "The Message of Ludingira to His Mother." For a discussion and bibliography see Frymer-Kensky, *In the Wake of the Goddesses*, 16, 35, and 229f. n. 3.

52. Çig and Kramer, "A Sumerian Portrait," 414.

53. See Westenholz, "Metaphorical Language in the Poetry of Love in the Ancient Near East."

54. Sefati, "An Oath of Chastity in a Sumerian Love Song (SRT 31)?" 50.

55. Golden (in *Children and Childhood in Classical Athens*, 100) cites a fragment of Euripedes' *Erechtheus* that urged children "to feel a lover-like passion" for their mother. See also Hallett's suggestion (in *Fathers and Daughters in Roman Society*, 246–259) that there may have been libidinal attachments between mother and son in Rome too.

56. Leick, *Sex and Eroticism in Mesopotamian Literature*, 153–156.

57. See, for example, Bever, "Old Age and Witchcraft in Early Modern Europe," especially 176f. See also Banner, *In Full Flower*, 189–197; and N. Foner, *Ages in Conflict*, 172–183.

58. Henderson, "Older Women in Attic Old Comedy," 126.

59. Larner, *Witchcraft and Religion*, 84.

60. For an analysis of the Akkadian incantations and prayers concerned with witchcraft see Abusch, *Babylonian Witchcraft Literature* and idem, "The Demonic Image of the Witch in Standard Babylonian Literature." See also Rollins, "Women and Witchcraft in Ancient Assyria (c. 900–600 B.C.)." Rollins's scope is much broader than her title suggests. See also Leick's chapter "Witches, Demons, and the Ambivalence of Love" in *Sex and Eroticism in Mesopotamian Literature*, 220–231. That there are more references to female than male witches see Abusch, "The Demonic Image of the Witch in Standard Babylonian Literature," 31. See also the many more references to *kaššaptu* (female witch) than to *kaššapu* (male sorcerer) in CAD K 291f.

61. See Abusch, "*Maqlu.*"

62. In none of the treatments (see above) on Mesopotamian witchcraft is any linkage made between old age and witchcraft.

63. Berlin, ed., *Enmerkar and Ensuḫkešdanna*. That she, and not he, is named points to her higher status and importance.

64. See Walters, "The Sorceress and Her Apprentice." According to Walters (in ibid., 28), "Many cases of suspected sorcery may have been handled at lower levels of authority or even sub rosa." For the various laws dealing with witchcraft down the millennia see the index in Roth, *Law Collections* s.v. "witchcraft."

65. Walters, "The Sorceress and Her Apprentice," 37.

66. Foster, *Before the Muses*, vol. 2, 882.

67. For witchcraft as a cause of impotency among young men see Biggs, *ša.zi.ga: Ancient Mesopotamian Potency Incantations*, 3f.

68. See Scurlock, "Baby-Snatching Demons, Restless Souls, and the Dangers of Childbirth," 156.

69. For a discussion of and bibliography on the "Old Woman" see Fontaine, "A Heifer from Thy Stable."

70. For this role of women see Cooper, *The Return of Ninurta to Nippur*, 136–137.

71. Herlihy, *Medieval Households*, 121.

72. See CAD Ṣ 24–25 s.v. *ṣabātu*. It is an idiom frequently found in prayers.

73. See Civil, "On Mesopotamian Jails and Their Lady Warden," 78 n. 21.

74. See Frymer-Kensky, *In the Wake of the Goddesses*, 14f., 32, 45, and passim.

75. Sauren, "Nammu and Enki," 200.

76. See Kramer, "Ninurta's Pride and Punishment."

77. Hallo, "Individual Prayer in Sumerian," 86.

78. Avalos, *Illness and Health Care in the Ancient Near East*, 189. For the association of motherhood and intercession see also the hymn to Gula in Foster, *Before the Muses*, vol. 2, 582f.

79. See van der Toorn, *From Her Cradle to Her Grave*, 141. Research in the United States also finds the linking of old women and religion. See Learn, *Older Women's Experience of Spirituality*.

80. Gordon, *Sumerian Proverbs*, 110 1.142.

81. Dalley, *Mari and Karana*, 100f.

82. Parpola, *Letters from Assyrian and Babylonian Scholars*, 190f.

83. For references to men, as well as to women, crying see CAD B 36–38 s.v. *bakû*. For crying in Greece see Segal, *Euripides and the Poetics of Sorrow*, 62–73.

84. Civil (in "On Mesopotamian Jails and Their Lady Warden") makes some interesting comments as to why the warden deity of Mesopotamian jails was a woman and not a strong male deity who might have been considered more capable of controlling the inmates. See also Foster, "Letters and Literature," 101:20, where a man writing to a queen of a small Old Babylonian kingdom says, "You felt nothing of a woman's pity (*rīmam ša sinništim ul taršim*)."

85. Kovacs, *The Epic of Gilgamesh*, 69:13.

86. Frymer-Kensky, *In the Wake of the Goddesses*, 37. For goddesses lamenting like mothers see Cohen, *Canonical Lamentations of Ancient Mesopotamia*, vol. 1, 111:146; and Michalowski, *The Lamentation over the Destruction of Sumer and Ur*, 43:117; 45:137, 141; 47:174; and passim. Kramer has written extensively on the "Mater Dolorosa" goddess type. For bibliography see Frymer-Kensky, *In the Wake of the Goddesses*, 233 n. 20. For more examples see also ibid., 36–39.

87. Cohen, *Canonical Lamentations of Ancient Mesopotamia*, vol. 1, 185: a+ 40–a+ 42.

88. See Deimel, *Sumerische Tempelwirtschaft zur Zeit Urukaginas und seiner Vorganger*, 33f. Elderly women worked as professional mourners in ancient Greece to earn a pittance. See Garland, *The Greek Way of Life*, 258.

89. For references to the *kalû* see CAD K 91–94.

90. Frymer-Kensky, *In the Wake of the Goddesses*, 43.

91. For references to *lallarītu* see CAD L 47f; for *ama'irakku* see CAD A/2 s.v. *ama'irrû*.

92. Shaffer, "From the Bookshelf of a Professional Wailer."

93. For *maliktu* see CAD M/1 164a; for *mudû* see CAD M/2 165f; for *nēmequ* see CAD N/2 162a.

94. See chapter 9. But Denning-Bolle, *Wisdom in Akkadian Literature*, apart from Siduri's advice to Gilgamesh (pp. 94–96, 156), makes no mention of women. However, see the comments (too sanguine, in my opinion) by Frymer-Kensky on Mesopotamian women's learning in *In the Wake of the Goddesses*, 32–44, especially 36–42.

95. Cited in CAD N/2 162a.

96. Cooper, *The Curse of Agade*, 50 I:29–30. This passage describes the happy times in Agade before Naram-Sin had sinned. For another reference to advice being characteristic of old women (*buršuma*) see also Farber-Flügge, *Der Mythos "Inanna und Enki,"* 50:34.

97. Jacobsen, *The Harps*, 110:160.

98. Ibid., 141:224–227.

99. For this translation see Cooper, "Review of *Enlil and Ninlil*," 184f:13–22.

100. For comments on these myths see Frymer-Kensky, *In the Wake of the Goddesses*, 48–49.

101. Jacobsen, *The Harps*, 21 ii 4–10.

102. Civil, "Enlil and Ninlil," 60:141.

103. Kramer, "The Marriage of Martu," 17:45–48.

104. Ibid., 12.

105. Kovacs, *The Epic of Gilgamesh*, 85 n. 1. Her profession as tavern-keeper implies that she is an independent woman. See chapter 7 for the importance of women in the hero's life.

106. Dalley, *Myths from Mesopotamia*, 212, 224.

107. Jacobsen, *The Harps*, 317:589–630.

108. See Jacobsen, "The Myth of Inanna and Bilulu."

109. See Camp, "The Wise Women of 2 Samuel." I was less certain of their existence when chapter 9 was first published.

110. Jacobsen, *The Harps*, 450:28f.

111. Westenholz, "The Clergy of Nippur," 303.

112. Hallo and Van Dijk, *The Exaltation of Inanna*, 4. See also Hallo, "Women of Sumer."

113. Foster, "Women in Sargonic Texts," 53. See ibid., note 1 for bibliography.

114. For the most recent publication and discussion of this text, as well as for bibliography, see Hallo, "The Royal Correspondence of Larsa," 388:39f.

115. Ibid., 381.

116. One cannot assume a large number of Mesopotamian authoresses. One must remember that only three rulers—Shulgi, Lipit-Ishtar, and Ashurbanipal—in all of Mesopotamian history boasted about their literacy! Darnton's estimate (in "Cherchez la Femme," 22) of the proportion of French writers who were women varies from 2% in 1757 to 5% in 1784.

117. Jacobsen, *The Harps*, 26. For more on some of the problems of the authorship of these courtly love songs see Leick, *Sex and Eroticism in Mesopotamian Literature*, 113–116.

118. For Kubatum and Watartum see Frymer-Kensky, *In the Wake of the Goddesses*, 42. Kramer (in "Ua-aua: A Sumerian Lullaby," 652 n. 2) suggests that the lullaby was probably composed by a court poet "at the queen's behest."

119. The *vox feminae* remains to be fully explored. See the insightful comments by Sasson on women's letters in Mari in "The Posting of Letters with Divine Messages." Paul (in "The 'Plural of Ecstasy' in Mesopotamian and Biblical Love Poetry") has noted a grammatical feature that he believes characterizes women's "ecstatic amatory discourse."

120. The comments by Leick (in *Sex and Eroticism in Mesopotamian Literature*, 68) on the Sumerian bridal songs also assume female authorship.

121. Frymer-Kensky, *In the Wake of the Goddesses*, 40. Note below in the discussion of queen mothers that it was not until after her mother-in-law's death that Shiptu, wife of Zimri-Lim, came into her own. See below too for tensions between mothers-in-law and daughters-in-law.

122. See Limet, "The Cuisine of Ancient Sumer," 140. For the many references to male cooks and only three to female cooks see CAD N/2 313–316a s.v. *nuḫatimmatu* and *nuḫatimmu*.

123. Michalowski, *Letters from Early Mesopotamia*, 78.

124. See the index under "Female employment" in Lesko, ed., *Women's Earliest Records*; and Frymer-Kensky, *In the Wake of the Goddesses*, 22–24, 32–36.

125. Cited in Jacobsen, *Toward the Image of Tammuz*, 349 n. 68. The Sumerian equivalent for old woman here is *um.ma* "mother."

126. Idem, *The Harps*, 322–323:15–23. For references to the *sābītu*, translated as tavernkeeper/innkeeper, see CAD S 8.

127. Frymer-Kensky, *In the Wake of the Goddesses*, 32f., 35. Interestingly, Bennett (in *Women in Medieval English Countryside*, 123) notes that brewers (ale-wives) of Brigstock were "particularly active during the middle years of married life."

128. Oppenheim, *The Interpretation of Dreams*, 221–222. On the "tools" of the practitioners see ibid., 222–225. See also Asher-Greve, "The Oldest Female Oneiromancer." Hallo (in "Women of Sumer," 30) discusses *entu* high priestesses who function as dream interpreters, an example then of the interrelation between the cultic and the mantic. For this see also Asher-Greve, ibid., 31–32.

129. On the *šā'iltu* see CAD Š/1 109–110. For the reference to an elderly woman (*šībtum*) who is a diviner in an Old Assyrian text see ibid., 110.

130. CAD B 112 s.v. *bārītu*. CAD Š/1 110b suggests what, in my view, is the more likely difference between the *šā'iltu* and the *bārītu*: the former remained a popular diviner, the latter was the professional diviner.

131. Oppenheim, *The Interpretation of Dreams*, 190. For symbolic dreams of women see ibid. For *šabrâtu* see CAD Š/1 15a.

132. Jacobsen, *Toward the Image of Tammuz*, 220.

133. For references to the midwife see CAD Š/1 16 s.v. *šabsūtu*. See also von Soden, "Die Hebamme in Babylonien und Assyrien."

134. Plato, *Thaetetus*, 26:149b. For old women as midwives in classical Greece see Garland, *The Greek Way of Life*, 62.

135. For the link in Hittite between "midwife" and "old woman" see Beckman, *Hittite Birth Rituals*, 233.

136. Jacobsen, *The Harps*, 95 n. 2.

137. The *Homeric Hymn to Demeter* recounts how the goddess responded to the loss of her daughter by leaving the divine sphere of Olympus, disguising herself as an old woman, and hiring herself out to a mortal family to care for their son. See Foley, *The Homeric Hymn to Demeter*, 6:101–104: "Like a very old woman cut off from childbearing . . . such are the nurses of the law-giving king."

138. On health care in Mesopotamia see Avalos, *Illness and Health Care*, 99–231. See Gelb, "The Arua Institution."

139. For references to the *šakintu* see CAD Š/1 165–166. For her activities see Dalley and Postgate, *The Tablets from Fort Shalmanesser*, 9–14.

140. What follows is only a brief overview. An in-depth examination by period (and place, if possible) is the desideratum. Exemplary is Roth's recently published article, "The Neo-Babylonian Widow." For a bibliography on earlier treatments on the widow see ibid., notes 1 and 2. On p. 3 she discusses the problems faced by Assyriologists in dealing with this subject.

141. Golden, *Children and Childhood in Classical Athens*, 139. Roth (in "The Neo-Babylonian Widow," 5) estimates that "at least one quarter and perhaps as many as one half" of the documented households she examined were headed by widows. Hers is a very small sampling of texts.

142. CAD A/1 364a.

143. Gordon, *Sumerian Proverbs*, 197. For the sad plight of widows see also Fensham, "Widow, Orphan, and the Poor in Ancient Near Eastern Legal and Wisdom Literature."

144. Gordon, *Sumerian Proverbs*, 273.

145. Roth, *Law Collections*, 76. The same goal of their laws is voiced by other rulers of Mesopotamia.

146. Jacobsen, "A Maidenly Inanna," 65:154–157. Jacobsen suggests (in ibid., 67) that just as a mother often arranged the marriage for her son or daughter, so too Utu would arrange a remarriage so that the widow would be "under someone's authority and protection."

147. Jacobsen, *The Harps*, 128:30–31 and 137:159–161, respectively.

148. For the passages that concern the widow see the index in Roth, *Law Collections*.

149. Ibid., 165 § 33. On the widow in the Middle Assyrian period see Saporetti, *The Status of Women in the Middle Assyrian Period*, 17–20.

150. For a pre-Sargonic text see Glassner, "Women, Hospitality, and the Honor of the Family," 85. But there is a gender bias here, for the widows are "classified among the 'mothers' that is to say married women whose husbands are still alive." For the Sargonic period see the archive of Ur-Shara and his wife Ama-e in Foster, *Umma in the Sargonic Period*, 75. For the Ur III period see Owen, "Widows' Rights in Ur III Sumer," 175. For the Old Babylonian period see Donbaz and Yoffee, *Old Babylonian Texts from Kish*, 62f. For Assyria see Postgate, "On Some Assyrian Ladies," 94. For the Neo-Babylonian period see Roth, "The Neo-Babylonian Widow."

151. See Harris, "The Organization and Administration of the Cloister in Ancient Babylonia." For the example of the childless Hana's way of providing for herself, frequently used by widows, by adopting a slave as son and heir see A. Kuhrt, "Non-Royal Women in the Late Babylonian Period," 229f.

152. Translated by Oppenheim in *Letters from Mesopotamia*, 92.

153. For such contracts see Westbrook, *Old Babylonian Marriage Law*.

154. For the Old Babylonian text from Ur see van de Mieroop, *Structure and Enterprise in Old Babylonian Ur*, 117.

155. For this text see Greenfield, "Adi Baltu—Care for the Elderly and Its Rewards," 309f.

156. Lambert, "Prostitution," 134f.

157. Parpola, *The Correspondence of Sargon II*, 21–22.

158. Roth, "The Neo-Babylonian Widow," 7 and 25–26.

159. See Gelb, "The Arua Institution."

160. Roth, "The Neo-Babylonian Widow," 24 n. 101.

161. On the remarriage of widows in Mesopotamia see Wilcke, "Familiengrundüng im Alten Babylonien," 303–313.

162. But for a negative view toward remarriage outside of Mesopotamia, in Emar, Nuzi, and Hana, see van der Toorn, "Gods and Ancestors in Emar and Nuzi," 51f. For references to earlier discussions see ibid., 51 n. 62, and idem, "The Significance of the Veil in the Ancient Near East," 336–338.

163. On the *univira* as a Roman ideal see Pomeroy, *Goddesses, Whores, Wives, and Slaves*, 206–208.

164. Postgate, *Early Mesopotamia*, 148.

165. Stafford, *Queens, Concubines, and Dowagers*, 197. Although little work has been done on queen mothers in Mesopotamia, cogent comments on the subject can be found in Andreason, "The Role of the Queen Mother in Israelite Society"; and Ben-Baraq, "The Queen Consort and the Struggle for Succession to the Throne."

166. See Ben-Baraq, ibid., 38f.

167. The outstanding example is that of the famous Sammuramat, wife of Shamshi-Adad V (823–811 B.C.E.) and mother of Adad-nirari III (810–783 B.C.E.). See ibid., 35 n. 16.

168. Andreason, "The Role of the Queen Mother in Israelite Society," 194. On the special relationship between brother and sister in Mesopotamia see the example of Dumuzi and his sister Geshtinanna in Frymer-Kensky, *In the Wake of the Goddesses*, 36, 38, 167.

169. For a general survey on queens see Seux, "Königtum." For queen mothers see ibid., 162; Hallo, "The Women of Sumer"; and the index under "Queens" in Lesko, ed., *Women's Earliest Records*. See also Michalowski, "Royal Women of the Ur III Period," parts I, II, and III. Dalley (in *Mari and Karana*) focuses on the lives of the queens of these two cities, Shiptu and Iltani, respectively.

170. When the former queen Baranamtara, wife of Lugalbanda, died (her husband had died earlier), the reigning queen organized "grand funeral ceremonies with 177 female mourners [and], 92 male lamenters, as well as 48 'wives of notables' . . . representing the whole community," who accompanied her to her final resting place. Glassner, "Women, Hospitality, and the Honor of the Family," 89.

171. On Abi-simti see Michalowski, "Durum and Uruk during the Ur III Period." See also van de Mieroop, "Women in the Economy of Sumer," 57; see ibid., 57 n. 30 for the list of texts that mention her and p. 59 for bibliography.

172. Jacobsen, "Two Bal-Bal-e Dialogues."

173. Frayne, *Old Babylonian Period (2003–1595 B.C.)*, 59.

174. See Batto, *Studies on Women at Mari*, 64–73. Zimri-Lim had no brothers or sons but a large extended and immediate family of women, including wives, daughters, concubines, and sisters.

175. See Lafont, "Les femmes du palais de Mari," 182.

176. N. Foner, *Ages in Conflict*, 84–88.

177. See Batto, *Studies on Women at Mari*, 159 in the index for Adduduri's letters.

178. See ibid., 64–72; and more recently the stimulating discussion by Sasson, "The Posting of Letters with Divine Messages," especially 304f, 307, and 307 n. 27.

179. Dalley, *Mari and Karana*, 71.

180. Oppenheim, *Ancient Mesopotamia*, 359 n. 33. Westenholz questions the long-held view that women of the Assyrian court lived highly circumscribed lives. See her important essay "Toward a New Conceptualization of the Female Role in Mesopotamian Society," 515f.

181. For the attribution of a Syro-Palestinian background for Semiramis see Weinfeld, "Semiramis: Her Name and Her Origin." See most recently Roux, "Semiramis la reine mystérieuse d'Orient"; see ibid., 192–195 for a discussion of the Assyrian sources.

182. Taşyürek, "Some New Assyrian Rock Reliefs in Turkey," especially 180.

183. Reade, "Was Sennacherib a Feminist?" 139.

184. For the inscribed statues see Strommenger, *5000 Years of the Art of Mesopotamia*, 443 illus. 215.

185. See Hallo and Simpson, *The Ancient Near East*, 130; and CAD K 81a.

186. van Driel, "Wine Lists and Beyond," 272.

187. For treatment of this dowager see Reade, 142–145; and for more recent comments about her see Porter, *Images, Power, and Politics*, 16f., 74, 153 n. 313.

188. For this oracle see Biggs, "Akkadian Oracles and Prophecies," 605.

189. van de Mieroop, "An Inscribed Bead of Queen Zakutu."

190. Reade, "Was Sennacherib a Feminist?" 143; for a photograph of this bronze see ibid., Fig. 4. Bullae with stamp seal impressions may also include Naqi'a behind the king. See ibid., 144f.

191. On Adad-guppi see Weisberg, "Royal Women in the Neo-Babylonian Period"; Weisman, *Nebuchadnezzar and Babylon*, 7–12; and Beaulieu, *The Reign of Nabonidus, King of Babylon, 556–539 B.C.*, 967–979.

192. See Beaulieu, "Women in Neo-Babylonian Society," 9.

193. Pomeroy, *Women in Hellenistic Egypt*, 11.

194. Bin-Nun cited *apud* Arbeli in "The Removal of the Tawananna from Her Position," 81. For examples of Hittite queens and queen mothers who held the title of Tawananna see ibid., 79–85, passim.

195. See N. Foner, *Ages in Conflict*, 84–88. In chapter 4 I treat the far better attested conflict between older and younger men, fathers and sons.

196. Frankena, ed., *Briefe aus dem British Museum (LIH and CT 2–33)*, vol. 2, 150:14.

197. Reiner, *Šurpu: A Collection of Sumerian and Akkadian Incantations*, vol. 2, 13:24–25.

198. CAD E 149a s.v. *emētu*.

199. Whiting, *Old Babylonian Letters from Tell Asmar*, 15:32.

200. See, for example, Waetzoldt, "Compensation of Craft Workers and Officials in the Ur III Period," 131 n. 141: among the labor force is a woman with two grown daughters; the likely elder of the two has two children. From the rations of the last, Waetzoldt infers that one is between five and ten years old; the other not yet five. The second daughter has one son, not yet five. For other examples of grandmothers in the labor force see ibid., note 142. Prosopography and epistolary sources may increase the information on the relationships between grandmothers and other family members.

201. Foster, *Before the Muses*, vol. 1, 357:89f. and 105f., respectively.

202. For the most recent treatments of this text see Leichty, "Feet of Clay"; and Zaccagnini, "Feet of Clay at Emar and Elsewhere."

CHAPTER 7. IMAGES OF WOMEN IN THE *GILGAMESH EPIC*

1. Moran, "Review of *Altorientalische Lituraturen*.

2. Segal, "Ancient Texts and Modern Literary Criticism," 7. Like Moran, Segal pressed for openness to literary-critical analyses of classical

texts. Since this article he and other classicists have been highly productive in this direction, especially in treating women in myth and drama.

3. Tigay, *The Evolution of the Gilgamesh Epic*, 232f. The problem, of course, is whether the contractions and expansions of women's speeches really incorporate changing attitudes or are simply literary structural changes. But I am aware that my not carefully separating the images in the different versions can create some confusion. What is sorely needed is a composite critical edition of the *Gilgamesh Epic*. E. A. Speiser's translation of the *Gilgamesh Epic* in ANET (pp. 72–99) is used throughout this chapter unless otherwise noted. Kovacs' edition was not available at the time of its writing.

4. Ibid., 74–75. There is also more stress put on her wisdom in the Late Version. She is not only *mūdât kalâma* "one who knows everything," but also is wise (*emqet*).

5. Gold, *The Lady and the Virgin*, 2. My thinking on images of women was greatly stimulated by Gold's study, especially by her comments in the preface. Despite the vast differences between Mesopotamian and medieval French society, what Gold has to say about the often uncritical presuppositions of feminist historians in her field has been very helpful to me.

6. This is true even of Ishtar. Note the brevity of her proposal compared with the length of Gilgamesh's refusal of her proposal.

7. Gold, *The Lady and the Virgin*, xviii.

8. Herein lie both the challenges and the pitfalls confronting the modern scholar studying an ancient text. To what extent can ancient fantasies and realities be sorted out without imposing modern Western views on an alien culture? Oppenheim was acutely sensitive to this problem. See especially "Introduction: Assyriology—What and How?" in his *Ancient Mesopotamia*, 7–30.

9. Babcock, ed., *The Reversible World*, 14–15. In the introduction to this highly stimulating collection of essays, Babcock offers an excellent analysis of the various forms of inversion, their history and functions. She traces inversion back to "Greek parody of the Homeric journey to Hades" (p. 16). In my opinion, and this is at the heart of this chapter, the *Gilgamesh Epic* is a far earlier source of inversion.

10. Donaldson, *The World Upside-Down*, 6. I am well aware of the need for caution in applying a literary technique common in Western literature to the *Gilgamesh Epic*. But, as Babcock points out in *The Reversible World*, viewing the world as "upside-down" and topsy-turvy seems to have universal comic appeal. Foster (in "Humor and Cuneiform Literature")

makes no specific mention of inversion. However, the *aluzinnu* text discussed by Foster (in ibid., 74f.) (he very aptly translates *aluzinnu* as "trickster") may well belong to a genre associated with Ishtar festivities, which, as noted in chapter 9, were very much involved with inversion. I suspect that "The Poor Man of Nippur" also fits the inversion pattern.

11. See *rīmtu(m)* in AHw 986. For the cow as nourishing mother and goddess in Hindu tradition see O'Flaherty, *Women, Androgynes, and Other Mythical Beasts*, 33, 42, 91, and passim.

12. Oppenheim, *The Interpretation of Dreams*, 221f. The interpretation of dreams by mothers is often an aspect of their reassuring a troubled child.

13. This is an interesting parallel with Achilles and his mother, Thetis. With both heroes, the father is very much in the background, and there exists an intense relationship with another male.

14. The term *ḫarimtu* (used to describe Shamhat in the Enkidu episode) is, in my view, a nonjudgmental term for a woman who uses her sexuality to support herself. In Enkidu's curse the *ḫarimtu* becomes an object of male control and male violence. Perhaps translating it "harlot" or "whore" in the latter case might more accurately reflect the negative judgment. The feminist historian Gerda Lerner, in her highly speculative and problematic article "The Origin of Prostitution in Ancient Mesopotamia," treats the *ḫarimtu*-Enkidu episode as a historical datum. She disregards the fact that the *Gilgamesh Epic* is a literary work and therefore historical data must be separated from literary motifs and themes. There is no evidence in the *Gilgamesh Epic* of a "temple" prostitute to contrast with a "commercial" prostitute. Indeed, I think the existence and extent of cultic prostitution requires reconsideration and more careful study of the primary sources. It is obvious that prostitution was a social fact. The question is how, when, and where it was transformed into an organized and institutionalized phenomenon of urban life. In Sippar, as one text suggests, a group of prostitutes (several of them from elsewhere) lived in a group under the supervision, in some way, of the *kalamāḫu* of the Shamash temple (see R. Harris, *Ancient Sippar*, 332). Yet the expected association should rather be with the Ishtar temple that existed in Sippar (see Lambert, "Prostitution"). It may have been a matter of administration but in no way was it a question of cultic function.

15. For other references linking prostitution and taverns see CAD A/2 473 s.v. *aštammu* and CAD Ḫ 101 s.v. *ḫarimtu*. Note that *aštammu* and not *bīt sābīti* is used for "tavern." Enkidu's curse also brings "prostitute" and "tavern" together.

16. See, for example, Lambert, *Babylonian Wisdom Literature*, 102:73–79. Westbrook (in "The Enforcement of Morals in Mesopotamian Law") examines evidence suggesting that public authorities might intervene to restrain a husband's extramarital liaison with a prostitute.

17. Friedrich, *The Meaning of Aphrodite*, 14.

18. Farber-Flügge, *Der Mythos "Inanna und Enki,"* 56:38f.

19. Gottwald (in *The Tribes of Yahweh*, 557f.) discusses Rahab's social position as a prostitute. Note that she may have "operated an inn," again the common association of the prostitute with the inn or tavern.

20. Ortner, "Is Female to Male as Nature Is to Culture?" 84, 70, and 80, respectively.

21. The masculine preoccupation with sexuality can be seen in the uses of *šamḫiš* and *qašdu* cited in Edzard, "Kleine Beiträge zum Gilgameš-Epos," 53f. The *šamḫākuma attanallak* of Gilgamesh's dream in Gilg. P. i 4 should also be added. Note, as Edzard does, that Uruk is also described as the city of *kezrēti šamḫāti u ḫarimāti*, in "lovely-locks, joy-girls, and harlots" (translation in Kovacs, *The Gilgamesh Epic*, 56).

22. Here we find perhaps the binary opposition of the raw and the cooked: milk of wild animals versus bread and beer, which are cooked and processed. Note too that the hunter and shepherds who live in contact with animals are also liminal figures in the *Gilgamesh Epic*.

23. Given the confines of this chapter I will only note in passing the consummate artistry with which the author delineates the subtle and significant changes in the relationship, from wordlessness to dialogue; the importance of Enkidu's looking at and listening to Shamhat, beautifully replicating a child's development which ends with leaving mother and home and entering a man's world. Renger, "Gilg. P. ii 32 [PBS 10/3]."

24. For *kirimmu* see CAD K 406.

25. For a discussion, with literature, of the readings suggested for the simile, see Renger, "Gilg. P. ii 32 [PBS 10/3]." He opts for "like a god/deity." This too would present a role reversal: the prostitute functioning as a deity and Enkidu as a mere mortal! Note that when they eventually go to Uruk, their roles have changed; Enkidu walks "ahead and Shamhat behind him" (Gilg. P. v 8f.), in conventional(?) male-female fashion. For this reading see Kovacs, *The Epic of Gilgamesh*, 15 II 43. The Old Babylonian version reads "like a child." Ibid., note 1.

26. There may have been the topos of wise woman in Mesopotamia, as Camp (in "The Wise Women of 2 Samuel") suggests was the case for ancient Israel: see my notes to chapter 9. What seems to me likely is that the proverbial language of the *ḫarimtu* (and of the *sābītu*) is an important

element of inversion: from the mouths of these marginal and, I presume, uneducated, perhaps uncouth, women issue forth words of learning. For the simile "its (the bird's) mouth hurled invectives like a prostitute" see Kramer, "Sumerian Similes," 10.

27. I opt for the translation "tavernkeeper" rather than "barmaid," for it seems more in keeping with the economic status of the *sābītu* in the Old Babylonian period. Also, Siduri has the equipment of the brewer (*kannu*, *namzītu* in Gilg. X i 3), so she is more than a barmaid. The importance of the *sābītu* in the Old Babylonian period emerges from her mention in the laws. For references see Roth, *Law Collections*, 281 s.v. "innkeeper." For other references to *sābītu* see CAD S 8 s.v. *sābû*. The *(bīt) aštammi* and the *bīt sābīti* were presumably not one and the same place, although there was certainly an overlap in their functions. Both provided drinks, entertainment, and a place to meet prostitutes. Although the *aštammu* probably was also an inn, providing overnight lodging to travellers, there is no such evidence for the *bīt sābīti*. Both appear to have had "bad" reputations (for references see CAD A/2 473 s.v. *aštammu* and CAD S 9 s.v. *sābû* in *bīt sābî*). For references to the literature and discussion of both and the Arzana House in Hittite sources see Hoffner, "The Arzana House." An important aspect of the *aštammu* is its relationship to the cult of Ishtar. See CAD A/2 473b, where *èš.dam* refers to the entire temple of Ishtar. Games were "played" in Ishtar's cult, and the *aštammu* and the *bīt sābīti* were places of "games." For references see CAD M/2 15 and 16 s.v. *mēlultu* and *mēlulu*.

28. For comments on Siduri as a name of Ishtar see Lambert, "The Hymn to the Queen of Nippur," 208. It seems to me that for both Siduri and the *harimtu* Shamhat, the association with Ishtar is significant. But just what its implication is, remains unclear.

29. Speiser, "The Epic of Gilgamesh," 89 n. 152.

30. According to the Laws of Hammurapi, section 110, a *nadītu* or *ugbatu* who opened or entered a tavern would be punished by being burnt to death, presumably because her chastity would be called into question (Roth, "Law Collections," 101). It is noteworthy that this rare harsh punishment was also meted out for incest between mother and son (Ibid., 111).

31. For a discussion of her "philosophy" see Tigay, *The Evolution of the Gilgamesh Epic*, 167–169, 211–212.

32. For these verses from the Old Babylonian Version see Kovacs, *The Epic of Gilgamesh*, 85 n. 1.

33. It is a striking contrast that men are always addressed by name in the Utnapishtim story.

34. See the examples noted below of Aya and the women of Uruk. See also the roles of mothers in the *Anzu* and *Enki and Ninmah* myths. For more on such examples see chapter 6.

35. In the *Gilgamesh Epic*, women speaking proverbially are consoling. Note also the harsh proverbial discourse of Gilgamesh with Ishtar.

36. A close study of letters to and by women focusing on women's rhetoric in light of recent analytical methods and comparative studies in this area might yield important results. Siduri's speech might also be described as "specific" in character. For more comments on feminine rhetoric, see my notes to chapter 9.

37. If this is indeed the case, it would be strong confirmation of one of the basic theses of this chapter.

38. "The gods kept hearing their [the women's] complaints" (*tazzim-tašina ištenemme* [I ii 29]).

39. There seems to be an echo from everyday life in the wife's having to remind the busy, forgetful husband of some family matter or member.

40. It is amazing that in the *Gilgamesh Epic*, Ishtar's name has been substituted for Mami and Nintu of the Old Babylonian Atrahasis flood versions (see Tigay, *The Evolution of the Gilgamesh Epic*, 224f.), given the antipathy toward her in Gilg. VI 1–79. There was no attempt to reconcile the contradiction. Though never a mother goddess in the Mesopotamian pantheon, Ishtar as the "mother" of kings is well attested to. And yet paradox is very much a part of her nature (see chapter 10).

41. Jacobsen, *The Treasures of Darkness*, 135.

42. Abusch's "Ishtar's Proposal and Gilgamesh's Refusal" is a comprehensive and in-depth analysis, the focus of which is very different from mine. This, once again, demonstrates the multivalence of the *Gilgamesh Epic*, surely the touchstone of a classic.

43. Yet even she proposes marriage and not an affair. So despite the inversion she too reinforces the social norms, as do other women in the *Gilgamesh Epic*.

44. The *nādu* "waterskin" of line 38 and the *šēnu* "shoe" of line 41, I suggest, are perhaps masculine symbols. For the best translation of these metaphors see Kovacs, *The Epic of Gilgamesh*, 52.

45. For the bisexuality of Ishtar see Hoffner, "Symbols for Masculinity and Femininity," 333f. n. 54. In addition to his references to CAD, see now CAD M/2 15 s.v. *mēlultu*, lexical section, for the dual nuances of this term as "play" and "battle," in connection with Inanna-Ishtar. What is an integral part of Ishtar's nature, her "manliness," is rejected in the *Gilgamesh Epic*.

46. Lambert, *Babylonian Wisdom Literature*, 102:72. Would the *šāra* of Gilg. VI 34 perhaps call to mind to the listener the *šāri* of the proverb?

47. O'Flaherty, *Women, Androgynes, and Other Mythical Beasts*, 72ff. There is much merit in looking to other polytheistic traditions and the scholarly work done with these to better understand Mesopotamian attitudes toward the gods. This is not to dismiss political or historical issues, which must be considered. More questionable is the view that the "immorality" of Ishtar was rejected. See the pertinent comments of Diakonoff in "Review of *Het Gilgamesj Epos. . .*" 65f. Application of O'Flaherty's "banalization of the gods" deserves far more space than I devote to it here.

48. For *a-ḫa-ab-bu-ub* see Tigay, *The Evolution of the Gilgamesh Epic*, 9 n. 20, 274 n.

49. Jacobsen, *The Treasures of Darkness*, 218.

50. Homosexuality is banned only in the Middle Assyrian Laws (see Roth, *Law Collections*, 160 A § 20), and so it may well have been a social reality. For a detailed discussion see Bottéro and Petschow, "Homosexualität." However, it seems hardly to have been institutionalized as it was in classical Athens (see Dover, *Greek Homosexuality*). Pertinent perhaps is a proverb cited by Lambert (in *Babylonian Wisdom Literature*, 259:10–11): "(Personal) friendship lasts for a day, being a colleague forever" (*ibrūtam ša ūmakkal kinattūtu ša dārâti*). Enkidu is often referred to as "comrade, companion" (*ibru*) by Gilgamesh, and on occasion Enkidu so refers to Gilgamesh. The competition of intense friendship with kin and other ties may have been addressed in this proverb. The theme of failed friendship also appears in the epics of Lugalbanda and Etana.

51. Kilmer, "A Note on an Overlooked Word-Play."

52. See Kovacs, *The Epic of Gilgamesh*, 11 I 237, 248, and 263. See also the simile describing the mourning Gilgamesh in Gilg. VIII ii 19: "Like a lioness deprived of her cubs he keeps pacing to and fro" (*kīma nēšti ša šuddat mēraniša ittanasḫur ana pānišu u arkišu*). This has a maternal association and perhaps is an extension of the husband/wife motif. Note too that all descriptions of physical beauty in the *Gilgamesh Epic* are confined to Gilgamesh and Enkidu.

53. See, for example, Kilmer, "A Note on an Overlooked Word-Play," 130f.; Alster, "The Paradigmatic Character of Mesopotamian Heroes," 55f; and Abusch, "Ishtar's Proposal and Gilgamesh's Refusal."

54. Incredibly, even in the netherworld unexpected mention is made of a mother, "the mother of Ninazu" (Gilg. XII 29, 47). Also noteworthy is the mention of "her breast" (*iratsa*), with its maternal association (in Gilg. XII 31, 49).

55. Donaldson, *The World Upside-Down*, 15.

56. Wolf (in "Chinese Women," 168) notes that the Chinese mother made "full use of her husband's isolation from his children to strengthen their bond to her." For the close mother-son relationship and the importance of sons to mothers in the politics of the Indian family, see Kakar, *The Inner World*, 57.

57. This phrase is used by Kakrides in *Homeric Researches*. On pp. 152ff. he discusses the ascending scale of affection in ancient Indian tales in which siblings and parents rank above spouse; in other words, brotherly love is valued more highly than conjugal or filial love. The Inanna/ Dumuzi laments might also be reexamined in light of this perspective.

CHAPTER 8. GENDER AND SEXUALITY IN THE MYTH OF *NERGAL AND ERESHKIGAL*

1. Estimations of the length of the two versions differ. I here follow Dalley, *Myths from Mesopotamia*, 163. Vogelzang (in "Some Aspects of Oral and Written Tradition in Akkadian") estimates 88 lines for the Amarna version and 440 lines for the Sultantepe version; for a discussion of the differences between the two versions see ibid., 271–278. See also Reiner, "Nergal and Ereškigal." I will be using throughout this chapter the translation of Dalley (in *Myths from Mesopotamia*, 163–177) unless otherwise designated.

2. Very helpful is the "interpretive outline" by Foster that attempts to integrate the different texts in *Before the Muses*, vol. 1, 410–428. Foster fills in some of the gaps with various suggestions.

3. "Mistress of the Great Land" is the translation of her Sumerian name. Messengers are free from travel limitations. For a discussion of the messenger in the later version of *Nergal and Ereshkigal* see Meier, *The Messenger in the Ancient Semitic World*, 147–150. Meier (in ibid., 147) describes this myth as "perhaps the most detailed literary text recounting the reception of messengers."

4. In the Uruk fragment they kneel.

5. Dalley (in *Myths from Mesopotamia*, 163), however, explains the significance of the chair as an attempt "to ensure that he can escape from the underworld and elude death," connecting it to the "ghost's chair" in lexical texts.

6. See Foster, *Before the Muses*, vol. 1, 410; Reiner, "Nergal and Ereškigal," 50; and Oppenheim, "Mesopotamian Mythology III," 147 and passim. Jacobsen (in *The Treasures of Darkness*, 229f.) expresses some uncertainty about the "ultimate meaning" of the myth. For him, "it appears almost impenetrable."

7. Dalley, *Myths from Mesopotamia*, 163f. This is also Lambert's view in "Studies in Nergal," 357. J. Bottéro (in *Mesopotamia: Writing, Reasoning, and the Gods*, 299) states that the name Nergal comes from Sumerian and means "Authority of the Great-City," i.e., the netherworld.

8. Bottéro, "Intelligence and the Technical Function of Power," 152b. This was his observation in earlier publications as well.

9. Frymer-Kensky, *In the Wake of the Goddesses*, 46 and 235 n. 5.

10. Reiner, "Nergal and Ereškigal"; and Jacobsen, *The Treasures of Darkness*, 229f.

11. Hutter, *Altorientalische Vorstellungen von der Unterwelt*, 84–100. In his view, the myth primarily served to "tame" death, thus rendering it less frightening to the ancients (ibid., 166–172).

12. Specialists in the field are just beginning to address the issue of gender in ancient Mesopotamia. See Frymer-Kensky, "The Ideology of Gender in the Bible and the Ancient Near East" and *In the Wake of the Goddesses*, especially 12–13, 30–31; M. I. Marcus, "Incorporating the Body"; and Pollock, "Women in a Men's World." Pollock (in ibid., 383) speaks of the "prevailing male dominated discourse of mid-third millennium Sumerian society." Her comment strongly suggests that there was little if any change in the androcentric character of Mesopotamian society throughout its history.

On sexuality in Mesopotamia see Bottéro, "L'amour à Babylone." See also the chapter "'Free Love' and Its Disadvantages," in his *Mesopotamia: Writing, Reasoning, and the Gods*, 130–153. Especially stimulating and suggestive is the article by Cooper entitled "Enki's Member." The first book-length study on sexuality is the recent publication *Sex and Eroticism in Mesopotamian Literature* by Leick, which is rich in insights and sources. She treats *Nergel and Ereshkigal* (pp. 249–253) far more briefly and from a different perspective than I do. The book appeared after I had completed this essay.

13. Crane, *Sexuality and Gender in Early Modern Europe*, 4.

14. Ibid., 18. I therefore differ with Frymer-Kensky (in "The Ideology of Gender in the Bible and the Ancient Near East," 188), who finds that "the only clear evidence of gendered thinking we have from Akkadian language texts are the Aguŝaya hymn and the Gilgamesh epic." The evidence is more implicit than explicit in *Nergal and Ereshkigal* but is nevertheless there.

15. This same concern is expressed in chapters 4 and 5. One must check the data of the myths against other sources, which I will do to some degree later in this chapter.

16. Alster, "Marriage and Love in the Sumerian Love Songs," 15.

17. This form of address signifies the equal status between Ereshkigal and Nergal. For references see CAD A/1 200f. s.v. *aḫu*. There is also a conciliatory note here.

18. The last line (*adu kīnanna*) presents problems. Moran (in "Review of *Altorientalische Vorstellungen, . . .*" 115) suggests the translation "'so far, thus,' i.e., this is the story up to this point, the end of the reverse side." Moran considers the phrase a scribal remark. Foster (in *Before the Muses*, vol. 1, 416) accepts Moran's suggestion. The story certainly seems incomplete.

19. This is contrary to Hutter's view (in *Altorientalische Vorstellungen von der Unterwelt*, 91).

20. Oppenheim, "Mesopotamian Mythology III," 154.

21. CAD Q 45.

22. Foster, *Before the Muses*, vol. 1, 413. As Reiner notes (in "Nergal and Ereškigal," 51), from the very beginning "a series of instructions, repeated messages, and other ceremonial[s]" characterize the much longer later version. I will overlook the numerous problems in the text and focus only on what can be gathered about the subjects of gender and sexuality.

23. For *aḫameš* see CAD A/1 164a; for *šitmuriš* see CAD Š/1 296f.

24. Foster, *Before the Muses*, vol. 1, 413:13.

25. Ibid., 424:52–53.

26. Hutter, *Altorientalische Vorstellungen von der Unterwelt*, 84. For a similar linking of love with the pleasure of food and drink in ancient Greece see Parker, "Love's Body Anatomized," 98; and Henderson, *The Maculate Muse*, 47–48, 52, 60–61, and 74.

27. For a stimulating discussion of the Greek view that women were more prone to erotic emotion than men "and sexually insatiable once aroused," see Carson, "Putting Her in Her Place."

28. In CAD M/2 317b: *mu-[tú] ka-[lu (?)]-ma ul e-sik ul adâni dīni ša ilī rabûte.*

29. Foster, *Before the Muses*, vol. 1, 425.

30. Dalley, *Myths from Mesopotamia*, 155.

31. Foster (in *Before the Muses*, vol. 1, 426) translates the line as "bald, with a tic, lame." Nergal apparently did not kneel with the other gods.

32. Hutter, *Altorientalische Vorstellungen von der Unterwelt*, 90. For this nuance of laughing see also CAD Ṣ 65a s.v. *ṣaḫû.*

33. Grayson, *Assyrian Royal Inscriptions*, 59:6. I owe this reference to Jerrold Cooper. Of interest too are the many incantations to counter impotency that are erotic in content and are "obstensibly recited by a woman

often addressing a man in the second person to enable him to make love."
For these see Biggs, *ša.zi.ga: Ancient Mesopotamian Potency Incantations*, 2.

34. I am grateful to Anna Guinan for permitting me to cite from her
unpublished English paper, translated and published in Dutch: "De Houding
Ten Aanzien van Sexualiteit." It examines the first-millennium Tablet 104
Šumma Ālu, a collection of omens taken from human sexual behavior.

35. Oppenheim, "Mesopotamian Mythology III," 154.

36. See, for example, van de Mieroop, "Women in the Economy of
Sumer"; and W. W. Hallo, "Women of Sumer." For the situation in ancient
Egypt see most recently Robins, *Women in Ancient Egypt*, 42–55.

37. See Edzard, "Ku(g)-Baba"; and Hallo, "Women of Sumer," 28.

38. Leichty, *The Omen Series šumma izbu*, 8.

39. See CAD S 290 s.v. *sinništu*.

40. See CAD K 27 b s.v. *ṣabātu*.

41. See Dossin, *Archives royales de Mari*, 69 r. 10–11. See also Dalley, *Myths
from Mesopotamia*, 285, where the passivity of the god Erra is underlined
by his staying in bed and enjoying himself with his spouse Mami. Dallying
amorously undermines the desideratum of masculine aggressive activism.

42. Guinan, "De Houding Ten Aanzien van Sexualiteit" (English ms.).
68–81.

43. Held, "A Faithful Lover in an Old Babylonian Dialogue."

44. Cooper, "Enki's Member." The growing corpus of published
religious and secular Mesopotamian love poetry provides a rich source of
material for learning more about the topic of gender and sexuality. For
cogent observations on this genre see Alster, "Marriage and Love in the
Sumerian Love Songs." See also Leick, *Sex and Eroticism in Mesopotamian
Literature*, especially 64–138.

45. For women as composers if not the writers of love songs see Fox,
The Song of Songs and the Ancient Egyptian Love Songs, 56. However, see the
reservations about this point expressed by Lichtheim in *Ancient Egyptian
Literature*, vol. 2, 8.

46. And yet there is almost a virginal quality about Ereshkigal as if it
was Nergal who awakened her to her sexuality. This may point up the
masculine ambiguity toward women: woman as both virgin and prostitute.
For the Greek view see Carson, "Putting Her in Her Place." There are basic
differences, however, between the Mesopotamian and Greek views, which
remain to be examined.

47. McKinstry, "The Plot of Gender," 30.

48. For a discussion of the issue of women's autonomy in Mesopotamia see R. Harris, "Independent Women in Ancient Mesopotamia?"

49. Gordon, *Sumerian Proverbs*, 115 1.147.

50. See Westbrook, "Adultery in Ancient Near Eastern Law," 557f.

51. Lambert, *Babylonian Wisdom Literature*, 232.

52. Cooper, "Enki's Member," 88.

53. See Zweig, "The Mute Nude Female Characters in Aristophanes' Plays." She observes (in ibid., 83) that "few of these scenes [in vase paintings] demonstrate mutual affection . . . and the majority seem concerned only with male pleasure."

54. Konstan, *Games of Venus*, 1–3.

55. Reiner, "Nergal and Ereškigal," 85–93. Leick (in *Sex and Eroticism in Mesopotamian Literature*, 71 and 79) observes in far earlier texts that "sexual intimacy, spontaneously desired by both partners, is practically a prerequisite for the decision to marry" and "the importance of erotic satisfaction within marriage (and before) was recognized."

56. Ibid., 87:5–89:19.

57. CAD L 51a s.v. *lalû*.

58. CAD H 31 s.v. *ḫā'iru*.

59. Westbrook, "The Enforcement of Morals in Mesopotamian Law."

60. Kramer, *The Sumerians*, 255. For the "ups and downs" of marriage see also idem, "The Woman in Ancient Sumer," 110–111. For a wonderful visual depiction of the love and affection between spouses see idem, *The Sumerians* (between pp. 160 and 161) for the sculpted seated couple from Nippur (fig. 2 here).

61. Lambert, *Babylonian Wisdom Literature*, 147: 48–52. To what extent, if any, changes in views toward gender and sexuality took place in the three thousand years of Mesopotamian history is at this time impossible to chart. My guess is that by and large there was a fairly consistent perspective throughout. It is noteworthy that Ereshkigal is frequently invoked in Greek magical love incantation papyri of the Greco-Roman period. See Biggs, "Liebeszauber," 18.

CHAPTER 9. THE FEMALE "SAGE" IN MESOPOTAMIAN LITERATURE

1. These traditional roles are best summed up in Lambert, "The Gula Hymn of Bulluṭsa-rabi," 121:65: "I am daughter, I am daughter-in-law, I am spouse, I am housekeeper."

2. Skinner, "Introduction," 3. This comment by Skinner, a classicist, is as applicable to ancient Near Eastern women as to Greek and Roman women.

3. Ibid.

4. Oppenheim, *Ancient Mesopotamia*, 301.

5. For example, *Frauen in altsumerischer Zeit* by Asher-Greve is an exhaustive study of women, focusing on the approximately nine hundred years of Uruk IV through Early Dynastic III periods. On ancient Near Eastern women (Egypt, Mesopotamia, Israel) see Lesko, ed., *Women's Earliest Records*; and Robins, *Women in Ancient Egypt*. The kinds of sources available on Mesopotamian woman for any given period skew the information. In my judgment, women's position probably changed far less than is frequently assumed.

6. These "definitions" are given by Buccellati in "Wisdom and Not," 42.

7. For references to *apkallatu* see CAD A/2 171. For more on the Akkadian terms for "sage," see Sweet, "The Sage in Akkadian Literature."

8. See R. Harris, "Review of *The Female and the Nature of the Divine*."

9. For an excellent entrée into Mesopotamian wisdom literature, its terminology, and problems, see Denning-Bolle, *Wisdom in Akkadian Literature*. But apart from Siduri of the *Gilgamesh Epic*, she mentions no other woman. Given the social structure and ideals of Mesopotamian and Egyptian societies I find it unlikely that women, with the exception of those who like Enheduanna lived outside of the traditional norms, would be permitted or even wish to devote themselves full-time to scholarship and learning. At the same time one must not be too dogmatic if one bears in mind the results of recent studies on ancient Greek women. For example, Wider (in "Women Philosophers in the Ancient Greek World") demonstrates that women were consistently involved with philosophy throughout antiquity, ancient and modern views notwithstanding.

10. For *nēmequ* see CAD N/2 160; for *emqu* see CAD E 151.

11. Detienne and Vernant, *Cunning Intelligence in Greek Culture and Society*, 3. These authors note (pp. 4–5) that although philosophical thinking marked a break with the earlier understanding of *mētis*, it nevertheless continued "to operate in large areas such as politics, the military art, medicine, and the skills of the artisan." Even Adapa, the Mesopotamian sage par excellence, was wise in practical matters as well as outstanding in scholarly achievement, as shown by Foster (in "Wisdom and the Gods in Ancient Mesopotamia").

12. See Crenshaw, "Prolegomenon," 4.

13. Oppenheim, "The Position of the Intellectual in Mesopotamian Society."

14. So too was a goddess, Seshat, the patroness of writing in ancient Egypt. Note that the patron saint of the faculty of the medieval faculty of arts was Saint Katherine, and yet medieval women were not permitted to enroll in institutions of higher learning. See Shank, "A Female University Student in Late Medieval Krakow," 373.

15. Sjöberg, "The Old Babylonian Eduba," 175, 173.

16. For references see AHw 1395.

17. Oppenheim, *Catalogue of the Cuneiform Tablets of the Wilberforce Eames Babylonian Collection*, 21–22.

18. For the names and functions of these scribes, see R. Harris, "The Organization and Administration of the Cloister in Ancient Babylonia," 138–139; and idem, *Ancient Sippar*, 196–197, 288.

19. This is important, for it suggests the possibility that scribes in the Old Babylonian period and later too may have taught their craft to their daughters, as well as to their sons. The question is whether women, apart from the special instances discussed, ever put their knowledge to professional use. Male scribes may have deliberately chosen Sumerian names to demonstrate their learning, but whether this was so for the *nadîtu* scribe is difficult to say.

20. R. Harris, "The Organization and Administration of the Cloister," 131–138, 141. For more on this remarkable institution see R. Harris, ibid., *Ancient Sippar*, and "The *nadîtu* Woman."

21. Batto (in *Studies on Women at Mari*, 5) states that the woman at Mari "might receive an extensive education and serve as a scribe." Dalley (in *Mari and Karana*, 110) comments that the number of female scribes "is enough to show that men did not hold a monopoly on literate skills." I contend that "extensive education" was rare for anyone, but especially so for women. In Mari it was for slave-girls who were trained for the specific concern of their owners: to limit access to harem women by non-kin males.

22. These scribes are named in Birot, "Textes économiques de Mari IV." Dalley (in *Mari and Karana*, 110) refers to them as female secretaries. But their slave status is significant and should not be forgotten.

23. See Durand, "Trois études sur Mari," 167 n. 41. See also idem, "Les dames du palais de Mari," 419, where a female scribe is considered as part of the household of the princess of Qatna.

24. See the English summary in Dandamaev, *Vavilouskie Pisci*, 237. It must be stressed that this datum should not be taken as evidence of the deterioration of women's legal and economic status. Women continued throughout all of Mesopotamian history to participate in the economic life of their community. They also continued, I maintain, to be excluded from

educational opportunities. Nor should we assume that they regarded this negatively.

25. Hallo and van Dijk, *The Exaltation of Inanna*, 4.

26. Ibid., 33:138.

27. The extent to which Enheduanna's work reveals a specifically female style and rhetoric remains to be explored. Appearances to the contrary, was she locked into traditional male canons and forms?

28. For details of this text see Hallo, "The Royal Correspondence of Larsa." The possibility remains, however, that, although Ninshatapada was the author of the letter, she may have dictated it.

29. Hallo, "Women of Sumer," 32.

30. See Kramer, "Sumerian Love-Song." However, in his later publication he is less certain of female authorship. See idem, "Sumerian Sacred Marriage Texts," 644–645.

31. Note, for example, the Sumerian proverb, "My mouth makes me comparable with men," which as Lambert rightly observes (in *Babylonian Wisdom Literature*, 236, 238) "suggests that a woman may be speaking" and emphasizes the oral eloquence of women.

32. See Landsberger and Civil, *The Series Ḫar-ra=ḫubullu*, 9:148–149. She does not appear in any other Sippar text.

33. Waterman, *Royal Correspondence of the Assyrian Empire*, 453:1367–1368. This self-deprecation by a woman also is found below in the letter by princess Kiru to her father. The question remains whether she actually wrote these texts. In tone, they are reminiscent of Shiptu's concern for her husband in a similar context.

34. The case of the palace attendant (*sal suhur.lal*) who was the author or coauthor of several Luwian purification rituals in the Hittite material is also of interest. See Güterbock, "A Hurro-Hittite Hymn to Ishtar," 159. Her low status is significant and parallels the Mari examples above.

35. Castellino, *Two Šulgi Hymns*, 47:155ff. For music as part of school instruction see also Sjöberg, "The Old Babylonian Eduba," 168–170. But again it must be noted that women would not receive their learning in this masculine institution. Pomeroy (in *Goddesses, Whores, Wives, and Slaves*, 17–18) points out that being well-read in Greek literature is associated with playing the lyre and dancing.

36. For references see Sjöberg, "The Old Babylonian Eduba," 170 n. 39.

37. See Dossin, *Archives royales de Mari*, 64 (discussed by Batto in *Studies on Women at Mari*, 51), where Shamshi-Adad advises his son to send his grown daughters to Shubat-Enlil to learn the art of singing (*nārūtu*). CAD Z 40 notes that the *zammeru* connotes "either an untrained

singer or a singer of popular songs," in contrast to the *nāru*, "who performed in palace and temple, singing to the accompaniment of various musical instruments." A group of Kassite letters report on the illnesses of young women in a music academy attended by princes and princesses. See Ritter, "Magical Expert (= *Āšipu*) and Physician (= *Asû*)," 317–318. For a discussion of songstresses in Zimri-Lim's harem see Durand, "Les dames du palais de Mari," 390–394.

38. Sharp, "Folk Medicine," 247–248.

39. Oppenheim, *Ancient Mesopotamia*, 292.

40. For a discussion of their different methods of healing see ibid., 290–292.

41. Ibid., 385 n. 14.

42. Dalley (in *Mari and Karana*, 122) implies that a "medical practitioner might be of either sex." I doubt there were very many female physicians. Female practitioners were most likely limited to treating women.

43. Oppenheim, *Ancient Mesopotamia*, 304–305.

44. See, for example, Hock-Smith and Spring, eds., *Women in Ritual and Symbolic Roles*, 21.

45. For information on the tasks of the midwife see Jacobsen, "Notes on Nintur," 290–293. See also von Soden, "Die Hebamme in Babylonien und Assyrien."

46. Pringle, "Hittite Birth Rituals," 133. Lefkowitz and Fante (in *Women's Life in Greece and Rome*, 162–163) include Roman texts that demonstrate the "elaborate professional skill involved in an exclusively female profession." Of interest too is the case of the biblical midwives in Exodus 1:15 who outwitted the Egyptian authorities. Detienne and Vernant (in *Cunning Intelligence in Greek Culture and Society*, 309) mention that Aristotle was impressed with the "quickwittedness" needed by the midwife "when she cuts through the umbilical cord. . . . The skill of the midwife is no different from the subtlety of the politician."

47. See R. Harris, "The *nadītu* Woman," 135.

48. The *qadištu* woman is customarily associated with wetnursing (see CAD Q 48–49) but may have been a midwife too.

49. Denning-Bolle (in *Wisdom in Akkadian Literature*, 75) discusses at length the "intermeshing of cult with the more speculative problems of existence that renders any definition of 'wisdom' in Mesopotamia fairly tenuous." The consequence and biases of Greek philosophical thinking make this problematic for us. Detienne and Vernant in *Cunning Intelligence in Greek Culture and Society* are very helpful in clarifying the issues.

50. CAD B 112 s.v. *bārītu*. This too points to the distance of the world of goddesses from the world of human women.

51. For a discussion of this text see Oppenheim, *The Interpretation of Dreams in the Ancient Near East*, 221–222.

52. Ibid.

53. Ibid., 225.

54. Hallo and van Dijk, *The Exaltation of Inanna*, 59–60.

55. On Nanshe see Frymer-Kensky, *In the Wake of the Goddesses*, 35, 37, 38–39, and 222–223.

56. Batto, *Studies on Women at Mari*, 119ff.

57. Oppenheim, *Ancient Mesopotamia*, 221–222.

58. For a discussion of some of the issues see Rollins, "Women and Witchcraft in Ancient Assyria (c. 900–600 B.C.)."

59. For some examples of ambivalence see R. Harris, "Women in the Ancient Near East," 963.

60. Camp, "The Wise Women of 2 Samuel."

61. For a discussion of her letter see Batto, *Studies on Women at Mari*, 44.

CHAPTER 10. INANNA-ISHTAR AS PARADOX AND A COINCIDENCE OF OPPOSITES

1. Much has been written about Inanna-Ishtar by people outside of the field of ancient Near Eastern studies. The tendency in these writings is to flatten and level the distinctively Mesopotamian features of the goddess. For example, O'Brien (in "Review of *Inanna, Queen of Heaven and Earth*," 60) states that "Inanna's resemblances to various Greek deities and to the Aegean nature deities of the Bronze Age [is] currently being resurrected by archaeologists and students of Greek religion." See also the observation by Pope (in *The Song of Songs*, 562): "The combination of beauty and terror which distinguishes the Lady of the Canticle also characterizes the goddess of Love and War throughout the ancient world, from Mesopotamia to Rome, particularly the goddess Inanna or Ishtar of Mesopotamia, Anat of the West Semites, Athena or Victoria of the Greeks and Romans, Britannia, and most striking of all, Kali of India." The telling comments by Hackett (in "Can a Sexist Model Liberate Us?" 75) serve as a corrective. She notes that "the fullness and breadth of the power of these goddesses represented in the ancient world is boiled down to one or two aspects." I will therefore largely bypass the works by nonspecialists and focus on the primary sources and the studies by specialists.

The history of the syncretism and fusion of the Sumerian Inanna with the Akkadian Ishtar is complex and problematic. Scholars have attempted to resolve the problem in different ways. See the study by Heimpel, "A Catalog of Near Eastern Venus Deities." See also Jacobsen, *The Treasures of Darkness*, 135–143. For the purposes of this article I will treat the two goddesses as one, ignore the numerous historical issues and problems, and instead focus on presenting a theoretical framework for understanding the special features of the goddess. The Sumerian Inanna already incorporates many of the distinctive aspects of the Akkadian Ishtar.

2. Jacobsen, *The Treasures of Darkness*, 143. Jacobsen (in "Mesopotamian Religion," 459) suggests that the fact that "the offices attributed to her show little unity or coherent pattern" may be due to "the syncretistic image of Inanna." I hope to show that, on the contrary, there does exist a coherency in her attributes.

3. Kramer, *From the Poetry of Sumer*, 77.

4. Oppenheim, *Ancient Mesopotamia*, 197.

5. Wilcke, "Inanna-Ishtar," especially 81.

6. Alster, "An Aspect of 'Enmerkar and the Lord of Arrata,'" 109.

7. Bottéro (in "La femme, l'amour et la guerre en Mésopotamie ancienne") suggests various possible explanations for the special character of the goddess, which include ethnographical, historical, and psychological factors. For him, because the gods are man writ large, the human model for the deity is the prostitute, advocate of free love, a marginal person in society. But there is, in my opinion, much more to the goddess.

8. Vanstiphout, "Inanna/Ishtar as a Figure of Controversy," especially 233. Vanstiphout discusses the various scholarly interpretations suggested down the years to account for her manifoldness.

9. There are, for example, many parallels between Ishtar and the Hurrian goddess Ishtar-Shawushka. See Wegner, *Gestalt und Kult des Ishtar-Shawuška*, 1–9.

10. Ortner, "Is Female to Male as Nature Is to Culture?" 85.

11. Jacobsen (in *The Treasures of Darkness*, 135) observes that her many different aspects (which make for the ambiguities) incline one "to wonder whether several, originally different deities have not here coalesced in one, the many faceted goddess Inanna." For a historical reconstruction of the fusion of Inanna and Ishtar see Heimpel, "A Catalog of Near Eastern Venus Deities."

12. As Jacobsen concludes his discussion of the goddess (in *The Treasures of Darkness*, 143). So, too, Kramer (in *From the Poetry of Sumer*, 96) misses the menacing complexity of the goddess when he says that "Inanna

is the very epitome of the liberated woman, the ideal divine patroness for the current women's lib movement. Bright, brave and desirable, nonetheless she allowed no one, neither man nor god, to stand in her way."

13. The study of her myths is still in its infancy. But see Kirk, *Myth*, 103–105, 108–115. For an analysis by one of the few scholars in the field with interest in and knowledge of the study of mythology see Alster, "On the Interpretation of the Sumerian Myth 'Inanna and Enki.'" For valid criticism of historical interpretations of her myths see Cooper, *The Curse of Agade*, 9–10. For folkloristic methodology being applied to Inanna's myths see Fontaine, "The Deceptive Goddess in Ancient Near Eastern Myth." For surveys of the goddess's myths see Kramer, *The Sumerians*, 153–163; and Edzard, "Mesopotamien."

14. ANET 94 xi:116. This is not to say that Inanna-Ishtar is a mother goddess. She is not. Although the mother of sons (see Wilcke, "Inanna-Ishtar," 80), her maternity is of no consequence in her myths.

15. ANET 84 vi:1–79. For another interpretation of the encounter of Ishtar and Gilgamesh, see Abusch, "Ishtar's Proposal and Gilgamesh's Refusal." It is important to note that the mother-goddess, Mami, of the earlier flood story in the Old Babylonian *Atrahasis* was replaced by Ishtar. See Tigay, *The Evolution of the Gilgamesh Epic*, 224–225. Kramer (in *From the Poetry of Sumer*, 74) comments on the positive relationship between Gilgamesh and Inanna in the Sumerian Gilgamesh episodes in contrast to the Akkadian epic.

16. Kramer, "BM 23631: Bread for Enlil, Sex for Inanna Tab. II–IV," especially 127, lines 138–139.

17. Turner, *The Ritual Process*, 95.

18. Hallo and van Dijk, *The Exaltation of Inanna*, 19 v:40; 15 ii:9.

19. See the moving laments of the bereaved young widow Inanna after the death of her husband, Dumuzi, in Jacobsen, *The Treasures of Darkness*, 49–52. And yet the goddess is responsible for his seizure in her stead by the demons of the netherworld in the Sumerian myth "Inanna's Descent to the Netherworld."

20. Sjöberg, "*in-nin šà-gur₄-ra*: A Hymn to the Goddess Inanna," 189–195.

21. Alster, "An Aspect of 'Enmerkar and the Lord of Aratta,'" 108.

22. Reiner and Güterbock, "The Great Prayer to Ishtar and Its Two Versions from Boğazköy," 259.

23. Güterbock, "A Hurro-Hittite Hymn to Ishtar," 157–158. Though other gods also act in cruel and unpredictable fashion, none seems to do so as characteristically as this goddess.

24. Stewart, *Nonsense*, 61.

25. Kramer, "BM 29616: The Fashioning of the *gala*." This is an instance, then, of music as therapy as it is in an episode of the biblical David and Saul story (1 Samuel 16:23). Gelb (in "Homo Ludens in Early Mesopotamia," 73) comments, "It also seems quite clear that the *gala*, while men, had certain feminine characteristics which connect them with women." This is especially interesting in light of the sexual ambiguity of the goddess's cultic personnel.

26. For an excellent treatment of this myth and references to studies of the text see Foster, "Ea and Ṣaltu."

27. I don't think there are any grounds for assuming that the Mesopotamians had a view of two kinds of strife, as one finds, for example, among the Greeks. See Vernant, *Myth and Thought among the Greeks*, 40–41. So, too, in the Middle Ages there was a good Venus and a bad Venus. Economou, "The Two Venuses and Courtly Love."

28. ANET 56:219. These creatures, like Inanna-Ishtar, are liminal, being neither male nor female. In the Akkadian *Descent of Ishtar*, Ea creates an *assinnu*, who is a cultic member of the goddess's temple.

29. Foster, "Ea and Ṣaltu," 84. For mention of Inanna's "untamable anger" see Hallo and van Dijk, *The Exaltation of Inanna*, 52. See ibid., 19:38–39 for the passage, "Who can temper your raging heart. Your malevolent heart is beyond tempering."

30. The Akkadian word for this whirling dance is *guštu*, a pun on Ishtar's name, Gušea. In this hymn Ishtar is described as "dancing the whirl as a man does."

31. Hallo and van Dijk, *The Exaltation of Inanna*, 48.

32. See ibid., 49–50. Hallo and van Dijk translate the *me*s as "divine attributes." For a full analysis of the *me*s see G. Farber-Flügge, *Der Mythos "Inanna und Enki*," 116–164. I find that the translation by Alster, "the cultural norms," is the most fitting. See his "On the Interpretation of the Sumerian Myth 'Inanna and Enki,'" especially 21.

33. Wolkstein and Kramer, *Inanna, Queen of Heaven and Earth*, 15–18. For the Sumerian and somewhat different translation (in German), see Farber-Flügge, *Der Mythos "Inanna und Enki*," 56–59.

34. Zeitlin, "Playing the Other," 79. I find that Dionysus in the deepest sense approaches the very special and elusive quality of Inanna-Ishtar, far more than does any goddess in any other tradition.

35. Heimpel (in "A Catalog of Near Eastern Venus Deities") disagrees with the view that a case can be made for Inanna-Ishtar's androgyny. But see the thorough and excellent article by Groneberg, "Die sumerisch-

akkadische Inanna/Ištar," in which she criticizes Heimpel's view (pp. 30–33). She concludes that in Mesopotamia, Ishtar's bisexuality was viewed in mythological terms rather than as a reality. Groneberg finds the male warlike aspects of the goddess attested to between ca. 2500 and ca. 700 B.C.E. Iconographically, Inanna-Ishtar is frequently represented as a woman-in-arms. On her iconography (with bibliography) see Seidel, "Inanna-Ishtar." Ochshorn (in "Ishtar and Her Cult," 20) errs when she speaks of "the startlingly androgynous vision of ancient near Eastern polytheism." Apart from Inanna-Ishtar (and Hurrian Ishtar-Shawushka), the gender boundaries are strictly adhered to in Mesopotamia. So, too, is she mistaken when she suggests that "victory in war was not viewed as an essentially feminine or masculine trait" (ibid., 20). War was a masculine occupation and preoccupation. Although Mesopotamian society was not the sexually dimorphic society of classical Athens, the public sphere, with the exception of very limited functions, was closed to women. For this see Winter, "Women in Public." It is noteworthy that Fontaine (in "The Deceptive Goddess in Ancient Near Eastern Myth," 91), applying folkloristic methodology to the Sumerian myths of Inanna, comments that "Inanna fills with ease the typical action roles ascribed to male characters in traditional compositions. . . . *At the same time, Inanna resists total 'masculinization' and retains her feminine nature* [my emphasis]." In short, the goddess is both masculine and feminine.

36. CAD M/2 306 s.v. *muttallu*, lexical section.

37. Reisman, *Two Neo-Sumerian Royal Hymns*, 167:18, 24.

38. Cohen, "The Incantation-Hymn," 606:14–22.

39. The father of the children is not Dumuzi, and her sons play no role in her mythology or worship.

40. The analogical link between love and war is not uncommon in ancient Near Eastern texts. For "the military structures set forth in relation to the woman" see Meyers, "Gender Imagery in the Song of Songs," 221. Of interest is the comment by Eichler (in "Of Slings, Shields, Throw Sticks, and Javelins," 99 n. 1) on the passage in the exordium of Inanna and Ebih, describing Inanna as "the one who darts forth in the great battles pressing the siege shield upon the ground." The Sumerian term for "darting forth" occurs elsewhere in association with prostitution.

41. Just as "to go to war is a festival for young men": see CAD I/J 197 s.v. *isinnu*.

42. Sjöberg and Bergmann, *The Collection of Sumerian Temple Hymns*, 47 no. 40:515.

43. Cooper, *The Curse of Agade*, 251:188–189.

44. See CAD K 406 for *kirimmu* "as a characteristic and functional position of a mother's arm assumed in order to hold a child safely."

45. ANET 451. The maternal love and concern of Ishtar of Arbela for Esarhaddon and his son Ashurbanipal are especially prominent in the messages sent by the goddess to these rulers via a "prophet" who might be either male or female. On these, see ANET 449–451.

46. Groneberg, "Die sumerisch-akkadische Inanna/Ištar," 42–43.

47. Sjöberg, "*in-nin šà-gur₄-ra:* A Hymn to the Goddess Inanna," 225. Sjöberg gives references and discusses the meaning of the transformation implied here. In his opinion, the passage does not suggest "a changing of sexes when referring to the Inanna-Ishtar cult. The passages refer only to the changing roles of women and men in the cult ceremonies." In the reference (p. 225) to Ishtar changing Esarhaddon's enemy from a man into a woman, in my view, the hope is that the enemy will become powerless like a woman. Note the association in Mesopotamia, as elsewhere, of the left side with the female and the right side with the male. On the "pure right" hand and the "impure left" hand see Civil, "Enlil and Ninlil," especially 46–47.

48. Cagni, *The Poem of Erra,* 52: "*ana šupluḫ niši.*" The well-attested sexuality and femininity of Inanna-Ishtar, and her powers of fertility for humans and animals as well as the land, are vividly depicted in the rich poetry of the sacred marriage rites. See Kramer, *The Sacred Marriage Rite.* What I want to emphasize here is the paradoxical juxtaposition of her manliness/maleness alongside her femininity/femaleness, the bipolarity that is the special character of the goddess.

49. See the very relevant observation by Macdonald (in "Drawing the Line—Gender, Peace, and War," 6): "Where war is defined as a male activity and where highly valued masculine characteristics are often associated with war, a female warrior must be seen as inherently unsettling to the social order." War, contra Ochshorn (in "Ishtar and Her Cult), is a masculine activity in Mesopotamia. See the provocative but problematic comments of Foster (in "Women in Sargonic Texts," 55–56), where he speaks of "the feminine aspect of war." Crucial is the very significant role that Ishtar plays in the Akkad dynasty, a period of transition and ideological transformations in Mesopotamian society.

50. Hallo and Simpson, *The Ancient Near East,* 54. Hallo and van Dijk (in *The Exaltation of Inanna,* 6–7) suggest that the linking of Ishtar with the Sumerian Inanna that persists in all the traditions about Sargon may reflect his association (perhaps sexual) with a priestess of the goddess.

51. Foster, "Women in Sargonic Texts," 55–56. On the much later analogy between war and childbirth see Huston, "The Matrix of War."

52. Tigay, *The Evolution of the Gilgamesh Epic*, 135.
53. Jacobsen, *The Treasures of Darkness*, 140. See below Jacobsen's new interpretation of the Burney Relief as an Ishtar icon that may have been on display in a brothel.
54. Lambert, *Babylonian Wisdom Literature*, 218:7. This proverb is immediately preceded by proverbs concerning prostitutes, male and female: the goddess's devotees.
55. For a stimulating discussion of the space/time structure of Gilgamesh's speech see Abusch, "Ishtar's Proposal and Gilgamesh's Refusal," 165–173.
56. See Seidel, "Inanna-Ishtar," 88. See also Fauth, "Ištar als Löwengöttin."
57. CAD L 23 s.v. *labbatu*.
58. Jacobsen, "Pictures and Pictorial Language (The Burney Relief)." For the earlier interpretation, see Frankfort, *The Art and Architecture of the Ancient Orient*, 110–112.
59. It is not my intention to give here the details of these festivals but, rather, to provide a framework for the understanding the dynamics of the festivals, which in turn shed light on the distinctive nature of the goddess. To date, no theologico-historical study of these festivals has been made.
60. I am most grateful to Anne Kilmer for very generously putting her important manuscript "An Oration on Babylon" at my disposal. It is now published; see bibliography.
61. Caillois, *Man, Play, and Games*, 36.
62. For references to play in relationship to Inanna-Ishtar see CAD M/2 16 s.v. *mēlulu*. On the symbolic association of war and sports (games) see Blanchard and Cheska, *The Anthropology of Sport*, 57–58.
63. CAD M/2 196.
64. See CAD M/2 15b and lexical section s.v. *mēlultu*.
65. On the history of theories of play see Stewart, *Nonsense*, 44 n. 91. See also Handelman's excellent article, "Play."
66. Ibid., 366.
67. Eco, "The Frames of Comic Freedom," 6.
68. Goldwasser, "Carnival."
69. For a discussion of the terminology for abusive language see Farber-Flügge, *Der Mythos "Inanna und Enki,"* 108f.
70. Lambert, "The Problem of the Love Lyrics," 99.
71. Legman, *Rationale of the Dirty Joke*, 14. Kilmer also notes that sounds such as "chirping" and "twittering" were made by the goddess's personnel, which also suggests a departure from conventional patterns of speech.

There may well have been one or more sacred clowns in her personnel, but to date no firm data on such a person or persons have been found.

72. Ellis (in "Lion-Men in Assyria," 75) tentatively suggests a link between the lion men on cylinder seals and the Ishtar cult.

73. See note 30 above.

74. Babcock, *The Reversible World*, 32.

75. See Wilcke, "Inanna-Ishtar," 85–86; and the excellent discussion with references by Groneberg, "Die sumerisch-akkadische Inanna/Ištar," 33–39.

76. CAD A/2 341–342 s.v. *assinnu*.

77. CD K 558–559 s.v. *kurgarrû*. This brings to mind the *bissu* priests of Java, who "possess both male and female attributes. . . . At annual dances . . . the *bissu* become possessed, enter a trance and plunge daggers into their larynxes." See Peacock, "Symbolic Reversal and Social History," 209–210.

78. Groneberg, "Die sumerisch-akkadische Inanna/Ištar," 39.

79. Reisman, "Iddin-Dagan's Sacred Marriage Hymn," 187:45–64. For a different translation see Jacobsen, *The Harps*, 115–117. He translates *sag-ursag* as "guardsmen" rather than "male prostitutes" and suggests (p. 115 n. 8) that they were "a class of cult personnel in the service of Inanna. Originally apparently a corps of warriors, they developed into actors in ritual performance." The text suggests that the *sag-ursag* wore partly male and partly female clothing. Jacobsen understands the clothing passage differently (p. 116 n. 10). But he too interprets it as signifying "a reversal of normal usage." Sjöberg (in "A Hymn to Inanna and Her Self-Praise," 177f.) also opts for the warrior status of the *sag-ursag*, who is equated with the *assinnu*. This points up how much remains to be known about the goddess's personnel.

80. Eliade, *The Two and the One*, 113.

81. Cagni, *The Poem of Erra*, 52. He states (in ibid., 53 n. 133) that "in other contexts (where the Akkadian idiom *akālu asakka* 'eat a taboo item' is used) all refer to non-authorized people." Only in the case of Ishtar's devotees is the breaking of taboos permitted and even welcomed.

82. ANET 383. Yamuchi (in "The Descent of Ishtar," especially 145–150) critically discusses and disputes the view that traces the powerful Gnostic text *The Thunder, Perfect Mind*, ed. Robinson, in which "a female revealer, probably Sophia, expresses herself in all kinds of paradoxes and contradictions" (pp. 103f.) back to Mesopotamian origins, specifically, the Akkadian *Descent of Ishtar*.

83. Geertz, "Religion as a Cultural System," 173.

BIBLIOGRAPHY

Abusch, T. I. *Babylonian Witchcraft Literature: Case Studies*. Atlanta: Scholars Press, 1987.

———. "The Demonic Image of the Witch in Standard Babylonian Literature." *Religion, Science, and Magic: In Concert and in Conflict*. Ed. J. Neusner. New York: Oxford University Press, 1989. 27–58.

———. "Gilgamesh's Request and Siduri's Denial." *The Tablet and the Scroll*. 1–14.

———. "Ishtar's Proposal and Gilgamesh's Refusal: An Interpretation of the Gilgamesh Epic, Tablet 6, Lines 1–79." *History of Religions* 26 (1986): 143–187.

———. "*Maqlu*." RLA 7 (1987–1900): 346–351.

Achte, K., et al. "Themes of Death and Violence in Lullabies of Different Countries." *Omega* 20 (1989–1990): 193–204.

Albenda, P. "Woman, Child, and Family: Their Imagery in Assyrian Art." *La Femme*. 17–21.

Aldred, C. *Egyptian Art in the Days of the Pharaohs, 3100–320 B.C.* London: Thames Hudson, 1980.

———. "Some Royal Portraits of the Middle Kindgom in Ancient Egypt." *Ancient Egypt in the Metropolitan Museum Journal* vols. 1–11 (1968–1976): 1–24.

Alster, B. "An Aspect of 'Enmerkar and the Lord of Arrata.'" RA 67 (1973): 101–109.

———. *The Instructions of Suruppak: A Sumerian Proverb Collection*. Mesopotamia 2. Copenhagen: Akademisk Forlag, 1974.

―――. "Interaction of Oral and Written Poetry in Early Mesopotamian Literature." *Mesopotamian Epic Literature: Oral or Aural.* Ed. M. E. Vogelzang and H.L.J. Vanstiphout. Lewiston: Edwin Mellon, 1992. 23–70.

―――. "Marriage and Love in the Sumerian Love Songs." *The Tablet and the Scroll.* 15–27.

―――. "The Mythology of Mourning." *Acta Sumerologica* 5 (1983): 1–16.

―――. "On the Interpretation of the Sumerian Myth 'Inanna and Enki.'" *ZA* 4 (1975): 20–34.

―――. "The Paradigmatic Character of Mesopotamian Heroes." *RA* 68 (1974): 49–59.

―――. *Studies in Sumerian Proverbs.* Copenhagen: Akademisk Forlag, 1975.

―――, ed. *Death in Mesopotamia.* Copenhagen: Akademisk Forlag, 1980.

Alter, R. "Literary Refractions of the Jewish Family." *The Jewish Family: Metaphor and Memory.* Ed. D. Kraemer. New York: Oxford University Press, 1989. 225–234.

Amundsen, B. W., and C. J. Diers. "The Age of Menopause in Classical Greece and Rome." *Human Biology* 42 (1970): 79–86.

Andreason, N. "The Role of the Queen Mother in Israelite Society." *Catholic Biblical Quarterly* 45 (1983): 179–194.

Angel, J. L., and S. C. Bisel. "Health and Stress in Early Bronze Age Population." *Ancient Anatolia: Aspects of Change and Cultural Development: Essays in Honor of Machteld J. Mellink.* Ed. J. V. Canby et al. Madison: University of Wisconsin Press, 1986. 12–30.

Arbeli, S. "The Removal of the Tawananna from Her Position." *Society and Economy in the Eastern Mediterranean (1500–1000 B.C.).* Ed. M. Heltzer and E. Lipinski. Orientalia Lovaniensia Analecta 23. Louvain: Peeters, 1988. 79–85.

Arnett, W. S. "Growing Old in the Cradle: Old Age and Immortality among the Kings of Ancient Assyria." *International Journal of Aging and Human Development* 32:2 (1991): 135–141.

―――. "Only the Bad Died Young in the Ancient Middle East." *International Journal of Aging and Human Development* 21:2 (1985): 155–160.

Asher-Greve, J. M. *Frauen in altsumerischer Zeit.* Bibliotheca Mesopotamica 18. Malibu: Undena, 1985.

―――. "The Oldest Female Oneiromancer." *La Femme.* 27–32.

Avalos, H. *Illness and Health Care in the Ancient Near East: The Role of the Temple in Greece, Mesopotamia, and Israel.* Atlanta: Scholars Press, 1985.

Babcock, B. A., ed. *The Reversible World: Symbolic Inversion in Art and Society*. Ithaca: Cornell University Press, 1978.

Bamberger, J. "The Myth of Matriarchy: Why Men Rule in Primitive Society." *Women, Culture, and Society*. Ed. M. Z. Rosaldo and L. Lamphere. Stanford: Stanford University Press, 1974. 263–280.

Banner, L. W. *In Full Flower: Aging Women, Power, and Sexuality*. New York: Vintage, 1992.

Barnett, R. D. *The Sculpture of Aššur-naṣir-apli II, 883–859 B.C.* London: British Museum, 1962.

———. *Sculptures from the North Palace of Ashurbanipal at Nineveh, 668–627 B.C.* London: British Museum, 1976.

Barry H., III, and A. Schlegel. "Adolescent Initiation Ceremonies." *Cross-Cultural Samples and Codes*. Ed. H. Barry III and A. Schlegel. Pittsburgh: University of Pittsburgh Press, 1980. 277–288.

Batto, B. F. *Studies on Women at Mari*. Baltimore: Johns Hopkins University Press, 1974.

Bayliss, M. "Cult of the Dead in Assyria and Babylonia." *Iraq* 35 (1973): 115–126.

Beaulieu, P.-A. "New Light on Secret Knowledge in Late Babylonian Culture." *ZA* 82 (1992): 98–111.

———. *The Reign of Nabonidus, King of Babylon, 556–539 B.C.* New Haven: Yale University Press, 1989.

———. "Women in Neo-Babylonian Society." *Canadian Society for Mesopotamian Studies Bulletin* 26 (Nov. 1993): 7–14.

Beckman, G. M. *Hittite Birth Rituals*. Studien zu den Boğazköy-Texten 29. Wiesbaden: Harrassowitz, 1983.

Ben-Baraq, Z. "The Queen Consort and the Struggle for Succession to the Throne." *La Femme*. 33–40.

Bennett, J. M. *Women in the Medieval English Countryside: Gender and Household in Brigstock before the Plague*. New York: Oxford University Press, 1987.

Berlin, A., ed. *Enmerkar and Enšuḫkešdanna*. Philadelphia: The University Museum, 1979.

Bertelson, A. D. "Insomnia." *Sleep and Dreams: A Sourcebook*. Ed. J. Gackenbach. New York: Garland Press, 1986. 106–144.

Bertman, S. "The Ashes and the Flames: Passion and Aging in Classical Poetry." *Old Age in Greek and Latin Literature*. Ed. T. M. Falkner and J. de Luce. Albany: State University Press, 1989. 157–171.

Bever, E. "Old Age and Witchcraft in Early Modern Europe." *Old Age in Pre-industrial Society*. Ed. P. N. Stearns. New York: Holmes and Meier, 1982. 150–181.

Biggs, R. D. "Akkadian Oracles and Prophecies." *The Ancient Near East: Supplementary Text and Pictures Relating to the Old Testament.* Ed. J. B. Pritchard. Princeton: Princeton University Press, 1969. 604–607.

———. "The Human Body and Sexuality in Mesopotamian Medical Texts." (Forthcoming.)

———. "Liebeszauber." RLA 7 (1987): 17–18.

———. "Medicine, Surgery, and Public Health in Ancient Mesopotamia." CANE. Vol. 3, 1911–1924.

———. "Medizen A." RLA 7 (1990): 623–639.

———. *šà.zi.ga: Ancient Mesopotamian Potency Incantations.* Texts from Cuneiform Sources 2. Locust Valley, N.Y: J. J. Augustin, 1967.

Bing, J. D. "On the Sumerian Epic of Gilgamesh." JANES 7 (1975): 1–10.

Birot, M. "Textes economiques de Mari IV." RA 50 (1956): 57–72.

Black, J., and A. Green. *Gods, Demons, and Symbols of Ancient Mesopotamia: An Illustrated Dictionary.* Austin: University of Texas Press, 1992.

Blanchard, K., and A. Cheska. *The Anthropology of Sport: An Introduction.* South Hadley, Mass.: Bergin & Garvey, 1985.

Blazer, D. G. "Depression." *The Encyclopedia of Aging.* Ed. G. L. Maddox et al. New York: Springer, 1987. 169–170.

Borger, R. "Lullû in *Enuma eliš* IV 72." RA 74 (1980): 95–96.

Bottéro, J. "L'amour à Babylone." *Initiation à l'Orient ancien: De Sumer à la Bible.* Ed. J. Bottero. Série Histoire 170. Paris: Édition du Seuil, 1992. 185–198.

———. "La femme, l'amour et la guerre en Mesopotamie ancienne." *Poikilia études offertes à Jean-Pierre Vernan.* Paris: Éditions de L'école des Hautes Études, 1987. 165–183.

———. "La femme dans la Mesopotamie ancienne." *Histoire mondiale de la femme: préhistoire et antiquité.* Ed. P. Grimal. Paris: Nouvelle Librairie de France, 1965. 158–223.

———. "Intelligence and the Technical Function of Power." *Mythologies.* Comp. Y. Bonnefoy, trans. G. Honigsblum et al. Chicago: University of Chicago Press, 1991. Vol. 1, 145–155.

———. *Mesopotamia: Writing, Reasoning, and the Gods.* Trans. Z. Bahrani and M. van de Mieroop. Chicago: University of Chicago Press, 1992.

Bottéro, J., and H. Petschow. "Homosexualität." RLA 4 (1972–1975): 459–468.

Bremmer, J. N. "The Old Women of Ancient Greece." *Sexual Asymmetry: Studies in Ancient Society.* Ed. L. Blok and P. Mason. Amsterdam: J. C. Gieben, 1987. 191–215.

Breslau, L. D., and M. R. Hauge, eds. *Depression and Aging: Causes, Care, and Consequences.* New York: Springer, 1983.

Brinkman, J. A. "Forced Laborers in the Middle Babylonian Period." JCS 32 (1980): 17–22.

———. "Sex, Age, and Physical Condition Designations for Servile Laborers in the Middle Babylonian Period: A Preliminary Survey." *Zikir Šumim: Assyriological Studies Presented to F. R. Kraus.* Ed. G. van Driel et al. Leiden: E. J. Brill, 1982. 1–8.

Bryce, T. K. *Historical and Social Documents of the Hittite World.* St. Lucia: University of Queensland Press, 1982.

Buccellati, G. "Wisdom and Not: The Case of Mesopotamia." JAOS 101 (1981): 35–47.

Buckley, T., and A. Gottlieb. "A Critical Appraisal of Theories of Menstrual Symbolism." *Blood Magic: The Anthropology of Menstruation.* Ed. T. Buckley and A. Gottlieb. Berkeley: University of California, 1988. 3–50.

Bulkley, K. "The Evil Dreams of Gilgamesh: An Interdisciplinary Approach to Dreams in Mythological Texts." *The Dream and the Text: Essays on Literature and Language.* Ed. C. S. Rupprecht. Albany: State University of New York Press, 1993. 159–177.

Burrow, J. A. *The Ages of Man: A Study in Medieval Writing and Thought.* Oxford: Clarendon Press, 1986.

Butler, R. N. "Life Review: Reminiscence." *The Encyclopedia of Aging.* Ed. G. L. Maddox et al. New York: Springer, 1987. 397–398.

Cagni, L. *The Poem of Erra.* Sources from the Ancient Near East 1:3. Malibu: Undena, 1977.

Caillois, R. *Man, Play, and Games.* Trans. M. Barash. New York: Free Press, 1961.

Camp, C. V. "The Wise Women of 2 Samuel: A Role Model for Women in Early Israel." *Catholic Biblical Quarterly* 43 (1981): 14–29.

Canby, J. V. "The Child in Hittite Iconography." *Ancient Anatolia: Aspects of Change and Cultural Development, Essays in Honor of Machteld J. Mellink.* Ed. J. V. Canby et al. Madison: University of Wisconsin Press, 1986. 54–69.

Caquot, A., and M. Sznycer. *Ugaritic Religion.* Iconography of Religions 15:8. Leiden: J. E. Brill, 1980.

Carson, A. "Putting Her in Her Place: Women, Dirt, and Desire." *Before Sexuality: The Construction of Erotic Experience in the Ancient Greek World.* Ed. D. M. Halperin, J. J. Winkler, and F. I. Zeitlin. Princeton: Princeton University Press, 1990. 135–169.

Cassin, E. "The Death of the Gods." *Mortality and Immortality: The Anthropology and Archaeology of Death.* Ed. S. C. Humphreys and H. King. New York: Academic Press, 1981. 317–325.

————. "Mesopotamian Cosmogony." *Mythologies.* Comp. Y. Bonnefoy, trans. G. Honigsblum et al. Chicago: University of Chicago Press, 1991. Vol. 1, 155–162.

Castellino, G. R. *Two Šulgi Hymns.* Rome: Pontifical Institute, 1972.

Cicero, Marcus Tullius. *On Old Age. De senectute.* Trans. C. Bennett. Chicago: Bolchazy-Carducci, 1980.

Çig, M., and S. N. Kramer. "A Sumerian Portrait." *Bulletin Türk Tarih Kurumu* 40 (1976): 413–421.

Civil, M. "Enlil and Ninlil—The Marriage of Sud." *Studies in the Literature from the Ancient Near East Dedicated to S. N. Kramer.* Ed. J. M. Sasson. American Oriental Studies 65. New Haven: American Oriental Society, 1984. 43–64.

————. "The Message of Ludingira to His Mother, and a Group of Akkado-Hittite Proverbs." JNES 23 (1964): 1–11.

————. "On Mesopotamian Jails and Their Lady Warden." *The Tablet and the Scroll.* 72–78.

Clark, G. *Women in Late Antiquity: Pagan and Christian Life-Styles.* Oxford: Clarendon Press, 1994.

Cohen, M. E. *Canonical Lamentations of Ancient Mesopotamia.* Potomac, Md.: Capital Decisions, 1988.

————. "The Incantation-Hymn: Incantation or Hymn?" JAOS 95 (1975): 592–611.

Collon, D. "Clothing and Grooming in Ancient Western Asia." CANE. Vol. 1, 503–515.

Cool, L., and J. McCabe. "The 'Scheming Hag' and the 'Dear Old Thing': The Anthropology of Aging Women." *Growing Old in Different Societies.* Ed. J. Sokolovsky. Belmont, Calif.: Wadsworth, 1983. 56–68.

Cooper, J. S. *The Curse of Agade.* Baltimore: Johns Hopkins University Press, 1983.

————. "Enki's Member: Eros and Irrigation in Sumerian Literature." *Dumu-e₂-dub-ba-a.* 87–89.

————. "The Fate of Mankind: Death and Afterlife in Ancient Mesopotamia." *Death and Afterlife: Perspectives of World Religions.* Ed. H. Obayashi. New York: Greenwood Press, 1992. 19–33.

————. "Gilgamesh Dreams of Enkidu: The Evolution and Dilution of Narrative." *Essays on the Ancient Near East in Memory of Jacob Joel Finkelstein.* Ed. M. de Jong Ellis. Hamden, Conn.: Archon Books, 1982. 39–44.

————. "Kuss." RLA 6 (1983): 375–379.

————. *The Return of Ninurta to Nippur: An-gim dim-ma.* Analecta Orientalia 52. Rome: Pontifical Biblical Institute, 1978.

———. "Review of *Enlil and Ninlil*, by H. Behrens." In *JCS* 32:3 (1980): 175–188.

Covey, H. C. "The Definitions of the Beginning of Old Age in History." *The International Journal of Aging and Human Development* 34 (1992): 324–337.

———. *Images of Older People in Western Art and Society*. New York: Praeger, 1991.

———. "Perceptions and Attitudes toward Sexuality of the Elderly during the Middle Ages." *The Gerontologist* 29 (1989): 93–100.

Crane, S. *Sexuality and Gender in Early Modern Europe: Institutions, Texts, Images*. New York: Cambridge University Press, 1993.

Crenshaw, J. L., ed. "Prolegomenon." *Studies in Ancient Israelite Wisdom*. New York: Ktav, 1976.

———. "Youth and Old Age in Qoheleth." *Hebrew Annual Review* 10 (1986): 1–13.

Curchin, L. "Old Age in Sumer: Life Expectancy and Social Status of the Elderly." *Florilegium* [Carleton University Papers on Classical Antiquity] 2 (1980): 61–70.

Dalley, S. "The Gilgamesh Epic and Manichaean Themes." *Aram* 3 (1991): 23–33.

———. *Mari and Karana: Two Old Babylonian Cities*. London: Longman, 1984.

———. *Myths from Mesopotamia: Creation, the Flood, Gilgamesh, and Others*. New York: Oxford University Press, 1991.

Dalley, S. and J. N. Postgate. *The Tablets from Fort Shalmanesser*. London: British School of Archaeology in Iraq, 1984.

Dandamaev, M. A. "About Life Expectancy in Babylonia." *Death in Mesopotamia*. Ed. B. Alster. Copenhagen: Akademisk Forlag, 1980. 183–186.

———. *Slavery in Babylonia from Nabopolassar to Alexander the Great*. Ed. M. A. Powell and D. B. Weisberg, trans. V. A. Powell. Dekalb: Northern Illinois University Press, 1984.

———. *Vavilouskie Pisci* (English summary). Moscow: Nauka, 1983.

Darnton, R. "Cherchez la Femme." *The New York Review of Books* 42:13 (Aug. 10, 1995): 22–24.

David, M. "Adoption." RLA 1 (1932): 37–39.

———. *Die Adoption im altbabylonischen Recht*. Leipzig: T. Weicher, 1927.

Davies, E. N. "Youth and Old Age in the Thera Frescoes." *American Journal of Archaeology* 90 (1986): 399–406.

Davis, N. Z. *Society and Culture in Early Modern France*. Stanford: Stanford University Press, 1975.

Deimel, A. *Sumerische Tempelwirtschaft zur Zeit Urukaginas und seiner Vorganger*. Analecta Orientalia 2. Roma: Pontificio Instituto Biblico, 1931.

Denning-Bolle, S. *Wisdom in Akkadian Literature: Expression, Instruction, Dialogue*. Leiden: Ex Oriente Lux, 1992.

Detienne, M., and Vernant, J.-P. *Cunning Intelligence in Greek Culture and Society*. Atlantic Highland, N.J.: Humanities Press, 1978.

Diakonoff, I. M. "Extended Familics in Old Babylonian Ur." ZA 75 (1985): 47–65.

———. "Review of *Het Gilgamesj Epos*, by F.M.T. Bohl, and *Epos o Gilgamešovi*, by L. Matous." *Bibliotheca Orientalis* 18 (1961): 61–67.

———. "Slaves, Helots, and Serfs in Early Antiquity." *Acta Antiqua* 22 (1974): 45–78.

Donaldson, I. *The World Upside-Down: Comedy from Jonson to Fielding*. New York: Oxford University Press, 1970.

Donbaz, V., and N. Yoffee. *Old Babylonian Texts from Kish Conserved in the Istanbul Archaeological Museum*. Bibliotheca Mesopotamica 17. Malibu: Undena, 1986.

Dossin, G. *Archives royales de Mari*. Vol. 1. Paris: P. Geuthner, 1946.

Dover, K. *Greek Homosexuality*. New York: Vintage, 1978.

Drolet, J.-L. "Transcending Death during Early Adulthood: Symbolic Immortality, Death, Anxiety, and Purpose in Life." *Journal of Clinical Psychology* 46 (March 1990): 148–160.

Duncan-Jones, R. *Structure and Scale in the Roman Economy*. New York: Cambridge University Press, 1990.

Durand, J.-M. "Les dames du palais de Mari à l'epoque du royaume et de haute-Mesopotomie." *Mari—Annales de Recherches Interdisciplinaires* 4 (1985): 385–436.

———. "Trois études sur Mari." *Mari—Annales de Recherches Interdisciplinaires* 3 (1984): 127–179.

———, ed. *La femme dans le Proche-Orient antique*. Compte rendu de la 33e Rencontre Assyriologique Internationale. Paris: Éditions Recherche sur les Civilisations, 1987.

Eck, D. L. "Circumambulation." *Encyclopedia of Religion*. Ed. M. Eliade. New York: Macmillan, 1987. Vol. 3, 509–511.

Eco, U. "The Frames of Comic Freedom." *Carnival!* ed. T. A. Sebeok. Approaches to Semiotics 64. New York: Mouton, 1984. 1–9.

Economou, G. D. "The Two Venuses and Courtly Love." *In Pursuit of Perfection: Courtly Love in Medieval Literature*. Eds. J. M. Ferrante and G. D. Economou. Port Washington, N.Y.: Kennikat, 1975. 17–50.

Edzard, D. O. "Kleine Beiträge zum Gilgameš-Epos." *Orientalia* 54 (1985): 46–55.

———. "Ku(g)-Baba. " RLA 6 (1980–1983): 299.

Eichler, B. "Of Slings, Shields, Throw Sticks, and Javelins." *Studies in Literature from the Ancient Near East Dedicated to Samuel Noah Kramer.* Ed. J. M. Sasson. American Oriental Series 65. New Haven: American Oriental Society, 1984. 95–102.

Eliade, M. *Rites and Symbols of Initiation: The Mysteries of Birth and Rebirth.* Trans. W. R. Trask. New York: Harper and Row, 1965.

———. *The Two and the One.* Trans. J. M. Cohen. Chicago: University of Chicago Press, 1979.

———, ed. *Encyclopedia of Religion.* New York: Macmillan, 1987.

Ellis, R. S. *Foundation Deposits in Ancient Mesopotamia.* New Haven: Yale University Press, 1968.

———. "Lion-Men in Assyria." *Essays on the Ancient Near East in Memory of Jacob Joel Finkelstein.* Ed. M. de J. Ellis. Hamden, Conn.: Archon Books, 1977. 67–76.

Encyclopedia Americana. Danbury, Conn.: Grolier, 1992. S.v. "Perseus."

Esler, C. C. "Horace's Old Girls: Evolution of a Topos." *Old Age in Greek and Latin Literature.* Ed. T. H. Falkner and J. de Luce. Albany: State University of New York Press, 1989. 172–182.

Evans, G. "Ancient Mesopotamian Assemblies." JAOS 79 (1958): 1–11.

Eyben, E. *Restless Youth in Ancient Rome.* New York: Routledge, 1993.

———. "Roman Notes on the Course of Life." *Ancient Society* 4 (1973): 213–238.

Falkenstein, A. "Gilgameš." RLA 3 (1968): 357–363.

Falkner, T. M. "The Politics and the Poetics of Time in Solon's 'Ten Ages.'" *Classical Journal* 86 (1990): 1–15.

———. "The Wrath of Alcemene: Gender, Authority, and Old Age in Euripedes' *Children of Heracles.*" *Old Age in Greek and Roman Literature.* Ed. T. M. Falkner and J. de Luce. Albany: State University of New York Press, 1989. 114–131.

Falkner, T. M., and J. de Luce. "A View from Antiquity: Greece, Rome, and Elders." *Handbook of the Humanities and Aging.* Ed. T. Cole et al. New York: Springer, 1992. 3–39.

Faragher, J. "Old Women and Old Men in Seventeenth Century Wetherford, Connecticut." *Women's Studies* 4 (1976): 11–31.

Farber, G. "Another Old Babylonian Childbirth Incantation." JNES 43 (1984): 311–316.

Farber, W. "Forerunners and 'Standard Versions': A Few Thoughts about Terminology." *The Tablet and the Scroll.* 95–97.

———. "Lamaštu." RLA 6:5–6 (1983): 439–446.

———. "*lilû, lilîtu, ardat lilî.*" RLA 7:1–2 (1987): 23–24.

————. "Magic at the Cradle: Babylonian and Assyrian Lullabies."
    Anthropos 8 (1990): 139–148.

————. *Schlaf, Kindchen, Schlaf! Mesopotamische Baby-Beschworungen und-*
    Rituale. Winona, Ill.: Eisenbrauns, 1989.

Farber-Flügge, G. *Der Mythos "Inanna und Enki" unter besonderer Berück-*
    sichtigung der Liste der me. Studia Pohl 10. Rome: Biblical Institute Press,
    1973.

Fauth, V. W. "Ištar als Löwengöttin und die löwen köpfige Lamaštu." *Welt*
    des Orients 12 (1981): 21–36.

Fensham, F. C. "Widow, Orphan, and the Poor in Ancient Near Eastern
    Legal and Wisdom Literature." JNES 21 (1962): 129–139.

Feuer, L. S. "Generational Struggle in Plato and Aristotle." *The Conflict of*
    Generations in Ancient Greece and Rome. Ed. S. Bertman. Amsterdam:
    Gruner, 1976. 123–127.

Finet, A. "Le ṣuḫārum à Mari." *Bayerische Akademie der Wissenschaften* 75
    (1972): 65–72.

Finkelstein, J. J. "Documents from the Practice of Law." *The Ancient*
    Near East: Supplementary Texts and Pictures Relating to the Old Testa-
    ment. Ed. J. B. Pritchard. Princeton: Princeton University Press, 1969.
    542–547.

————. *"Late Old Babylonian Documents and Letters.* Yale Oriental Studies
    13. New Haven: Yale University Press, 1972.

Finley, M. I. "The Elderly in Classical Antiquity." *Old Age in Greek and Latin*
    Literature. Ed. T. M. Falkner and J. de Luce. Albany: State University of
    New York Press, 1989. 1–20.

Fischer, H. G. "Some Early Monuments from Busiris in the Egyptian
    Delta." *Ancient Egypt in the Metropolitan Museum Journal* vols. 1–11
    (1968–1976): 157–176.

Foley, H. *The Homeric Hymn to Demeter: Translation, Commentary, and*
    Interpretive Essays. Princeton: Princeton University Press, 1994.

————. "Review of *The Glory of Hera: Greek Mythology and the Greek Family,*
    by P. Slater." *Diacritics* 5 (1975): 31–36.

Foner, A. *Aging and Old Age: New Perspectives.* Englewood Cliffs, N.J.:
    Prentice Hall, 1986.

Foner, N. *Ages in Conflict: A Cross-Cultural Perspective on Inequality between*
    Old and Young. New York: Columbia University Press, 1984.

Fontaine, C. R. "The Deceptive Goddess in Ancient Near Eastern Myth:
    Inanna and Inaras." *Reasoning with the Foxes: Female Wit in a World of*
    Male Power. Ed. J. C. Exum and J.W.H. Bos. *Semeia* 42. Atlanta: Scholars
    Press, 1988. 84–102.

————. "A Heifer from Thy Stable: On Goddesses and the Status of Women in the Ancient Near East." *Union Theological Seminary Quarterly Review* 43 (1989): 67–91.

Foster, B. R. *Before the Muses: An Anthology of Akkadian Literature.* Vol. 1: Archaic, Classical Mature. Vol. 2: Mature, Late. Bethesda, Md.: CDL Press, 1993.

————. "Ea and Ṣaltu." *Essays on the Ancient Near East in Memory of Jacob Joel Finkelstein.* Ed. M. de J. Ellis. Hamden, Conn.: Archon Books, 1977. 79–84.

————. "Gilgamesh: Sex, Love, and the Ascent of Knowledge." *Love and Death in the Ancient Near East: Essays in Honor of Marvin H. Pope.* Ed. J. H. Marks and R. M. Good. Guilford, Conn.: Four Quarters, 1987. 21–42.

————. "Humor and Cuneiform Literature." *JANES* 6 (1974): 69–85.

————. "Letters and Literature: A Ghost's Entreaty." *The Tablet and the Scroll.* 98–102.

————. "On Authorship in Akkadian Literature." *Annuario del Instituto Orientali di Napoli* 51:1 (1991): 17–32.

————. "Review of *Das Gilgamesch-Epos,* ed. K. Oberhuber." *Bibliotheca Orientalis* 36 (May/July 1979): 185-188.

————. *Umma in the Sargonic Period.* Hamden, Conn.: Archon Books, 1982.

————. "Wisdom and the Gods in Ancient Mesopotamia." *Orientalia* 43 (1974): 344–354.

————. "Women in Sargonic Texts." *La Femme.* 53–61.

Fox, M. V. *The Song of Songs and the Ancient Egyptian Love Songs.* Madison: University of Wisconsin Press, 1985.

Frankena, R., ed. *Briefe aus dem Berliner Museum.* Altbabylonische Briefe 6. Leiden: E. J. Brill, 1974.

————, ed. *Briefe aus dem British Museum (LIH and CT 2–33)* Altbabylonische Briefe 2. Leiden: E. J. Brill, 1966.

Frankfort, H. *The Art and Architecture of the Ancient Orient.* Harmondsworth: Penguin, 1954.

————. *Sculpture of the Third Millennium B.C. from Tell Asmar and Khafajah.* Chicago: University of Chicago Press, 1939.

Frayne, D. R. *Old Babylonian Period (2003–1595 B.C.).* Royal Inscriptions of Mesopotamia 4. Toronto: University of Toronto Press, 1990.

Friedrich, P. *The Meaning of Aphrodite.* Chicago: University of Chicago Press, 1978.

Frymer-Kensky, T. "The Ideology of Gender in the Bible and the Ancient Near East." *Dumu-e₂-dub-ba-a.* 185–191.

————. *In the Wake of the Goddesses: Women, Culture, and the Biblical Transformation of Pagan Myth*. New York: Free Press, 1992.

Gaffney, P. "The Ages of Man in Old French Verse, Epic and Romance." *Modern Library Review* 85 (1990): 570–582.

Garber, M. B. *Coming of Age in Shakespeare*. New York: Methuen, 1981.

Gardner, J. "Aristophanes and Male Anxiety: The Defense of the *Oikos*." *Greece and Rome* 36 (1989): 31–62.

Gardner, J., and J. Maier. *Gilgamesh, Translated from the Sîn-leqi-unninnī Version*. NewYork: Knopf, 1984.

Garland, R. *The Greek Way of Life: From Conception to Old Age*. Ithaca: Cornell University Press, 1990.

Geertz, C. "Religion as a Cultural System." *Reader in Comparative Religion: An Anthropological Approach*. Ed. W. A. Lessa and E. Z. Vogt. 3rd ed. New York: Harper and Row, 1972. 167–178.

Gelb, I. J. "The Ancient Mesopotamian Ration System." JNES 24 (1965): 230–243.

————. "The Arua Institution." RA 66:1 (1972): 1–32.

————. "Homo Ludens in Early Mesopotamia." *Studia Orientalia* 46 (1975): 43–76.

————. "Household and Family in Early Mesopotamia." *State and Temple Economy in the Ancient Near East*. Ed. E. Lipinski. Orientalia Lovaniensia Analecta 5. Louvain: Department Orientalistiek, 1979. 1–97.

————. "Prisoners of War in Early Mesopotamia." JNES 32 (1973): 70–98.

Gilbert, C. "When Did Renaissance Man Grow Old?" *Studies in the Renaissance* 14 (1967): 7–32.

Glassner, J. J. "De Sumer à Babylone: Famille pour gérer, famille pour règner," *Histoire de la famille*. Ed. A. Burguierre et al. Paris: A. Colin, 1986. Vol. 1, 99–133.

————. "Women, Hospitality, and the Honor of the Family." *Women's Earliest Records*. 71–90.

Gold, P. S. *The Lady and the Virgin: Image, Attitude, and Experience in Twelfth Century France*. Chicago: University of Chicago Press, 1985.

Golden, M. *Children and Childhood in Classical Athens*. Baltimore: Johns Hopkins University Press, 1990.

————. "*Pais*, 'Child' and 'Slave.'" *L'Antiquité Classique* 54 (1985): 91–104.

Goldwasser, M. J. "Carnival." *Encyclopedia of Religion*. Ed. M. Eliade. New York: Macmillan, 1987. Vol. 3, 98–104.

Gordon, E. I. *Sumerian Proverbs: Glimpses of Everyday Life in Ancient Mesopotamia*. Philadelphia: University of Pennsylvania Press, 1959.

Gottwald, N. K. *The Tribes of Yahweh: A Sociology of the Religion of Liberated Israel, 1250–1050 B.C.E.* Maryknoll, N.Y.: Orbis, 1979.

Grayson, A. K. *Assyrian Royal Inscriptions, Part 2: From Tiglath Pileser I to Ashur-nasir-apli II.* Wiesbaden: O. Harrassowitz, 1976.

Green, L. "More Than a Fashion Statement: Clothing and Hairstyles as Indicators of Social Status in Ancient Egypt." *Canadian Society for Mesopotamian Studies Bulletin* 26 (Nov. 1993): 29–38.

Green, M. W. *Eridu in Sumerian Literature.* Ph.D. diss. University of Chicago, 1975.

Greenfield, J. "Adi Balṭu—Care for the Elderly and Its Rewards." *Archiv für Orientforschung* Beiheft 19 (1982): 309–316.

———. "Some Neo-Babylonian Women." *La Femme.* 75–80.

Greengus, S. "Bridewealth in Sumerian Sources." *Hebrew Union College Annual* 71 (1990): 25–88.

———. "Old Babylonian Marriage Ceremonies and Rites." JCS 20 (1966): 5–72.

———. *Old Babylonian Tablets from Ishchali and Vicinity.* Leiden: Nederlands Instituut, 1979.

Groneberg, B. "Die sumerisch-akkadische Inanna/Ištar: Hermaphroditos?" *Welt des Orients* 17 (1986): 25–46.

Grove, P. B., ed. *Webster's 3rd New International Dictionary.* Springfield, Mass.: Merriam-Webster, 1993. S.v. "father" and "mother."

Gruber, M. I. *Aspects of Nonverbal Communication in the Ancient Near East.* Studia Pohl 12. Rome: Biblical Institute Press, 1980. 2 vols.

———. "Breast-Feeding Practices in Biblical Israel and in Old Babylonian Mesopotamia." JANES 19 (1989): 61–83.

Guinan, A. K. "De Houding Ten Aanzien van Sexualiteit in Mesopotamie: Akkadische Gedragsomina." *Phoenix* 25:2 (1979): 68–81.

Gurney, A. R. and P. Hulin. *The Sultantepe Tablets.* Vol. 2. London: The British Museum of Archaeology at Ankara, 1964.

Güterbock, H. G. "A Hurro-Hittite Hymn to Ishtar." *Studies in Literature of the Ancient Near East Dedicated to Samuel Noah Kramer.* Ed. J. M. Sasson. American Oriental Series 65. New Haven: American Oriental Society, 1984. 155–164.

Gutmann, D. *Reclaimed Powers: Toward a New Psychology of Men and Women in Later Life.* New York: Basic Books, 1987.

Hackett, J. A. "Can a Sexist Model Liberate Us? Ancient Near Eastern 'Fertility' Goddess." *Journal of Feminist Studies in Religion* 5:1 (spring, 1989): 65–76.

Hallett, J. P. *Fathers and Daughters in Roman Society: Women and the Elite Family*. Princeton: Princeton University Press, 1984.

Hallisey, M. *Venomous Woman: Fear of the Female in Literature*. New York: Greenwood Press, 1987.

Hallo, W. W. "Individual Prayer in Sumerian: The Continuity of a Tradition." JAOS 88 (1968): 71–89.

————. "The Royal Correspondence of Larsa: III. The Princess and the Plea." *Marchands, diplomates, et empereurs: Études sur la Civilisation Mesopotamienne offertes à Paul Garelli*. Ed. D. Charpin and F. Joannès. Paris: Éditions Recherche sur les Civilisations, 1991. 377–388.

————. "Women of Sumer." *The Legacy of Sumer*. Ed. D. Schmandt-Besserat. Bibliotheca Mesopotamia 4. Malibu: Undena, 1976. 23–40.

Hallo, W. W., and W. K. Simpson. *The Ancient Near East: A History*. New York: Harcourt Brace Jovanovich, 1971.

Hallo, W. W. and J. J. van Dijk. *The Exaltation of Inanna*. New Haven: Yale University Press, 1968.

Halperin, D. M. *One Hundred Years of Homosexuality and Other Essays on Greek Love*. New York: Routledge, 1990.

Handelman, D. "Play." *Encyclopedia of Religion*. Ed. M. Eliade. New York: Macmillan, 1987. Vol. 11, 363–368.

Hansen, D. P., and G. F. Dales. "The Temple of Inanna, Queen of Heaven at Nippur." *Archaeology* 15 (1962): 75–84.

Harris, J. G. "Old Age." *The Anchor Bible Dictionary*. Ed. D. N. Freedman et al. New York: Doubleday, 1992. 10–12.

Harris, R. *Ancient Sippar: A Demographic Study of an Old Babylonian City (1894–1595 B.C.)*. Istanbul: Nederlands Historisch Archaeologish Instituut te Istanbul, 1975.

————. "Independent Women in Ancient Mesopotamia?" *Women's Earliest Records*. 145–156.

————. "The *naditu* Woman." *Studies Presented to A. Leo Oppenheim*. Chicago: Oriental Institute of the University of Chicago, 1964. 106–135.

————. "The Organization and Administration of the Cloister in Ancient Babylonia." *Journal of the Economic and Social History of the Orient* 6 (1963): 121–157.

————. "Representations of the Elderly in Ancient Mesopotamian Literature." *Ancient Egyptian and Mediterranean Studies in Memory of William A. Ward*. Ed. L. H. Lesko. Providence: Department of Egyptology, Brown University, 1998. 121–128.

————. "Review of *The Female and the Nature of the Divine*, by J. Ochshorn." *Biblical Archaeologist* 47 (1984): 124–125.

————. "Women in the Ancient Near East." *Interpreter's Dictionary of the Bible: Supplemental Volume.* Ed. K. Crim et al. Nashville: Abingdon, 1976. 960–963.

Heimpel, W. "A Catalog of Near Eastern Venus Deities." *Syro-Mesopotamian Studies* 4 (1982): 9–22.

Held, M. "A Faithful Lover in an Old Babylonian Dialogue." JCS 15 (1961): 1–26.

Henderson, J. *The Maculate Muse: Obscene Language in Attic Comedy.* New Haven: Yale University Press, 1975.

————. "Older Women in Attic Old Comedy." *Transactions of the American Philosophical Association* 117 (1987): 105–129.

Herlihy, D. "Growing Old in the Quattrocento." *Old Age in the Pre-Industrial Society.* Ed. P. Stearns. New York: Holmes and Meier, 1982. 104–118.

————. *Medieval Households.* Cambridge: Harvard University Press, 1985.

Hock-Smith, J., and A. Spring, eds. *Women in Ritual and Symbolic Roles.* New York: Plenum, 1978. "Introduction," 1–23.

Hoffner, H. A., Jr. "The Arzana House." *Anatolian Studies Presented to Hans Gustuv Güterback.* Ed. K. Bittel et al. Istanbul: Nederlands Historisch-Archaeologisch Instituut in Het Nabije Oosten, 1974. 113–121.

————. "Hittite Terms for the Life Span." *Love and Death in the Ancient Near East: Essays in Honor of Marvin H. Pope.* Ed. J. H. Marks and R. M. Good. Guilford, Conn.: Four Quarters, 1987. 53–55.

————. "Symbols for Masculinity and Femininity: Their Use in Ancient Near Eastern Sympathetic Magic Rituals." *Journal of Biblical Literature* 85 (1966): 326–334.

Hornung, E. *Conceptions of God in Ancient Egypt: The One and the Many.* Trans. J. Baines. Ithaca: Cornell University Press, 1982.

Humphreys, S. *The Family, Women, and Death: Comparative Studies.* Boston: Routledge Kegan Paul, 1983.

Huston, M. "The Matrix of War: Mothers and Heroes." *The Female Body in Western Culture: Contemporary Perspectives.* Ed. S.R. Suleiman. Cambridge: Harvard University Press, 1986. 131–135.

Hutter, M. *Altorientalische Vorstellungen von der Unterwelt: Literar-und religionsgeschichtliche Überlegungen zu Nergal und Ereškigal.* Orbis Biblicus et Orientalis 63. Gottingen: Vandenhoeck & Ruprecht, 1985.

Jacobsen, T. "Death in Mesopotamia (Abstract)." *Death in Mesopotamia.* Ed. B. Alster. Copenhagen: Akademisk Forlag, 1980. 19–23.

————. *The Harab Myth.* Sources from the Ancient Near East 2. Malibu: Undena, 1984.

————. *The Harps That Once . . . Sumerian Poetry in Translation*. New Haven: Yale University Press, 1987.

————. "A Maidenly Inanna." JANES 22 (1993): 63–68.

————. "Mesopotamian Religion." *Encyclopedia of Religion*. Ed. M. Eliade. New York: Macmillan, 1987. Vol. 9, 447–466.

————. "Note on the Word *lú*." *kinattūtu ša dārâti Raphael Kutscher Memorial Volume*. Tel Aviv 1. Tel Aviv: Institute of Archaeology, 1993. Vol. 1, 69–79.

————. "Notes on Nintur." *Orientalia* 42 (1973): 274–298.

————. "Pictures and Pictorial Language (The Burney Relief)." *Figurative Language in the Ancient Near East*. Ed. M. Mindlin et al. London School of Oriental and African Studies, 1987. 1–11.

————. "Primitive Democracy in Ancient Mesopotamia." JNES 3 (1943): 159–172.

————. *The Sumerian King List*. Chicago: University of Chicago Press, 1939.

————. *Toward the Image of Tammuz and Other Essays on Mesopotamian History and Culture*. Ed. W. L. Moran. Cambridge: Harvard University Press, 1970.

————. *The Treasures of Darkness: A History of Mesopotamian Religion*. New Haven: Yale University Press, 1976.

————. "Two Bal-Bal-e Dialogues." *Love and Death in the Ancient Near East: Essays in Honor of Marvin H. Pope*. Ed. J. H. Marks and R. M. Good. Guilford, N.H.: Four Quarters, 1987. 57–63.

Jacobsen, T., and S. N. Kramer. "The Myth of Inanna and Bilulu." JNES 12 (1953): 160–188.

Jalland, P., and J. Hooper, eds. *Women from Birth to Death: The Female Cycle in Britain, 1830–1914*. Brighton, Sussex: Harvester, 1986.

Janssen, R. M., and J. J. Janssen. *Growing Up in Ancient Egypt*. London: Rubicon, 1990.

Jeyes, U. "The *Nadītu* Women of Sippar." *Images of Women in Antiquity*. Ed. A. Cameron and A. Kuhrt. Detroit: Wayne State University Press, 1983. 260–272.

Kahn, C. H. *The Art and Thought of Heraclitus*. New York: Cambridge University Press, 1979.

Kakar, S. *The Inner World: A Psychoanalytic Study of Childhood and Society in India*. New Delhi: Oxford University Press, 1978.

Kakrides, J. T. *Homeric Researches*. Lund: Gleerup, 1949.

Katz, D. "Gilgamesh and Akka: Was Uruk Ruled by Two Assemblies?" RA 81 (1987): 105–112.

Kienast, B. "Kinderkauf." RLA 5 (1980): 598–601.

Kilmer, A. D. "Games and Toys in Ancient Mesopotamia." *Actes du 12ᵉ Congrès International des Sciences Préhistorique et Proto-historique* 4 (1993): 359–364.

———. "The Mesopotamian Concept of Overpopulation and Its Solution as Reflected in Mythology." *Orientalia* 41 (1972): 160–177.

———. "Music and Dance in Ancient Western Asia." CANE. Vol. 4, 2601–2613.

———. "A Note on an Overlooked Word-Play in the Akkadian Gilgamesh." *Zikir Šumim: Assyriological Studies Presented to F. R. Kraus on the Occasion of his Seventieth Birthday.* Ed. G. van Driel et al. Leiden: E. J. Brill, 1982. 128–132.

———. "An Oration on Babylon." *Altorientalische Forschungen* 18 (1991): 9–22.

———. "Speculations on Umul, the First Baby." *Kramer Anniversary Volume: Cuneiform Studies in Honor of Samuel Noah Kramer.* Ed. B. L. Eichler et al. Alter Orient und Altes Testament 25. Kevelaer: Butzon and Bercker, 1976. 265–270.

Kirk, G. S. *Myth: Its Meanings and Functions in Ancient and Other Cultures.* Berkeley and Los Angeles: University of California Press, 1973.

———. "Old Age and Maturity in Ancient Greece." *Eranos Jahrbuch* 40 (1971): 123–158.

Klein, J. "The 'Bane' of Humanity: A Lifespan of One Hundred Twenty Years." *Acta Sumerologica* 12 (1990): 57–70.

Klima, J. *Untersuchungen zum altbabylonischen Erbrecht.* Prague: Oriental-isches Institut, 1940.

Kluger, R. S. *The Archetypal Significance of Gilgamesh: A Modern Ancient Hero.* Ed. H. Y. Kluger. Einseideln, Switzerland: Daimon, 1991.

Konstan, D. *Games of Venus: An Anthology of Greek and Roman Erotic Verse from Sappho to Ovid.* New York: Routledge, 1991.

Kovacs, M. G. *The Epic of Gilgamesh.* Stanford: Stanford University Press, 1989.

Kramer, S. N. "BH 23631: Bread for Enlil, Sex for Inanna Tab. II–IV." *Orientalia* 54 (1985): 117–132.

———. "BM 29616: The Fashioning of the *gala.*" *Acta Sumerologica* 3 (1981): 1–9.

———. "BM 96927: A Prime Example of Ancient Scribal Redaction." *Lingering over Words: Studies in Ancient Near Eastern Literature in Honor of William L. Moran.* Ed. T. Abusch, J. Huehnergard, and P. Steinkeller. Harvard Semitic Studies 37. Atlanta: Scholars Press, 1990. 251–269.

———. "The Death of Ur-Nammu and the Descent to the Netherworld." JCS 21 (1967): 104–122.

———. *From the Poetry of Sumer*. Berkeley and Los Angeles: University of California Press, 1979.

———. *History Begins at Sumer: Thirty-Nine Firsts in Man's Recorded History*. 3rd rev. ed. Philadelphia: University of Pennsylvania Press, 1981.

———. "The Marriage of Martu." *Bar Ilan Studies in Assyriology Dedicated to Pinchas Artzi*. Ed. J. Klein and A. Skaist. Ramat-Gan: Bar Ilan University, 1990. 11–27.

———. "Modern Social Problems in Ancient Sumer." *Gesellschaftsklassen im Alten Zweistromland und in den Angrenzenden Gebieten*. Ed. D. O. Edzard. Munchen: Bayerische Akademie der Wissenschaften 75, 1970. 114–121.

———. "Ninurta's Pride and Punishment." *Aula Orientalia* 2 (1984): 231–237.

———. *The Sacred Marriage Rite: Aspects of Faith, Myth, and Ritual in Ancient Sumer*. Bloomington: Indiana University Press, 1969.

———. "Sumerian Love-Song." ANET 496.

———. *The Sumerians: Their History, Culture, and Character*. Chicago: University of Chicago Press, 1972.

———. "Sumerian Sacred Marriage Texts." *The Ancient Near East: Supplementary Texts and Pictures Relating to the Old Testament*. Ed. J. B. Pritchard. Princeton: Princeton University Press, 1969. 637–645.

———. "Sumerian Similes: A Panoramic View of Some of Man's Oldest Literary Images." JAOS 89 (1969): 1–10.

———. "Ua-aua: A Sumerian Lullaby." *The Ancient Near East: Supplementary Texts and Pictures Relating to the Old Testament*. Ed. J. B. Pritchard. Princeton: Princeton University Press, 1969. 651–652.

———. "The Woman in Ancient Sumer: Gleanings from Sumerian Literature." *La Femme*. 107–112.

Kramer, S. N., and J. Maier. *Myths of Enki, the Crafty God*. New York: Oxford University Press, 1989.

Kuhrt, A. "Non-Royal Women in the Late Babylonian Period: A Survey." *Women's Earliest Records*. 215–243.

Labat, R. "Geburt." RLA 3 (1964): 178–179.

———. *Traité akkadien de diagnostic et prognostic médicaux*. Paris: Academie Internationale d'Histoire des Sciences, 1951. Vol. 1, 217–231.

Lafont, B. "Les femmes du palais de Mari." *Initiation à l'Orient*. Ed. J. Bottéro. Paris: Édition du Seuil, 1992. 170–181.

La Fontaine, J. S. *Initiation*. Manchester: Manchester University Press, 1986.

Lambert, W. G. *Babylonian Wisdom Literature*. Oxford: Clarendon Press, 1960.

———. "A Catalogue of Texts and Authors." *JCS* 16 (1962): 59–77.

———. "Gilgamesh in Literature and Art: The Second and First Millennia." *Monsters and Demons in the Ancient and Medieval Worlds*. Ed. A. E. Farkas et al. Mainz on Rhine: Philipp von Zabern, 1987. 37–52.

———. "The Gula Hymn of Bulluṭsa-rabi." *Orientalia* 36 (1967): 105–132.

———. "The Hymn to the Queen of Nippur." *Zikir Šumim: Assyriological Studies Presented to F. R. Kraus on the Occasion of His Seventieth Birthday*. Ed. G. van Driel et al. Leiden: E. J. Brill, 1982. 173–218.

———. "The Problem of the Love Lyrics." *Unity and Diversity: Essays in the History, Literature, and Religion of the Ancient Near East*. Ed. H. Goedicke and J. J. Roberts. Baltimore: Johns Hopkins University Press, 1975. 98–135.

———. "Prostitution." *Aussenseiter und Randgruppen: Beiträge zu einer Socialgeschichte des alten Orients*. Ed. V. Haas. Xenia 32. Konstanz: Universitätverlag Konstanz, 1992. 127–158.

———. "Studies in Nergal." *Bibliotheca Orientalis* 30 (Sept.–Nov. 1973): 355–363.

———. "The Theology of Death." *Death in Mesopotamia*. Ed. B. Alster. Copenhagen: Akademisk Forlag, 1980. 53–66.

Landsberger, B., and M. Civil. *The Series Ḫar-ra=ḫubullu: Tablet XV*. Materials for the Sumerian Lexicon 9. Rome: Biblical Institute Press, 1967.

Larner, C. *Witchcraft and Religion: The Politics of Popular Belief*. Ed. A. MacFarlane. Oxford: Basil Blackwell, 1984.

Lattimore, R. A. *Greek Lyrics*. Chicago: University of Chicago Press, 1960.

Leach, E. R. "Magical Hair." *Myth and Cosmos: Readings in Mythology and Symbolism*. Ed. J. Middleton. Garden City, N.Y.: Natural History Press, 1967. 77–108.

Learn, C. D. *Older Women's Experience of Spirituality: Crafting the Quilt*. New York: Garland, 1996.

Leed, E. J. *The Mind of the Traveler: From Gilgamesh to Global Tourism*. New York: Basic Books, 1991.

Lefkowitz, M., and M. B. Fante. *Women's Life in Greece and Rome*. London: Duckworth, 1982.

Legman, G. *Rationale of the Dirty Joke*. New York: Grove Press, 1968.

Leichty, E. "Feet of Clay." *Dumu-e₂-dub-ba-a*. 349–356.

———. *The Omen Series šumma izbu*. Texts from Cuneiform Sources 4. Locust Valley, N.Y.: J. J. Augustin, 1970.

Leick, G. *Sex and Eroticism in Mesopotamian Literature*. London and New York: Routledge, 1994.

Lerner, G. "The Origin of Prostitution in Ancient Mesopotamia." *Signs* 11 (1986): 236–254.

Lesko, B. S., ed. *Women's Earliest Records from Ancient Egypt and Western Asia*. Brown Judaic Studies 66. Atlanta: Scholars Press, 1989.

Lichtheim, M. *Ancient Egyptian Literature*. Berkeley: University of California Press, 1980. 3 vols.

Limet, H. "La condition de l'enfant en Mésopotamie autour de l'an 2000 av. J.-C." *L'Enfant dans les Civilisations Orientales* (Het kind in de oosterse Beschavingen). Ed. A. Theodorides, P. N. Aster, and J. Ries. Louvain: Peeters, 1980. 5–17.

———. "The Cuisine of Ancient Sumer." *Biblical Archaeologist* 50 (Sept. 1989): 132–147.

———. "Le secret et les écrits: Aspects de l'esoterisme en Mesopotamie ancienne." *Les rites d'initiation*. Ed. J. Ries. Actes du Collège de Liege et de Louvain-la-Neuve. Louvain-la-Neuve: Centre d'Histoire des Religion, 1986. 243–254.

Lincoln, B. *Emerging from the Chrysalis: Rituals of Women's Initiation*. New York: Oxford University Press, 1991.

Livingstone, A. *Court Poetry and Literary Miscellanea*. Helsinki: Helsinki University Press, 1989.

———. *Mystical and Mythological Explanatory Works of Assyrian and Babylonian Scholars*. New York: Oxford University Press, 1986.

Lloyd-Jones, H. "Psychoanalysis and the Study of the Ancient World." *Freud and the Humanities*. Ed. P. Horden. New York: St. Martin's Press, 1985. 152–180.

Longman, T. *Fictional Akkadian Autobiography: A Generic and Comparative Study*. Winona Lake, Ind.: Eisenbrauns, 1991.

Macdonald, S. "Drawing the Line—Gender, Peace, and War: An Introduction." *Images of Women in Peace and War: Cross-Cultural and Historical Perspectives*. Ed. S. Macdonald et al. Madison: University of Wisconsin Press, 1988. 1–26.

Maddox, G. L., et al., eds. *The Encyclopedia of Aging*. New York: Springer, 1987.

Maekawa, K. "Female Weavers and Their Children in Lagash—Presargonic and Ur III." *Acta Sumerologica* 2 (1980): 81–125.

Maier, J., ed. *Gilgamesh: A Reader*. Wauconda, Ill.: Bolchazy-Carducci, 1997.

Malamat, A. "Longevity: Biblical Concepts and Some Ancient Near Eastern Parallels." *Archiv für Orientforschung* 19 (1982): 215–224.

Malul, M. "Adoption of Foundlings in the Bible and Mesopotamian
  Documents." *Journal for the Study of Old Testament* 46 (1990): 97–126.
Manniche, L. *An Ancient Egyptian Herbal.* Austin: University of Texas Press,
  1989.
Marcus, D. "Juvenile Delinquency in the Bible and the Ancient Near East."
  JANES 13 (1981): 31–52.
Marcus, M. I. "Dressed to Kill: Women and Pins in Early Iran." *Oxford Art
  Journal* 17 (1994): 3–15.
———. "Incorporating the Body: Adornment, Gender, and Social Identity
  in Ancient Iran." *Cambridge Archaeological Journal* 3:12 (1993): 157–178.
McKinstry, S. J. "The Plot of Gender: The How-to-Romance of *Pride and
  Prejudice.*" *Transcending Boundaries: Multi-disciplinary Approaches to the
  Study of Gender.* Ed. P. R. Frese and J. M. Coggeshall. New York: Bergin
  and Garvey, 1991. 29–40.
McManners, J. *Death and the Enlightenment.* New York: Oxford University
  Press, 1981.
McNeil, J. N., et al. "Helping Adolescents Cope with the Death of a Peer."
  Journal of Adolescent Research 6 (Jan. 1991): 132–145.
Medina, J. J. *The Clock of Ages: Why We Age—How We Age—Winding Back
  the Clock.* New York: Cambridge University Press, 1996.
Meier, S. A. *The Messenger in the Ancient Semitic World.* Harvard Semitic
  Monograph 45. Atlanta: Scholars Press, 1988.
Meyers, C. "Gender Imagery in the Song of Songs." *Hebrew Annual Review*
  10 (1987): 209–223.
Michalowski, P. "The Death of Šulgi." *Orientalia* 46 (1977): 220–225.
———. "Durum and Uruk during the Ur III Period." *Mesopotamia* 12
  (1977): 83–96.
———. *The Lamentation over the Destruction of Sumer and Ur.* Winona, Ind.:
  Eisenbrauns, 1989.
———. *Letters from Early Mesopotamia.* Ed. E. Reiner. Atlanta: Scholars
  Press, 1993.
———. "Presence at the Creation." *Lingering over Words: Studies in Ancient
  Near Eastern Literature in Honor of William L. Moran.* Harvard Semitic
  Studies 37. Atlanta: Scholars Press, 1990. 381–396.
———. "Royal Women of the Ur III Period, Part I: The Wife of Šulgi." JCS
  28 (1976): 169–172.
———. "Royal Women of the Ur III Period, Part II: Geme-Ninlila." JCS 31
  (1979): 171–176.
———. "Royal Women of the Ur III Period, Part III." *Acta Sumerologica* 4
  (1982): 129–142.

Moran, W. L. *The Amarna Letters: English Language Edition.* Baltimore: Johns Hopkins University Press, 1992.

————. "Atrahasis: The Babylonian Story of the Floods." *Biblica* 52 (1971): 51–61.

————. "Review of *Altorientalische Lituraturen,* by W. Röllig et al." JAOS 100 (1980): 189–190.

————. "Review of *Altorientalische vorstellungen von der Unterwelt: Literar- und religions geschichtliche Überlegungen zu Nergal und Ereškigal,* by M. Hutter." *Catholic Biblical Quarterly* 49 (1987): 114–115.

Murstein, B. I. "Love, Sex and Marriage through the Ages." *Rise of the Modern Woman.* Ed. P. N. Stearns. Arlington Heights, Ill.: Forum Press, 1978. 21–24.

Nougayrol, J. "Notes brèves." RA 64 (1968): 96.

O'Brien, J. "Review of *Inanna, Queen of Heaven and Earth: Her Stories and Hymns from Sumer,* by D. Wolkstein and S. N. Kramer." *Classical World* 79 (1985): 59–60.

Ochshorn, J. "Ishtar and Her Cult." *The Book of the Goddess Past and Present.* Ed. C. Olson. New York: Crossroad, 1983. 16–28.

O'Flaherty, W. D. *Women. Androgynes, and Other Mythical Beasts.* Chicago: University of Chicago Press, 1980.

Oleander, M. "Aspects of Baubo: Ancient Texts and Contexts." *Before Sexuality: The Construction of Erotic Experience in the Ancient Greek World.* Ed. D. M. Halperin, J. J. Winkler, and F. I. Zeitlin. Princeton: Princeton University Press, 1990. 83–113.

Oppenheim, A. L. *Ancient Mesopotamia: Portrait of a Dead Civilization.* Chicago: University of Chicago Press, 1964.

————. *Catalogue of the Cuneiform Tablets of the Wilberforce Eames Babylonian Collection in the New York Public Library.* American Oriental Series 32. New Haven: Yale University Press, 1948.

————. *The Interpretation of Dreams in the Ancient Near East.* Philadelphia: American Philosophical Society, 1956.

————. *Letters from Mesopotamia: Official Business and Private Letters on Clay Tablets from Two Millennia.* Chicago: University of Chicago Press, 1967.

————. "Mesopotamian Mythology I." *Orientalia* 16 (1947): 207–238.

————. "Mesopotamian Mythology II." *Orientalia* 17 (1948): 17–58.

————. "Mesopotamian Mythology III." *Orientalia* 19 (1950): 147–154.

————. "The Position of the Intellectual in Mesopotamian Society." *Daedalus* 104:2 (spring, 1975): 34–46.

————. "'Siege Documents' from Nippur." *Iraq* 17 (1955): 69–89.

Ortner, S. "Is Female to Male as Nature Is to Culture?" *Women, Culture, and Society*. Ed. M. Z. Rosaldo and L. Lamphere. Stanford: Stanford University Press, 1974. 67–87.

Osborne, R. "Women and Sacrifice in Classical Greece." *Classical Quarterly* 43 (1993): 392–405.

Owen, D. I. "Widow's Rights in Ur III Sumer." ZA 70 (1980): 170–184.

Pangle, T. L., ed. *The Laws of Plato*. Chicago: University of Chicago Press, 1980.

Parker, H. N. "Love's Body Anatomized: The Ancient Erotic Handbooks and the Rhetoric of Sexuality." *Pornography and Representation in Greece and Rome*. Ed. A. Richlin. New York: Oxford University Press, 1992. 90–111.

Parpola, S. "The Assyrian Tree of Life: Tracing the Origins of Jewish Monotheism and Greek Philosophy." JNES 52:3 (1993): 161–208.

―――. *The Correspondence of Sargon II, Part 1: Letters from Assyria and theWest*. State Archives of Assyria 1. Helsinki: Helsinki University Press, 1987.

―――. *Letters from Assyrian and Babylonian Scholars*. State Archives of Assyria 10. Helsinki: Helsinki University Press, 1993.

―――. "The Murderer of Sennacherib." *Death in Mesopotamia*. Ed. B. Alster. Copenhagen: Akademish Forlag, 1980. 171–181.

Partridge, E. *Origins: A Short Etymological Dictionary of Modern English*. New York: Macmillan, 1959.

Paul, S. M. "The 'Plural of Ectasy' in Mesopotamian and Biblical Love Poetry." *Solving Riddles and Untying Knots: Biblical, Epigraphic, and Semitic Studies in Honor of Jonas C. Greenfield*. Ed. Z. Zevit, S. Gitin, and M. Sokoloff. Winona Lake, Ind.: Eisenbrauns, 1995. 585–597.

Peacock, J. L. "Symbolic Reversal and Social History: Transvestites and Clowns of Java." *The Reversible World: Symbolic Inversion in Art and Society*. Ed. B. Babcock. Ithaca: Cornell University Press, 1978. 209–224.

Pearce, L. E. "The Scribes and Scholars of Ancient Mesopotamia." CANE. Vol. 4, 2265–2278.

―――. "Statements of Purpose: Why the Scribes Wrote." *The Tablet and the Scroll*. 185–193.

Perera, S. B. "The Descent of Inanna: Myth and Therapy." *Feminist Archetypal Theory*. Ed. E. Lauter and C. S. Rupprecht. Knoxville: University of Tennessee Press, 1985. 137–186.

Petschow, H.P.H. "Lehrvertrag." RLA 6 (1983): 556–570.

Plato. *Thaetetus*. Trans. R.A.H. Waterfield. Harmondsworth: Viking Penguin, 1987.

Pollock, S. "Women in a Men's World: Images of Sumerian Women." *Engendering Archaeology: Women and Prehistory.* Ed. J. M. Gero and M. Conkey. Cambridge, Mass.: B. Blackwell, 1991. 366–387.

Pomeroy, S. B. *Goddesses, Whores, Wives, and Slaves: Women in Classical Antiquity.* New York: Schocken, 1978.

————. *Women in Hellenistic Egypt: From Alexander to Cleopatra.* Detroit: Wayne State University Press, 1990.

Pope, M. *The Song of Songs: A New Translation with Introduction and Commentary.* Anchor Bible series. Garden City, N.Y.: Doubleday, 1977.

Porada, E. "An Emaciated Male Figure of Bronze in the Cincinnati Museum." *Studies Presented to A. Leo Oppenheim.* Ed. R. D. Biggs and J. A. Brinkman. Chicago: The Oriental Institute of the University of Chicago, 1964. 159–166.

Porter, B. N. *Images, Power, and Politics: Figurative Aspects of Esarhaddon's Babylonian Policy.* Philadelphia: American Philosophical Society, 1993.

Postgate, J. N. *Early Mesopotamia: State and Economy at the Dawn of History.* New York: Routledge, 1992.

————. "On Some Assyrian Ladies. " *Iraq* 41 (1979): 89–103.

Powell, M. A. "Economy of the Extended Family." *Oikumene* 5 (1986): 9–13.

Prévot, D. "L'épopée de Gilgamesh: Un scénario initiatique?" *Les rites d'initiation.* Ed. J. Ries. Actes du Collège de Liege et de Louvain-la-Neuve. Louvain-la-Neuve: Centre d'Histoire des Religions, 1986. 225–241.

Pringle, J. "Hittite Birth Rituals." *Images of Women in Antiquity.* Ed. A. Cameron and A. Kuhrt. Detroit: Wayne State University Press, 1983. 128–141.

Pritchard, J. B., ed. *Ancient Near Eastern Texts Relating to the Old Testament.* Princeton: Princeton University Press, 1950.

al-Rawi, F.N.H., and A. R. George. "Tablets from the Sippar Library." *Iraq* 52 (1990): 149–157.

Reade, J. *Assyrian Sculpture.* Cambridge: Harvard University Press, 1983.

————. "Was Sennacherib a Feminist?" *La Femme.* 139–145.

Reiner, E. "Nergal and Ereškigal: Epic into Romance." *Your Thwarts in Pieces, Your Mooring Rope Cut: Poetry from Babylonia and Assyria.* Ann Arbor: Horace H. Rackham School of Graduate Studies at the University of Michigan, 1985. 50–60.

————. *Šurpu: A Collection of Sumerian and Akkadian Incantations.* Archiv für Orientforschung Beiheft 11. Graz Austria: E. Weidner, 1958.

Reiner, E., and H. G. Güterbock. "The Great Prayer to Ishtar and Its Two Versions from Boğazköy." *JCS* 21 (1967): 255–266.

Reisman, D. D. "Iddin-Dagan's Sacred Marriage Hymn." JCS 25 (1973): 185–202.

———. *Two Neo-Sumerian Royal Hymns.* Ph.D. diss. University of Pennsylvania, 1969.

Renger, J. "Gilg. P ii 32 [PBS 10/3]." RA 66 (1972): 190.

———. "Untersuchungen zum Priestertum in der altbabylonischen Zeit." ZA 58 (1967): 110–188.

Reviv, H. *The Elders in Ancient Israel: The Study of a Biblical Institution.* Jerusalem: Magnes Press, 1989.

Richlin, A. *The Garden of Priapus: Sexuality and Aggression in Roman Humor.* New Haven: Yale University Press, 1983.

Riefstahl, E. "An Egyptian Portrait of an Old Man." JNES 10 (1951): 65–73.

Ritter, E. "Magical Expert (= *Āšipu*) and Physician (= *Asû*): Notes on Two Complementary Professions in Babylonian Medicine." *Studies in Honor of Benno Landsberger on his Seventy-Fifth Birthday.* Assyriological Studies 16. Chicago: University of Chicago Press, 1965. 299–321.

Robins, G. *Egyptian Painting and Relief.* Aylesburg: Shire, 1986.

———. "Some Images of Women in New Kingdom Art and Literature." *Women's Earliest Records.* 105–116.

———. *Women in Ancient Egypt.* Cambridge: Harvard University Press. 1993.

Robinson, J. M., ed. *The Thunder, Perfect Mind: The Nag Hammadi Library in English.* New York: Harper & Row, 1977.

Rollins, S. "Women and Witchcraft in Ancient Assyria (c. 900–600 B.C.)." *Images of Women in Antiquity.* Ed. A. Cameron and A. Kuhrt. Detroit: Wayne State University Press, 1983. 34–45.

Roth, M. T. "Age at Marriage and the Household: A Study of Neo-Babylonian and Neo-Assyrian Forms." *Comparative Studies in Society and History* 29 (1987): 715–747.

———. *Law Collections from Mesopotamia and Asia Minor.* Ed. P. Michalowski. SBL Writings from the Ancient World 6. Atlanta: Scholars Press, 1995.

———. "The Neo-Babylonian Widow." JCS 43–45 (1991–1993): 1–26.

Roux, G. "Semiramis la reine mystérieuse d'Orient." *Initiation à l'Orient.* Ed. J. Bottéro. Paris: Édition du Seuil, 1992. 194–203.

Sachs, A. "Temple Programs for the New Year's Festivals at Babylon." ANET 331–334.

Saller, R. "*Patria Potestas* and the Sterotype of the Roman Family." *Continuity and Change* 1:1 (1986): 7–22.

Saller, R., and B. D. Shaw. "Tombstones and Roman Family Relations in the Principate: Civilians, Soldiers, and Slaves." *Journal of Roman Studies* 84 (1984): 124–156.

Saporetti, C. *The Status of Women in the Middle Assyrian Period.* Monographs on the Ancient Near East 2/1. Malibu: Undena, 1979.

Sasson, J. M. "A King of Early Assyria: Shamshi-Adad." *History Today* 17 (Nov. 1968): 794–801.

———. "The Posting of Letters with Divine Messages." *Florilegium Marianum II Memorial M. Birot.* Ed. D. Charpin. Memoirs de NABU 3. Paris: Société pour l'Étude du Proche-Orient Ancien, 1994. 299–316.

Sauren, H. "Nammu and Enki." *The Tablet and the Scroll.* 198–207.

Schlegel, A., and H. Barry III. *Adolescence: An Anthropological Inquiry.* New York: Free Press, 1991.

———. "Adolescent Initiation Ceremonies." *Cross-Cultural Samples and Codes.* Ed. H. Barry III and A. Schlegel. Pittsburgh: University of Pittsburgh Press, 1980. 277–288.

Schlossman, B. L. "Portraiture in Mesopotamia in the Late Third and Early Second Millennium B.C. Part II." *Archiv für Orientforschung* 28 (1981/82): 145–170.

Schlossman, B. L., and H. J. York. "Women in Ancient Art." *Art Journal* 35 (1976): 345–351.

Scurlock, J. "Baby-Snatching Demons, Restless Souls, and the Dangers of Childbirth." *Incognita* 2 (1991): 137–185.

———. "Death and the Afterlife in Ancient Mesopotamia." CANE. Vol. 3, 1883–1893.

Sefati, Y. "An Oath of Chastity in a Sumerian Love Song (SRT 31)?" *Bar Ilan Studies in Assyriology Dedicated to Pinchas Artzi.* Ed. J. Klein and A. Skaist. Ramat-Gan: Bar Ilan University Press, 1990. 45–63.

Segal, C. "Ancient Texts and Modern Literary Criticism." *Arethusa* 1:1 (1968): 1–25.

———. *Euripides and the Poetics of Sorrow.* Durham: Duke University Press, 1993.

Seidel, U. "Inanna/Ishtar B. In der Bildkunst." RLA 5 (1976): 87–89.

Seux, M.-J. "Königtum." RLA 6 (1980–1983): 159–162.

Shaffer, A. "From the Bookshelf of a Professional Wailer." *The Tablet and the Scroll.* 208–210.

Shahar, S. *Childhood in the Middle Ages.* New York: Routledge, 1990.

Shakespeare, W. *As You Like It.* New York: Oxford University Press, 1993.

Shank, M. H. "A Female University Student in Late Medieval Krakow." *Signs* 12 (1987): 373–380.

Sharp, S. A. "Folk Medicine: Women as Keepers and Carriers of Knowledge." *Women's Studies International Forum* 9:3 (1986): 243–249.

Simic, A., and B. Myerhoff, eds. *Life's Career-Aging: Cultural Variations on Growing Old.* Beverly Hills, Calif.: Sage, 1978.

Simmons, L. W. *The Role of the Aged in Primitive Society.* Hamden, Conn.: Archon Books, 1970.

Simpson, W. K., ed. *The Literature of Ancient Egypt: An Anthology of Stories, Instructions, and Poetry.* New Haven: Yale University Press, 1973.

Sjöberg, Å. W. "Der Examenstat A." *ZA* 64 (1974): 137–176.

————. "A Hymn to Inanna and Her Self-Praise." *JCS* 40 (1988): 165–186.

————. "*in-nin šà-gur₄-ra:* A Hymn to the Goddess Inanna." *ZA* 65 (1976): 161–253.

————. "The Old Babylonian Eduba." *Sumerological Studies in Honor of Thorkild Jacobsen on his Seventieth Birthday.* Ed. S. Lieberman. Assyriological Studies 20. Chicago: University of Chicago Press, 1975. 159–179.

————. "Der Vater und sein Missratener Sohn." *JCS* 25 (1973): 105–169.

Sjöberg, Å. W., and E. Bergmann. *The Collection of Sumerian Temple Hymns.* Texts from Cuneiform 3. Locust Valley, N.Y.: J. J. Augustin, 1969.

Skaist, A. "The Ancestor Cult and Succession in Mesopotamia." *Death in Mesopotamia.* Ed. B. Alster. Copenhagen: Akademisk Forlag, 1980. 123–128.

Skinner, M. "Introduction." In *Rescuing Creusa: New Methodological Approaches to Women in Antiquity. Helios* 13/2 (1987): 1–8.

Smith, S. R. "Growing Old in Early Stuart England." *Albion* 8 (1976): 125–141.

Smith, W. S. *The Art and Architecture of Ancient Egypt.* Rev. ed. Ed. W. K. Simpson. New Haven: Yale University Press, 1981.

Snell, D. "Plagues and Peoples in Mesopotamia." *JANES* 14 (1985): 89–96.

von Soden, W. *The Ancient Orient: An Introduction to the Study of the Ancient Near East.* Trans. D. G. Schley. Grand Rapids: W. B. Eerdmans, 1993.

————. "Der grosse Hymnus an Nabu." *ZA* 61 (1971): 44–71.

————. "Die Hebamme in Babylonien und Assyrien." *Archiv für Orientforschung* 18 (1957): 119–121.

Spanel, D. *Through Ancient Eyes: Egyptian Portraiture.* Birmingham, Ala.: The Museum, 1988.

Speiser, E. A. "Atraḫasis." *ANET* 104–105.

————. "The Epic of Gilgamesh." *ANET* 72–99.

Sperling, S. D. "A šu-il-lá to Ishtar." *Welt des Orients* 12 (1981): 8–19.

Stafford, P. *Queens, Concubines, and Dowagers: The King's Wife in the Early Middle Ages.* Athens: University of Georgia Press, 1983.

Starr, B. D. "Sexuality." *The Encyclopedia of Aging*, ed. G. L. Maddox et al. New York: Springer, 1987. 606–608.

———. "Sexuality and Aging." *Annual Review of Gerontology and Geriatrics* 5 (1985): 97–126.

Stearns, P. N. "Old Women: Some Historical Observations." *Journal of Family History* 5 (spring, 1980): 44–57.

Steinkeller, P. "The Foresters of Umma: Toward a Definition of Ur III Labor." *Labor in the Ancient Near East*. Ed. M. A. Powell. New Haven: Yale University Press, 1987. 73–115.

Steinmetz, D. *From Father to Son: Kinship, Conflict, and Continuity in Genesis*. Louisville, Ky.: John Knox, 1991.

Stevenson, R. G. "The Fear of Death in Childhood." *Children and Death: Perspectives from Birth through Adolescence*. Ed. J. E. Schowalter et al. New York: Praeger, 1987. 123–131.

Stewart, S. *Nonsense: Aspects of Intertexuality in Folklore and Literature*. Baltimore: Johns Hopkins University Press, 1978.

Stol, M. "Private Life in Ancient Mesopotamia." CANE. Vol. 1, 485–501.

———. "Women in Mesopotamia." *Journal of the Economic and Social History of the Orient* 38 (1995): 123–144.

Strommenger, E. *5000 Years of the Art of Mesopotamia*. New York: H. N. Abrams, 1964.

———. "Kleidung B: Archäologish," RLA 6 (1983): 31–33.

Stone, E. C. *Nippur Neighborhoods*. Studies in Ancient Oriental Civilizations 44. Chicago: Oriental Institute, 1987.

Stone, E. C., and D. I. Owens, with J. Mitchell. *Adoption in Old Babylonian Nippur and the Archive of Mannum-mešu-liṣṣur*. Mesopotamian Civilizations 3. Winona Lake, Ind.: Eisenbrauns, 1991.

The Sumerian Dictionary of the University Museum of the University of Pennsylvania. Ed. Å. W. Sjöberg. Philadelphia: University Museum, 1984. Vol. 2:B.

Sweet, R. F. "The Sage in Akkadian Literature: A Philological Study." *The Sage in Israel and the Ancient Near East*. Ed. J. G. Gammie and L. G. Perdue. Winona Lake, Ind.: Eisenbrauns, 1990. 45–65.

Taşyürek, O. A. "Some New Assyrian Rock Reliefs in Turkey." *Anatolian Studies* 25 (1975): 169–180.

Thrasher, E. C., and S. I. Lamberg. "Hair." *The Encyclopedia of Aging*. Ed. G. L. Maddox et al. New York: Springer, 1987. 300–301.

Tigay, J. *The Evolution of the Gilgamesh Epic*. Philadelphia: University of Pennsylvania Press, 1982.

ⁿⁿⁿⁿ

Traube, E. "Incest and Mythology: Anthropological and Girardian Perspective." *Berkshire Review* 14 (1979): 37–53.

Tucker, N. "Lullabies." *History Today* 34 (Sept. 1984): 40–46.

Turner, V. *Dramas, Fields, and Metaphors: Symbolic Action in Human Society.* Ithaca: Cornell University Press, 1974.

———. *The Forest of Symbols: Aspects of Ndembu Ritual.* Ithaca: Cornell University Press, 1967.

———. *The Ritual Process: Structure and Anti-Structure.* Ithaca: Cornell University Press, 1969.

———. "Three Symbols of Passage in Ndembu Circumcision Ritual: An Interpretation." *Essays on the Ritual of Social Relations.* Ed. M. Gluckman. Manchester: Manchester University Press, 1962. 124–181.

van de Mieroop, M. "An Inscribed Bead of Queen Zakûtu." *The Tablet and the Scroll.* 259–261.

———. *Society and Enterprise in Old Babylonian Ur.* Berliner Beiträge zum Vordern Orient 12. Berlin: D. Reimer, 1992.

———. "Women in the Economy of Sumer." *Women's Earliest Records.* 56–39.

van der Toorn, K. *Family Religion in Babylonia, Ugarit, and Israel: Continuity and Change in the Forms of Religious Life.* Leiden: E. J. Brill, 1996.

———. *From Her Cradle to Her Grave: The Role of Religion in the Life of Israelite and Babylonian Women.* Trans. S. J. Denning-Bolle. Sheffield: Journal for the Study of the Old Testament Press, 1984.

———. "Gods and Ancestors in Emar and Nuzi." *ZA* 84 (1994): 38–59.

———. "The Significance of the Veil in the Ancient Near East." *Pomegranates and Golden Bells: Studies in Biblical Jewish and Near Eastern Ritual, Law, and Literature in Honor of Jacob Milgrom.* Ed. D. P. Wright, D. N. Freedman, and A. Hurvitz. Winona Lake, Ind.: Eisenbrauns, 1995. 327–339.

———. *Sin and Sanction in Israel and Mesopotamia.* Assen: Van Gorcum, 1985.

van Driel, G. "Wine Lists and Beyond." *Bibliotheca Orientalis* 38 (1981): 259–272.

van Driel, G., et al., eds. *Zikir Šumim: Assyriological Studies Presented to F. R. Kraus on the Occasion of His Seventieth Birthday.* Leiden E. J. Brill, 1982.

van Gennep, A. *The Rites of Passage.* trans. M. B. Vizedom and G. L. Caffee. London: Routledge and Kegan Paul, 1960.

Van Nortwick, T. "'Do Not Go Gently . . .' Oedipus at Colonus and the Psychology of Aging." *Old Age in Greek and Roman Literature.* Ed. T. M.

Falkner and J. de Luce. Albany: State University of New York Press, 1989. 132–156.

―――. *Somewhere I Have Never Travelled: The Second Self and the Hero's Journey in Ancient Epic*. New York: Oxford University Press, 1992.

Vanstiphout, H.L.J. "The Craftsmanship of Sin-leqi-unnini." *Orientalia Lovaniensia Periodica* 21 (1990): 45–79.

―――. "Inanna/Ishtar as a Figure of Controversy." *Struggles of the Gods: Papers of the Groninegen Work Group for the Study of the History of Religions*. Ed. H. G. Kippenberg. Berlin: de Gruyter, 1984. 225–237.

―――. "Memory and Literacy in Ancient Western Asia." CANE. Vol. 4, 2181–2196.

Vecsey, C. *Imagine Ourselves Richly: Mythic Narratives of North American Indians*. San Francisco: Harper Collins, 1991.

Veenhof, K. R. "A Deed of Manumission and Adoption from the Later Old Assyrian Period." *Zikir Šumim: Assyriological Studies Presented to F. R. Kraus on the Occasion of his Seventieth Birthday*. Leiden: E. J. Brill, 1982. 359–385.

―――. "Two šilip rēmim Adoptions from Sippar." *Cinquante-deux réflexions sur la Proche-Orient Ancien offertes en hommage à Leon de Meyer*. Ed. H. Gasche et al. Mesopotamian History and Environment Occasional Publications 2. Louvain: Peeters, 1994. 143–147.

Vernant, J.-P. *Myth and Thought among the Greeks*. London: Routledge and Kegan, 1983.

Vidal-Naquet, P. "The Black Hunter and the Origin of the Athenian Ephebia." *The Black Hunter: Forms of Thought and Forms of Society in the Greek World*. Trans. A. Szegedy-Maszak. Baltimore: Johns Hopkins University Press, 1986. 106–128.

―――. "Recipes for Greek Adolescence." *The Black Hunter: Forms of Thought and Forms of Society in the Greek World*. Trans. A. Szegedy-Maszak. Baltimore: Johns Hopkins University Press, 1986. 129–156.

Vogelzang, M. E. "Some Aspects of Oral and Written Tradition in Akkadian." *Mesopotamian Epic Literature: Oral or Aural*. Ed. M. E. Vogelzang and H.L.J. Vanstiphout. Lewiston: Edwin Mellon Press, 1992. 265–278.

Vulpe, N. "Irony and the Unity of the Gilgamesh Epic." JNES 53:4 (1994): 275–283.

Waetzoldt, H. "Compensation of Craft Workers and Officials in the Ur III Period." *Labor in the Ancient Near East*. Ed. M. A. Powell. New Haven: American Oriental Society, 1987. 117–141.

―――. "Kleidung A: Philologisch." RLA 6 (1983): 18–31.

Wagner, R. *Lethal Speech: Daribi Myth as Symbolic Obviation*. Ithaca: Cornell University Press, 1978.

Walters, S. D. "The Sorceress and Her Apprentice." JCS 23 (1970–1971): 27–38.

Waterman, L. *Royal Correspondence of the Assyrian Empire.* Vol. 2. Ann Arbor: University of Michigan Press, 1930.

Wegner, I. *Gestalt und Kult des Ishtar-Shawuška.* Kleinasien Hurritologische Studien 3. Kevelaer: Butzon & Zerker, 1981.

von Weiher, E. "Gilgameš und Enkidu: Die Idee einer Freundschaft." *Baghdader Mitteilungen* 11 (1980): 106–119.

Weinfeld, M. "The Phases of Human Life in Mesopotamian and Jewish Sources." *Priests, Prophets, and Scribes: Essays on the Formation and Heritage of Second Temple Judaism in Honor of Joseph Blenkinsopp.* Ed. E. Ulrich et al. Journal for the Study of Old Testament 149 Supplement Series. Sheffield: Sheffield Academy, 1992. 182–189.

———. "Semiramis: Her Name and Her Origin." *Ah Assyria . . . Studies in Assyrian History and Ancient Near Eastern Historiography Presented to Hayim Tadmar.* Ed. M. Cogan and I. Eph'al. Jerusalem: Magnes Press, 1991. 99–103.

Weisberg, D. B. "Royal Women in the Neo-Babylonian Period." *Le palais et la royaute.* Ed. P. Garelli. Paris: Geuther, 1972. 447–454.

Weisman, D. J. *Nebuchadnezzar and Babylon.* Oxford: Oxford University Press, 1985.

Westbrook, R. "Adultery in Ancient Near Eastern Law." *Revue Biblique* 4 (Oct. 1990): 542–580.

———. "The Enforcement of Morals in Mesopotamian Law." JAOS 104 (1984): 753–756.

———. *Old Babylonian Marriage Law.* Archiv für Orientforschung Beiheft 23. Horn, Austria: Ferdinand Berger und Sohne, 1988.

Westenholz, J. G. "The Clergy of Nippur: The Priestess of Enlil." *Nippur at the Centennial: Papers Read at the 35ᵉ Rencontre Assyriologique Internationale.* Philadelphia: The University Museum, 1992. 297–310.

———. "Metaphorical Language in the Poetry of Love in the Ancient Near East." *La circulation des biens, des personnes et des idées dans le Proche-Orient ancien.* Ed. D. Charpin and F. Joannès. Actes de la 38ᵉ Rencontre Assyriologiques Internationale. Paris: Éditions Recherche sur les Civilisations, 1991. 381–387.

———. "Toward a New Conceptualization of the Female Role in Mesopotamian Society." JAOS 110 (1990): 510–521.

Whiting, R. M. *Old Babylonian Letters from Tell Asmar.* Assyriological Studies 22. Chicago: Oriental Institute at the University of Chicago, 1987.

Wider, K. "Women Philosophers in the Ancient Greek World: Donning the Mantle." *Hypatia* 1 (spring, 1986): 21–62.

Wiedemann, T. E. *Adults and Children in the Roman Empire*. London: Routledge, 1989.

Wilcke, C. "Familiengrundüng im Alten Babylonien." *Geschlectsreife und Legitimation zur Zeugung*. Ed. E. W. Müller et al. Freiburg and Munich: Karl Alber, 1985, 213–317.

————. "Inanna-Ishtar A. Philologisch." RLA 5 (1976): 74–87.

Wilson, J. A. "The God and His Unknown Name of Power." ANET 12–14.

Winter, I. J. "Women in Public: The Disk of Enheduanna, the Beginning of the Office of Enpriestess and the Weight of Visual Evidence." *La Femme. 189–201.*

Wiseman, D. "Murder in Mesopotamia." *Iraq* 36 (1974): 249–260.

Wolf, M. "Chinese Women: Old Skills in a New Context." *Women, Culture, and Society*. Ed. M. L. Rosaldo and L. Lamphere. Stanford: Stanford University Press, 1974. 157–172.

Wolfe, H. *The Narrative Structure of Three Epic Poems: Gilgamesh, the Odyssey, Beowulf*. New York: Garland Press, 1987.

Wolff, H. W. "Problems between the Generations in the Old Testament." *Essays in Old Testament Ethics*. Ed. J. L. Crenshaw and J.T. Willis. New York: Ktav, 1974. 79–94.

Wolkstein, D., and S. N. Kramer. *Inanna, Queen of Heaven and Earth: Her Stories and Hymns from Sumer*. New York: Harper and Row, 1983.

Wood, W. G. "Alcoholism." *The Encyclopedia of Aging*. Ed. G. L. Maddox et al. New York: Springer, 1987. 25–27.

Woodruff, D. S. "Arousal, Sleep, and Aging." *Handbook of the Psychology of Aging*. Ed. J. E. Birren et al. New York: Van Nostrand Reinhold, 1985. 261–295.

Yamuchi, E. M. "The Descent of Ishtar, the Fall of Sophia, and the Jewish Roots of Gnosticism." *Tyndale Bulletin* 29 (1978): 143–175.

Zaccagnini, C. "Feet of Clay at Emar and Elsewhere." *Orientalia* 63 (1994): 1–4.

Zeitlin, F. "Playing the Other: Theater, Theatricality, and the Feminine in Greek Drama." *Representations* 11 (summer, 1985): 63–94.

Zettler, R. "The Genealogy of Ur-Meme: A Second Look." *Archiv für Orientforschung* 31 (1984): 1–9.

Zweig, B. "The Mute Nude Female Characters in Aristophanes' Plays." *Pornography and Representation in Greece and Rome*. Ed. A. Richlin. New York: Oxford University Press, 1992. 73–89.

INDEX